Mastering NLP from Foundations to LLMs

Apply advanced rule-based techniques to LLMs and solve real-world business problems using Python

Lior Gazit

Meysam Ghaffari

Mastering NLP from Foundations to LLMs

Group Product Manager: Ali Abidi

Publishing Product Manager: Ali Abidi

Book Project Manager: Hemangi Lotlikar

Content Development Editor: Priyanka Soam

Technical Editor: Rahul Limbachiya

Copy Editor: Safis Editing

Proofreader: Safis Editing

Indexer: Rekha Nair

Production Designer: Gokul Raj S.T

Senior DevRel Marketing Coordinator: Vinishka Kalra

First published: April 2024

Production reference: 2140524

Published by
Packt Publishing Ltd.
Grosvenor House
11 St Paul's Square
Birmingham
B3 1RB, UK.

ISBN: 978-1-80461-918-6

www.packtpub.com

To my parents, my siblings, and my boys.

Above all, to my Alla, whose support and faith paved the path to the creation of this book.

Thank you!

– Lior

To my beloved parents, Abbas, and Fereshteh, whose unwavering support and encouragement have been the cornerstone of my journey, this book is dedicated to you. Your endless love and belief in me have fueled my aspirations and guided me through the highs and lows of life.

To my esteemed professors and mentors, Prof. Ashok Srinivasan, Dr. Majid Afshar, Lior Gazit, and Dr. Natalia Summerville, your wisdom, guidance, and relentless dedication to nurturing intellect have sculpted my mind and broadened my horizons. Your teachings have illuminated my path, fostering in me a thirst for knowledge and a passion for exploration.

It is through the collective influence of my parents, professors, and mentors that I stand here today, humbled and grateful, ready to embark on this literary endeavor. Your invaluable contributions have shaped not only my intellect but also my character, and for that, I offer my deepest gratitude. This book is a reflection of the lessons learned, the challenges overcome, and the growth experienced, all made possible by your unwavering support and belief in me.

- Meysam Ghaffari

Foreword

Natural language processing (**NLP**) lies at the heart of a perplexing question – *how can two radically different entities – humans and computers – truly communicate with one another?* Human language is the complex, imperfect product of social and biological evolution. It's filled with illogical exceptions, subtle nuance, and multiple levels of abstract thinking. In contrast, computers communicate via mathematical models that, however complex, follow a logical, verifiable set of rules. As digital systems assume an ever greater role in human activity, they must be able to correctly interpret what humans actually mean from the words they say.

Lior Gazit and Meysam Ghaffari's new book, *Mastering NLP from Foundations to LLMs*, is a monumental resource for making that happen. Written for technology professionals who work with text – from beginners to seasoned NLP pros – the book lays out a practical strategy for one of this century's most daunting challenges. It charts a meticulous course through the intricate realms of NLP and **large language models** (**LLMs**), guiding you through fundamental concepts to the apex of contemporary artificial intelligence.

The book draws from Gazit's immersion in the fast-paced world of finance and Ghaffari's innovative NLP development in the healthcare sector. The result is a rare balance between technical depth and practical relevance. Their combined expertise shapes a book as rich in information as it is robust in practical insights. Each author's distinct influence enriches the narrative – combining Gazit's understanding of the power of **machine learning** (**ML**) to drive growth and Ghaffari's humanistic approach to applying ML for societal good.

Gazit and Ghaffari lay a solid foundation in the essential mathematical and statistical pillars supporting the complex algorithms of NLP. They employ a pedagogical strategy that progressively builds from basic principles to advanced applications, ensuring a clear trajectory of learning and comprehension.

As the narrative progresses, it delves deep into the engineering of ML models. You are guided through model construction, application, and the nuanced balance of fit versus generalizability. The exploration of text preprocessing is thorough, equipping you with essential tools to effectively prepare data for NLP tasks, from tokenization to the subtle art of named entity recognition.

The book's centerpiece – LLMs – is unveiled with a blend of care and deep expertise. The authors articulate the theoretical foundations, developmental challenges, and breakthroughs that mark the ascent of LLMs, guiding you to contemplate the direction of these formidable technologies. The authors also provide practical advice on setting up and accessing LLMs, providing you with actionable paths to harness these models in your work. This demystifies the sometimes daunting task of integrating advanced models into practical use cases.

In its visionary chapters, the book plunges into the functionalities of advanced technologies such as RAG and LangChain, providing a glimpse into an automated future where AI manages increasingly complex tasks. This narrative not only educates but inspires, mapping out the potential of LLMs to enhance performance and facilitate even greater innovation.

Concluding with a series of expert interviews, *Mastering NLP from Foundations to LLMs* offers a diverse array of perspectives that enrich the narrative with real-world applications across various industries. This remarkable book showcases the widespread transformation being driven by NLP and LLMs – giving technology professionals a detailed roadmap to a future in which they themselves can have a major role. It is a must-read for anyone who wants a seat at the LLM table.

Asha Saxena,

Entrepreneur, Professor, and AI Strategist

Bio: `https://ashasaxena.com/about-bio/`

Contributors

About the authors

Lior Gazit is a highly skilled ML professional with a proven track record of success in building and leading teams that use ML to drive business growth. He is an expert in NLP and has successfully developed innovative ML pipelines and products. He holds a master's degree and has published in peer-reviewed journals and conferences. As a senior director of a ML group in the financial sector and a principal ML advisor at an emerging start-up, Lior is a respected leader in the industry, with a wealth of knowledge and experience to share. With much passion and inspiration, Lior is dedicated to using ML to drive positive change and growth in his organizations.

Meysam Ghaffari is a senior data scientist with a strong background in NLP and deep learning. He currently works at MSKCC, where he specializes in developing and improving ML and NLP models for healthcare problems. He has over nine years of experience in ML and over four years of experience in NLP and deep learning. He received his PhD in computer science from Florida State University, his MS in computer science – artificial intelligence from Isfahan University of Technology, and his BS in computer science from Iran University of Science and Technology. He also worked as a post-doctoral research associate at the University of Wisconsin-Madison before joining MSKCC.

About the reviewers

Amreth Chandrasehar is an Engineering Leader in Cloud, AI/ML Engineering, Observability, Automation, and SRE. Over the last few years, Amreth has played a key role in Cloud Migration, Generative AI, AIOps, Observability, and ML adoption at various organizations. Amreth is also a co-creator of the Conduktor Platform Platform and a Tech/Customer Advisory board member at various companies on Observability. Amreth has also co-created and open-sourced Kardio.io, a service health dashboard tool. Amreth has been invited and spoken at several key conferences and has received several awards. I would like to thank my wife Ashwinya and my son Athvik for their patience and support during my review of this book.

Shivani Modi is a data scientist with a rich background in machine learning, deep learning, and NLP, having earned her Master's from Columbia University. Her career spans roles at IBM, SAP, C3 AI, and leadership at Konko AI, focusing on scalable AI models and innovative LLM tools. Shivani's dedication to mentoring and ethical AI application is evident through her advisory roles and commitment to the societal benefits of technology. Her upcoming projects aim to enhance LLM utilization for developers, prioritizing security and efficiency.

Disclaimer

This book has been created by authors, technical experts, and a professional publishing team.

The views, thoughts, examples, and opinions expressed in the book are of the authors and do not reflect those of the authors' employers.

Table of Contents

3

Unleashing Machine Learning Potentials in Natural Language Processing 33

4

Streamlining Text Preprocessing Techniques for Optimal NLP Performance 85

5

Empowering Text Classification: Leveraging Traditional Machine Learning Techniques   103

6

Text Classification Reimagined: Delving Deep into Deep Learning Language Models   139

7

Demystifying Large Language Models: Theory, Design, and Langchain Implementation   171

8

Accessing the Power of Large Language Models: Advanced Setup and Integration with RAG   197

9

Exploring the Frontiers: Advanced Applications and Innovations Driven by LLMs   219

10

Riding the Wave: Analyzing Past, Present, and Future Trends Shaped by LLMs and AI 245

11

Exclusive Industry Insights: Perspectives and Predictions from World Class Experts 279

Preface

This book provides an in-depth introduction to **natural language processing** (**NLP**) techniques, starting with the mathematical foundations of **machine learning** (**ML**) and working up to advanced NLP applications such as **large language models** (**LLMs**) and AI applications. As part of your learning experience, you'll get to grips with linear algebra, optimization, probability, and statistics, which are essential for understanding and implementing ML and NLP algorithms. You'll also explore general ML techniques and find out how they relate to NLP. The preprocessing of text data, including methods for cleaning and preparing text for analysis, will follow, right before you learn how to perform text classification, which is the task of assigning a label or category to a piece of text based on its content. The advanced topics of LLMs' theory, design, and applications will be discussed toward the end of the book, as will the future trends in NLP, which will feature expert opinions on the future of the field. To strengthen your practical skills, you'll also work on mocked real-world NLP business problems and solutions.

Who this book is for

This book is for technical folks, ranging from deep learning and ML researchers, hands-on NLP practitioners, and ML/NLP educators, to STEM students. Professionals working with text as part of their projects and existing NLP practitioners will also find plenty of useful information in this book. Beginner-level ML knowledge and a basic working knowledge of Python will help you get the best out of this book.

What this book covers

Chapter 1, *Navigating the NLP Landscape: A Comprehensive Introduction*, explains what the book is about, which topics we will cover, and who can use this book. This chapter will help you decide whether this book is the right fit for you or not.

Chapter 2, *Mastering Linear Algebra, Probability, and Statistics for Machine Learning and NLP*, has three parts. In the first part, we will review the basics of linear algebra that are needed at different parts of the book. In the next part, we will review the basics of statistics, and finally, we will present basic statistical estimators.

Chapter 3, *Unleashing Machine Learning Potentials in NLP*, discusses different concepts and methods in ML that can be used to tackle NLP problems. We will discuss general feature selection and classification techniques. We will cover general aspects of ML problems, such as train/test/validation selection, and dealing with imbalanced datasets. We will also discuss performance metrics for evaluating ML models that are used in NLP problems. We will explain the theory behind the methods as well as how to use them in code.

Chapter 4, Streamlining Text Preprocessing Techniques for Optimal NLP Performance, talks about various text preprocessing steps in the context of real-world problems. We will explain which steps suit which needs, based on the scenario that is to be solved. There will be a complete Python pipeline presented and reviewed in this chapter.

Chapter 5, Empowering Text Classification: Leveraging Traditional Machine Learning Techniques, explains how to perform text classification. Theory and implementation will also be explained. A comprehensive Python notebook will be covered as a case study.

Chapter 6, Text Classification Reimagined: Delving Deep into Deep Learning Language Models, covers the problems that can be solved using deep learning neural networks. The different problems in this category will be introduced to you so you can learn how to efficiently solve them. The theory of the methods will be explained here and a comprehensive Python notebook will be covered as a case study.

Chapter 7, Demystifying Large Language Models: Theory, Design, and Langchain Implementation, outlines the motivations behind the development and usage of LLMs, alongside the challenges faced during their creation. Through an examination of state-of-the-art model designs, you will gain comprehensive insights into the theoretical underpinnings and practical applications of LLMs.

Chapter 8, Accessing the Power of Large Language Models: Advanced Setup and Integration with RAG, guides you through setting up LLM applications, both API-based and open source, and delves into prompt engineering and RAGs via LangChain. We will review practical applications in code.

Chapter 9, Exploring the Frontiers: Advanced Applications and Innovations Driven by LLMs, dives into enhancing LLM performance using RAG, exploring advanced methodologies, automatic web source retrieval, prompt compression, API-cost reduction, and collaborative multi-agent LLM teams, pushing the boundaries of current LLM applications. Here, you will review multiple Python notebooks, each handling different advanced solutions to practical use cases.

Chapter 10, Riding the Wave: Analyzing Past, Present, and Future Trends Shaped by LLMs and AI, dives into the transformative impact of LLMs and AI on technology, culture, and society, exploring key trends, computational advancements, the significance of large datasets, and the evolution, purpose, and social implications of LLMs in business and beyond.

Chapter 11, Exclusive Industry Insights: Perspectives and Predictions from World Class Experts, offers a deep dive into future NLP and LLM trends through conversations with experts in legal, research, and executive roles, exploring challenges, opportunities, and the intersection of LLMs with professional practices and ethical considerations.

To get the most out of this book

All the code presented in this book is in the form of a Jupyter notebook. All the code was developed with Python 3.10.X and is expected to work on later versions as well.

Software/hardware covered in the book	Operating system requirements
Access to a Python environment via one of the following: • Accessing Google Colab, which is free and easy from any browser on any device (recommended) • A local/cloud development environment of Python with the ability to install public packages and access OpenAI's API	Windows, macOS, or Linux
Sufficient computation resources, as follows: • The previously recommended free access to Google Colab includes a free GPU instance • If opting to avoid Google Colab, the local/cloud environment should have a GPU for several code examples	

As the code examples in this book have a diversified set of use cases, for some of the advanced LLM solutions, you will need an OpenAI account, which will allow an API key.

If you are using the digital version of this book, we advise you to type the code yourself or access the code from the book's GitHub repository (a link is available in the next section). Doing so will help you avoid any potential errors related to the copying and pasting of code.

Download the example code files

You can download the example code files for this book from GitHub at `https://github.com/PacktPublishing/Mastering-NLP-from-Foundations-to-LLMs` If there's an update to the code, it will be updated in the GitHub repository.

Throughout the book we review complete code notebooks that represent solutions on a professional industry level:

Chapter	Notebook Name
4	Ch4_Preprocessing_Pipeline.ipynb Ch4_NER_and_POS.ipynb
5	Ch5_Text_Classification_Traditional_ML.ipynb
6	Ch6_Text_Classification_DL.ipynb
8	Ch8_Setting_Up_Close_Source_and_Open_Source_LLMs.ipynb Ch8_Setting_Up_LangChain_Configurations_and_Pipeline.ipynb

Chapter	Notebook Name
9	Ch9_Advanced_LangChain_Configurations_and_Pipeline.ipynb
	Ch9_Advanced_Methods_with_Chains.ipynb
	Ch9_Completing_a_Complex_Analysis_with_a_Team_of_LLM_Agents.ipynb
	Ch9_RAGLlamaIndex_Prompt_Compression.ipynb
	Ch9_Retrieve_Content_from_a_YouTube_Video_and_Summarize.ipynb

We also have other code bundles from our rich catalog of books and videos available at `https://github.com/PacktPublishing/`. Check them out!

Conventions used

There are a number of text conventions used throughout this book.

`Code in text`: Indicates code words in text, database table names, folder names, filenames, file extensions, pathnames, dummy URLs, user input, and Twitter handles. Here is an example: "Now, we add a feature for achieving the syntax. We define the `output_parser` variable, and we use a different function for generating the output, `predict_and_parse()`."

A block of code is set as follows:

```
import pandas as pd
import matplotlib.pyplot as plt
# Load the record dict from URL
import requests
import pickle
```

When we wish to draw your attention to a particular part of a code block, the relevant lines or items are set in bold:

```
qa_engineer (to manager_0):
exitcode: 0 (execution succeeded)
Code output:
Figure(640x480)
programmer (to manager_0):
TERMINATE
```

Bold: Indicates a new term, an important word, or words that you see onscreen. For instance, words in menus or dialog boxes appear in **bold**. Here is an example: "While we chose one particular database, you can refer to the **Vector Store** page to read more about the different choices."

> **Tips or important notes**
> Appear like this.

Get in touch

Feedback from our readers is always welcome.

General feedback: If you have questions about any aspect of this book, email us at customercare@ packtpub.com and mention the book title in the subject of your message.

Errata: Although we have taken every care to ensure the accuracy of our content, mistakes do happen. If you have found a mistake in this book, we would be grateful if you would report this to us. Please visit www.packtpub.com/support/errata and fill in the form.

Piracy: If you come across any illegal copies of our works in any form on the internet, we would be grateful if you would provide us with the location address or website name. Please contact us at copyright@packt.com with a link to the material.

If you are interested in becoming an author: If there is a topic that you have expertise in and you are interested in either writing or contributing to a book, please visit authors.packtpub.com.

Reviews

Please leave a review. Once you have read and used this book, why not leave a review on the site that you purchased it from? Potential readers can then see and use your unbiased opinion to make purchase decisions, we at Packt can understand what you think about our products, and our authors can see your feedback on their book. Thank you!

For more information about Packt, please visit www.packtpub.com.

Share Your Thoughts

Once you've read *Mastering NLP from Foundations to LLMs*, we'd love to hear your thoughts! Scan the QR code below to go straight to the Amazon review page for this book and share your feedback.

https://packt.link/r/1-804-61918-3

Your review is important to us and the tech community and will help us make sure we're delivering excellent quality content.

Download a free PDF copy of this book

Thanks for purchasing this book!

Do you like to read on the go but are unable to carry your print books everywhere?

Is your eBook purchase not compatible with the device of your choice?

Don't worry, now with every Packt book you get a DRM-free PDF version of that book at no cost.

Read anywhere, any place, on any device. Search, copy, and paste code from your favorite technical books directly into your application.

The perks don't stop there, you can get exclusive access to discounts, newsletters, and great free content in your inbox daily

Follow these simple steps to get the benefits:

1. Scan the QR code or visit the link below

https://packt.link/free-ebook/978-1-80461-918-6

2. Submit your proof of purchase

3. That's it! We'll send your free PDF and other benefits to your email directly

1

Navigating the NLP Landscape: A Comprehensive Introduction

This book is aimed at helping professionals apply **natural language processing** (**NLP**) techniques to their work, whether they are working on NLP projects or using NLP in other areas, such as data science. The purpose of the book is to introduce you to the field of NLP and its underlying techniques, including **machine learning** (**ML**) and **deep learning** (**DL**). Throughout the book, we highlight the importance of mathematical foundations, such as linear algebra, statistics and probability, and optimization theory, which are necessary to understand the algorithms used in NLP. The content is accompanied by code examples in Python to allow you to pre-practice, experiment, and generate some of the development presented in the book.

The book discusses the challenges faced in NLP, such as understanding the context and meaning of words, the relationships between them, and the need for labeled data. The book also mentions the recent advancements in NLP, including pre-trained language models, such as BERT and GPT, and the availability of large amounts of text data, which has led to improved performance on NLP tasks.

The book will engage you by discussing the impact of language models on the field of NLP, including improved accuracy and effectiveness in NLP tasks, the development of more advanced NLP systems, and accessibility to a broader range of people.

We will be covering the following headings in the chapter:

- What is natural language processing?
- Initial strategies in the machine processing of natural language
- A winning synergy – the coming together of NLP and ML
- Introduction to math and statistics in NLP

Who this book is for

The target audience of the book is professionals who work with text as part of their projects. This may include NLP practitioners, who may be beginners, as well as those who do not typically work with text.

What is natural language processing?

NLP is a field of **artificial intelligence** (**AI**) focused on the interaction between computers and human languages. It involves using computational techniques to understand, interpret, and generate human language, making it possible for computers to understand and respond to human input naturally and meaningfully.

The history and evolution of natural language processing

The history of NLP is a fascinating journey through time, tracing back to the 1950s, with significant contributions from pioneers such as Alan Turing. Turing's seminal paper, *Computing Machinery and Intelligence*, introduced the Turing test, laying the groundwork for future explorations in AI and NLP. This period marked the inception of symbolic NLP, characterized by the use of rule-based systems, such as the notable Georgetown experiment in 1954, which ambitiously aimed to solve machine translation by generating a translation of Russian content into English (see `https://en.wikipedia.org/wiki/Georgetown%E2%80%93IBM_experiment`). Despite early optimism, progress was slow, revealing the complexities of language understanding and generation.

The 1960s and 1970s saw the development of early NLP systems, which demonstrated the potential for machines to engage in human-like interactions using limited vocabularies and knowledge bases. This era also witnessed the creation of conceptual ontologies, crucial for structuring real-world information in a computer-understandable format. However, the limitations of rule-based methods led to a paradigm shift in the late 1980s towards statistical NLP, fueled by advances in ML and increased computational power. This shift enabled more effective learning from large corpora, significantly advancing machine translation and other NLP tasks. This paradigm shift not only represented a technological and methodological advancement but also underscored a conceptual evolution in the approach to linguistics within NLP. In moving away from the rigidity of predefined grammar rules, this transition embraced corpus linguistics, a method that allows machines to "perceive" and understand languages through extensive exposure to large bodies of text. This approach reflects a more empirical and data-driven understanding of language, where patterns and meanings are derived from actual language use rather than theoretical constructs, enabling more nuanced and flexible language processing capabilities.

Entering the 21st century, the emergence of the web provided vast amounts of data, catalyzing research in unsupervised and semi-supervised learning algorithms. The breakthrough came with the advent of neural NLP in the 2010s, where DL techniques began to dominate, offering unprecedented accuracy in language modeling and parsing. This era has been marked by the development of sophisticated models such as Word2Vec and the proliferation of deep neural networks, driving NLP towards more natural and effective human-computer interaction. As we continue to build on these advancements, NLP stands at the forefront of AI research, with its history reflecting a relentless pursuit of understanding and replicating the nuances of human language.

In recent years, NLP has also been applied to a wide range of industries, such as healthcare, finance, and social media, where it has been used to automate decision-making and enhance communication between humans and machines. For example, NLP has been used to extract information from medical documents, analyze customer feedback, translate documents between languages, and search through enormous amounts of posts.

Initial strategies in the machine processing of natural language

Traditional methods in NLP consist of text preprocessing, which is synonymous with text preparation, which is then followed by applying **ML** methods. Preprocessing text is an essential step in NLP and ML applications. It involves cleaning and transforming the original text data into a form that can be easily understood and analyzed by ML algorithms. The goal of preprocessing is to remove noise and inconsistencies and standardize the data, making it more suitable for advanced NLP and ML methods.

One of the key benefits of preprocessing is that it can significantly improve the performance of ML algorithms. For example, removing stop words, which are common words that do not carry much meaning, such as "the" and "is," can help reduce the dimensionality of the data, making it easier for the algorithm to identify patterns.

Take the following sentence as an example:

I am going to the store to buy some milk and bread.

After removing the stop words, we have the following:

going store buy milk bread.

In the example sentence, the stop words "**I**," "**am**," "**to**," "**the**," "**some**," and "**and**" do not add any additional meaning to the sentence and can be removed without changing the overall meaning of the sentence. It should be emphasized that the removal of stop words needs to be tailored to the specific objective, as the omission of a particular word might be trivial in one context but detrimental in another.

Additionally, **stemming** and **lemmatization**, which reduce words to their base forms, can help reduce the number of unique words in the data, making it easier for the algorithm to identify relationships between them, which will be explained completely in this book.

Take the following sentence as an example:

The boys ran, jumped, and swam quickly.

After applying stemming, which reduces each word to its root or stem form, disregarding word tense or derivational affixes, we might get:

The boy ran, jump, and swam quick.

Stemming simplifies the text to its base forms. In this example, "**ran**," "**jumped**," and "**swam**" are reduced to "**ran**," "**jump**," and "**swam**," respectively. Note that "ran" and "swam" do not change, as stemming often results in words that are close to their root form but not exactly the dictionary base form. This process helps reduce the complexity of the text data, making it easier for machine learning algorithms to match and analyze patterns without getting bogged down by variations of the same word.

Take the following sentence as an example:

The boys ran, jumped, and swam quickly.

After applying lemmatization, which considers the morphological analysis of the words, aiming to return the base or dictionary form of a word, known as the lemma, we get:

The boy run, jump, and swim quickly.

Lemmatization accurately converts "**ran**," "**jumped**," and "**swam**" to "**run**," "**jump**," and "**swim**." This process takes into account the part of speech of each word, ensuring that the reduction to the base form is both grammatically and contextually appropriate. Unlike stemming, lemmatization provides a more precise reduction to the base form, ensuring that the processed text remains meaningful and contextually accurate. This enhances the performance of NLP models by enabling them to understand and process language more effectively, reducing the dataset's complexity while maintaining the integrity of the original text.

Two other important aspects of preprocessing are data normalization and data cleaning. **Data normalization** includes converting all text to lowercase, removing punctuation, and standardizing the format of the data. This helps to ensure that the algorithm does not treat different variations of the same word as separate entities, which can lead to inaccurate results.

Data cleaning includes removing duplicate or irrelevant data and correcting errors or inconsistencies in the data. This is particularly important in large datasets, where manual cleaning is time-consuming and error-prone. Automated preprocessing tools can help to quickly identify and remove errors, making the data more reliable for analysis.

Figure 1.1 portrays a comprehensive preprocessing pipeline. We will cover this code example in *Chapter 4*:

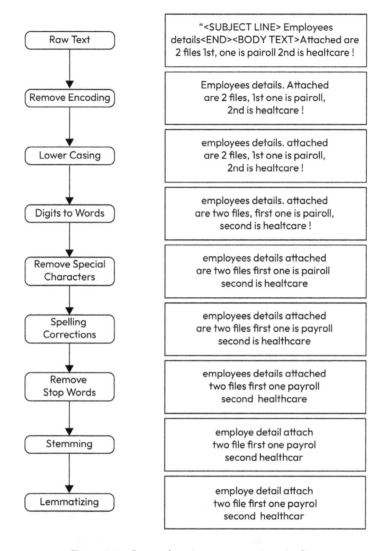

Figure 1.1 – Comprehensive preprocessing pipeline

In conclusion, preprocessing text is a vital step in NLP and ML applications; it improves the performance of ML algorithms by removing noise and inconsistencies and standardizing the data. Additionally, it plays a crucial role in data preparation for NLP tasks and in data cleaning. By investing time and resources in preprocessing, one can ensure that the data is of high quality and is ready for advanced NLP and ML methods, resulting in more accurate and reliable results.

As our text data is prepared for further processing, the next step typically involves fitting an ML model to it.

A winning synergy – the coming together of NLP and ML

ML is a subfield of AI that involves training algorithms to learn from data, allowing them to make predictions or decisions without those being explicitly programmed. ML is driving advancements in so many different fields, such as computer vision, voice recognition, and, of course, NLP.

Diving a little more into the specific techniques of ML, a particular technique used in NLP is **statistical language modeling**, which involves training algorithms on large text corpora to predict the likelihood of a given sequence of words. This is used in a wide range of applications, such as speech recognition, machine translation, and text generation.

Another essential technique is **DL**, which is a subfield of ML that involves training artificial neural networks on large amounts of data. DL models, such as **convolutional neural networks** (**CNNs**) and **recurrent neural networks** (**RNNs**), have been shown to be adequate for NLP tasks such as language understanding, text summarization, and sentiment analysis.

Figure 1.2 portrays the relationship between AI, ML, DL, and NLP:

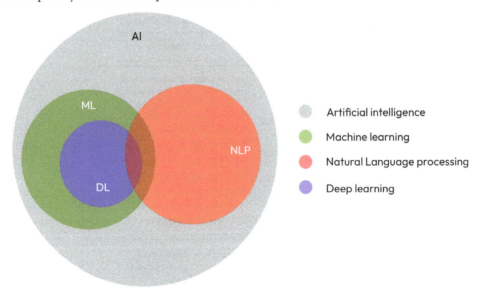

Figure 1.2 – The relationship between the different disciplines

Introduction to math and statistics in NLP

The solid base for NLP and ML is the mathematical foundations from which the algorithms stem. In particular, the key foundations are linear algebra, statistics and probability, and optimization theory. *Chapter 2* will survey the key topics you will need to understand these topics. Throughout the book, we will present proofs and justifications for the various methods and hypotheses.

One of the challenges in NLP is dealing with the vast amount of data that is generated in human language. This includes understanding the context, as well as the meaning of the words and relationships between them. To deal with this challenge, researchers have developed various techniques, such as embeddings and attention mechanisms, which represent the meaning of words in a numerical format and help identify the most critical parts of the text, respectively.

Another challenge in NLP is the need for labeled data, as manually annotating large text corpora is expensive and time-consuming. To address this problem, researchers have developed unsupervised and weakly supervised methods that can learn from unlabeled data, such as clustering, topic modeling, and self-supervised learning.

Overall, NLP is a rapidly evolving field that has the potential to transform the way we interact with computers and information. It is used in various applications, from chatbots and language translation to text summarization and sentiment analysis. The use of ML techniques, such as statistical language modeling and DL, has been crucial in developing these systems. Ongoing research addresses the remaining challenges, such as understanding context and dealing with the lack of labeled data.

One of the most significant advances in NLP has been the development of pre-trained language models, such as **bidirectional encoder representations from transformers (BERTs)** and **generative pre-trained transformers (GPTs)**. These models have been trained on massive amounts of text data and can be fine-tuned for specific tasks, such as sentiment analysis or language translation.

Transformers, the technology behind the BERT and GPT models, revolutionized NLP by enabling machines to understand the context of words in sentences more effectively. Unlike previous methods that processed text linearly, transformers can handle words in parallel, capturing nuances in language through attention mechanisms. This allows them to discern the importance of each word relative to others, greatly enhancing the model's ability to grasp complex language patterns and nuances and setting a new standard for accuracy and fluency in NLP applications. This has enhanced the creation of NLP applications and has led to improved performance on a wide range of NLP tasks.

Figure 1.3 details the functional design of the Transformer component.

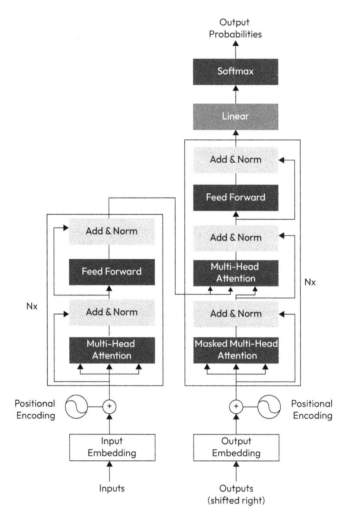

Figure 1.3 – Transformer in model architecture

Another important development in NLP has been the increase in the availability of large amounts of annotated text data, which has allowed for the training of more accurate models. Additionally, the development of unsupervised and semi-supervised learning techniques has allowed for the training of models on smaller amounts of labeled data, making it possible to apply NLP in a wider range of scenarios.

Language models have had a significant impact on the field of NLP. One of the key ways that language models have changed the field is by improving the accuracy and effectiveness of natural language processing tasks. For example, many language models have been trained on large amounts of text data, allowing them to better understand the nuances and complexities of human language. This has led to improved performance in tasks such as language translation, text summarization, and sentiment analysis.

Another way that language models have changed the field of NLP is by enabling the development of more advanced, sophisticated NLP systems. For example, some language models, such as GPT, can generate human-like text, which has opened up new possibilities for natural language generation and dialogue systems. Other language models, such as BERT, have improved the performance of tasks such as question answering, sentiment analysis, and named entity recognition.

Language models have also changed the field by making it more accessible to a broader range of people. With the advent of pre-trained language models, developers can now easily fine-tune these models to specific tasks without the need for large amounts of labeled data or the expertise to train models from scratch. This has made it easier for developers to build NLP applications and has led to an explosion of new NLP-based products and services.

Overall, language models have played a key role in advancing the field of NLP by improving the performance of existing NLP tasks, enabling the development of more advanced NLP systems, and making NLP more accessible to a broader range of people.

Understanding language models – ChatGPT example

ChatGPT, a variant of the GPT model, has become popular because of its ability to generate human-like text, which can be used for a broad range of natural language generation tasks, such as chatbot systems, text summarization, and dialogue systems.

The main reason for its popularity is its high-quality outputs and its ability to generate text that is hard to distinguish from text written by humans. This makes it well-suited for applications that require natural-sounding text, such as chatbot systems, virtual assistants, and text summarization.

Additionally, ChatGPT is pre-trained on a large amount of text data, allowing it to understand human language nuances and complexities. This makes it well-suited for applications that require a deep understanding of language, such as question answering and sentiment analysis.

Moreover, ChatGPT can be fine-tuned for specific use cases by providing it with a small amount of task-specific data, which makes it versatile and adaptable to a wide range of applications. It is widely used in industry, research, and personal projects, ranging from customer service chatbots, virtual assistants, automated content creation, text summarization, dialogue systems, question answering, and sentiment analysis.

Overall, ChatGPT's ability to generate high-quality, human-like text and its ability to be fine-tuned for specific tasks makes it a popular choice for a wide range of natural language generation applications.

Let's move on to summarize the chapter now.

Summary

In this chapter, we introduced you to the field of NLP, which is a subfield of AI. The chapter highlights the importance of mathematical foundations, such as linear algebra, statistics and probability, and optimization theory, which are necessary to understand the algorithms used in NLP. It also covers the challenges faced in NLP, such as understanding the context and meaning of words, the relationships between them, and the need for labeled data. We discussed the recent advancements in NLP, including pre-trained language models, such as BERT and GPT, and the availability of large amounts of text data, which has led to improved performance in NLP tasks. We touched on the importance of text preprocessing as you gains knowledge of the importance of data cleaning, data normalization, stemming, and lemmatization in text preprocessing. We then talked about how the coming together of NLP and ML is driving advancements in the field and is becoming an increasingly important tool for automating tasks and improving human-computer interaction.

After learning from this chapter, you will be able to understand the importance of NLP, ML, and DL techniques. you will be able to understand the recent advancements in NLP, including pre-trained language models. you will also have gained knowledge of the importance of text preprocessing and how it plays a crucial role in data preparation for NLP tasks and in data cleaning.

In the next chapter, we will cover the mathematical foundations of ML. These foundations will serve us throughout the book.

Questions and answers

1. What is natural language processing (NLP)?

    *   Q: What defines NLP in the field of artificial intelligence?

    *   A: NLP is a subfield of AI focused on enabling computers to understand, interpret, and generate human language in a way that is both natural and meaningful to human users.

2. Initial strategies in machine processing of natural language.

    *   Q: What is the importance of preprocessing in NLP?

    *   A: Preprocessing, including tasks such as removing stop words and applying stemming or lemmatization, is crucial for cleaning and preparing text data, thereby improving the performance of machine learning algorithms on NLP tasks.

3. The synergy of NLP and machine learning (ML).

    *   Q: How does machine learning contribute to advancements in NLP?

    *   A: ML, especially techniques such as statistical language modeling and deep learning, drives NLP forward by enabling algorithms to learn from data, predict word sequences, and perform tasks such as language understanding and sentiment analysis more effectively.

4.   Introduction to math and statistics in NLP

- Q: Why are mathematical foundations important in NLP?

- A: Mathematical foundations such as linear algebra, statistics, and probability are essential for understanding and developing the algorithms that underpin NLP techniques, from basic preprocessing to complex model training.

5.   Advancements in NLP – the role of pre-trained language models

- Q: How have pre-trained models such as BERT and GPT influenced NLP?

- A: Pre-trained models, trained on vast amounts of text data, can be fine-tuned for specific tasks such as sentiment analysis or language translation, significantly simplifying the development of NLP applications and enhancing task performance.

6.   Understanding transformers in language models

- Q: Why are transformers considered a breakthrough in NLP?

- A: Transformers process words in parallel and use attention mechanisms to understand word context within sentences, significantly improving a model's ability to handle the complexities of human language.

2

Mastering Linear Algebra, Probability, and Statistics for Machine Learning and NLP

Natural language processing (NLP) and **machine learning** (ML) are two fields that have significantly benefited from mathematical concepts, particularly linear algebra and probability theory. These fundamental tools enable the analysis of the relationships between variables, forming the basis of many NLP and ML models. This chapter provides a comprehensive introduction to linear algebra and probability theory, including their practical applications in NLP and ML. The chapter commences with an overview of vectors and matrices and covers essential operations. Additionally, the basics of statistics, required for understanding the concepts and models in subsequent chapters, will be explained. Finally, the chapter introduces the fundamentals of optimization, which are critical for solving NLP problems and understanding the relationships between variables. By the end of this chapter, you will have a solid foundation in linear algebra and probability theory and understand their essential applications in NLP and ML.

In this chapter, we'll be covering the following topics:

- Introduction to linear algebra
- Eigenvalues and eigenvectors
- Basic probability for machine learning

Introduction to linear algebra

Let's start by first understanding scalars, vectors, and matrices:

- **Scalars**: A scalar is a single numerical value that usually comes from the real domain in most ML applications. Examples of scalars in NLP include the frequency of a word in a text corpus.

- **Vectors**: A vector is a collection of numerical elements. Each of these elements can be termed as an entry, component, or dimension, and the count of these components defines the vector's dimensionality. Within NLP, a vector could hold components related to elements such as word frequency, sentiment ranking, and more. NLP and ML are two domains that have reaped substantial benefits from mathematical disciplines, particularly linear algebra and probability theory. These foundational tools aid in evaluating the correlation between variables and are at the heart of numerous NLP and ML models. This segment presents a detailed primer on linear algebra and probability theory, along with their practical usage in NLP and ML. For instance, a text document's three-dimensional vector representation might be expressed as a real-number array, such as [word frequency, sentiment ranking, complexity].

- **Matrices**: A matrix can be perceived as a rectangular collection of numerical elements composed of rows and columns. To retrieve an element from the matrix, one needs to denote its row and column indices. In the field of NLP, a data matrix might include rows that align with distinct text documents and columns that align with different text attributes, such as word frequency, sentiment, and so on. The dimensions of such a matrix are represented by the notation $n \times d$, where n is the number of rows (i.e., text documents), and d is the number of columns (i.e., attributes).

Let's move on to the basic operations for scalars, vectors, and matrices next.

The basic operations for scalars, vectors, and matrices—addition and subtraction—can be carried out on vectors with the same dimensions. Let's have two vectors:

$$\mathbf{x} = [x_1, x_2, \ldots, x_n]$$

$$\mathbf{y} = [y_1, y_2, \ldots, y_n]$$

$$\mathbf{x} - \mathbf{y} = [x_1 - y_1, x_2 - y_2, \ldots, x_n - y_n]$$

For example, if we have two vectors, a = [4,1] and b = [2,4], then *a + b = [6,5]*.

Let's visualize this as follows:

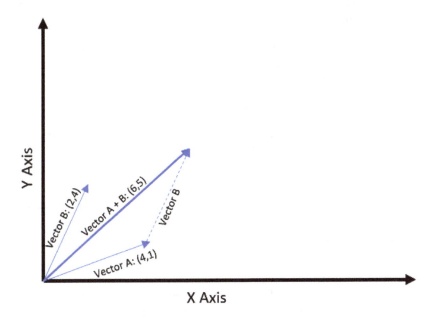

Figure 2.1 – Adding two vectors (a = [4,1] and b = [2,4]) means that a + b = [6,5]

It is possible to scale a vector by multiplying it by a scalar. This operation is performed by multiplying each component of the vector by the scalar value. For example, let's consider a n-dimensional vector, $\mathbf{x} = [x_1, x_2, ..., x_n]$. The process of scaling this vector by a factor of a can be represented mathematically as follows:

$$\mathbf{x} = [x_1, x_2, ..., x_n]$$

$$a \cdot \mathbf{x} = [a x_1, a x_2, ..., a x_n]$$

This operation results in a new vector that has the same dimensionality as the original vector but with each component multiplied by the scalar value a.

There are two types of multiplications between vectors: dot product ($\cdot$) and cross product ($\times$). The dot product is the one we use often in ML algorithms.

The dot product is a mathematical operation that can be applied to two vectors, $\mathbf{x} = [x_1, x_2, ..., x_n]$ and $\mathbf{y} = [y_1, y_2, ...y_n]$. It has many practical applications, one of which is to help determine their similarity. It is defined as the sum of the product of the corresponding elements of the two vectors. The dot product of x and y is represented by the symbol $x \cdot y$ (having a dot in the middle) and is defined as follows:

$$\mathbf{x} \cdot \mathbf{y} = \sum_{i=1}^{n} x_i \cdot y_i$$

where n represents the dimensionality of the vectors. The dot product is a scalar quantity and can be used to measure the angle between two vectors, as well as the projection of one vector onto another. It also serves a vital function in numerous ML algorithms, including linear regression and neural networks.

The dot product is commutative, meaning that the order of the vectors does not affect the result. This means that $x \cdot y = y \cdot x$. Furthermore, the dot product maintains the distributive property of scalar multiplication, implying the following:

$$\mathbf{x} \cdot (\mathbf{y} + \mathbf{z}) = \mathbf{x} \cdot \mathbf{y} + \mathbf{x} \cdot \mathbf{z}$$

The dot product of a vector with itself is also known as its squared norm or Euclidean norm. The norm, symbolized by $norm(x)$, signifies the length of the vector and is computed as

$$norm(\mathbf{x})^2 = \mathbf{x} \cdot \mathbf{x} = \sum_{i=1}^{n} x_i^2$$

The normalization of vectors can be achieved by dividing them by their norm, also known as the Euclidean norm or the length of the vector. This results in a vector with a unit length, denoted by x'. The normalization process can be shown as

$$\mathbf{x}' = \frac{\mathbf{x}}{\|\mathbf{x}\|} = \frac{\mathbf{x}}{\sqrt{\mathbf{x} \cdot \mathbf{x}}}$$

where $\mathbf{x}$ is the original vector and $\|\mathbf{x}\|$ represents its norm. It should be noted that normalizing a vector has the effect of retaining its direction while setting its length to 1, allowing the meaningful comparison of vectors in different spaces.

The cosine similarity between two vectors $x = [x_1, x_2, \ldots, x_n]$ and $y = [y_1, y_2, \ldots, y_n]$ is mathematically represented as the dot product of the two vectors after they have been normalized to unit length. This can be written as follows:

$$Cos(\mathbf{x}, \mathbf{y}) = \frac{(\mathbf{x} \cdot \mathbf{y})}{(\|\mathbf{x}\| \cdot \|\mathbf{y}\|)} = \frac{(\mathbf{x} \cdot \mathbf{y})}{(\sqrt{\mathbf{x} \cdot \mathbf{x}} \cdot \sqrt{\mathbf{y} \cdot \mathbf{y}})}$$

where $\|\mathbf{x}\|$ and $\|\mathbf{y}\|$ are the norms of the vectors x and y, respectively. This computed cosine similarity between x and y is equivalent to the cosine of the angle between the two vectors, denoted as θ.

Vectors with a dot product of 0 are deemed orthogonal, implying that in the case of having both non-0 vectors, the angle between them is 90 degrees. We can conclude that a 0 vector is orthogonal to any vector. A group of vectors is considered orthogonal if each pair of them is orthogonal and each vector possesses a norm of 1. Such orthonormal sets prove to be valuable in numerous mathematical contexts. For instance, they come into play when transforming between different orthogonal co-ordinate systems, where the new co-ordinates of a point are computed in relation to the modified direction set. This approach, known as co-ordinate transformation in the field of analytical geometry, finds widespread application in the realm of linear algebra.

Basic operations on matrices and vectors

Matrix transpose is the process of obtaining the transpose of a matrix and involves interchanging its rows and columns. This means that the element originally at the (i, j)th position in the matrix now occupies the (j, i)th position in its transpose. As a result, a matrix that was originally of size $n \times m$

becomes an $m \times n$ matrix when transposed. The notation used to represent the transpose of matrix X is $\mathbf{X}^T$. Here's an illustrative example of a matrix transposition operation:

$$\mathbf{X} = \begin{bmatrix} x_{1,1} & x_{1,2} \\ x_{2,1} & x_{2,2} \\ x_{3,1} & x_{3,2} \end{bmatrix}$$

$$\mathbf{X}^T = \begin{bmatrix} x_{1,1} & x_{2,1} & x_{3,1} \\ x_{1,2} & x_{2,2} & x_{3,2} \end{bmatrix}$$

Crucially, the transpose $(\mathbf{X}^T)^T$ of matrix $\mathbf{X}^T$ reverts to the original matrix X. Moreover, it is clear that row vectors can be transposed into column vectors and vice versa. Additionally, the following holds true for both matrices and vectors:

$$(\mathbf{X} + \mathbf{Y})^T = \mathbf{X}^T + \mathbf{Y}^T$$

It's also noteworthy that dot products are commutative for matrices and vectors:

$$\mathbf{X}^T \cdot \mathbf{Y} = \mathbf{Y}^T \cdot \mathbf{X}$$

$$\mathbf{x}^T \cdot \mathbf{y} = \mathbf{y}^T \cdot \mathbf{x}$$

Matrix definitions

In this section, we'll cover the different type of matrix definitions:

- **Symmetric matrix**: A symmetric matrix is a type of square matrix where the transpose of the matrix is equal to the original matrix. In mathematical terms, if a matrix X is symmetric, then $\mathbf{X} = \mathbf{X}^T$. For example,

$$\mathbf{X} = \begin{bmatrix} 1 & 2 & 3 \\ 2 & 4 & 5 \\ 3 & 5 & 7 \end{bmatrix}$$

  is symmetric.

- **Rectangular diagonal matrix**: This is a matrix that is $m \times n$ in dimensions, with non-0 values only on the main diagonal.

- **Upper (or Lower) triangular matrix**: A matrix is called an upper (triangular) matrix if all the entries (i,j) below (above) its main diagonal are 0. Next, we are going to describe matrix operations.

Determinants

The determinant of a square matrix provides a notion of its impact on the volume of a d-dimensional object when multiplied by its co-ordinate vectors. The determinant, symbolized as $det(A)$, represents the (signed) volume of the parallelepiped formed by the row or column vectors of the matrix. This interpretation holds consistently, as the volume determined by the row and column vectors is mathematically identical. When a diagonalizable matrix A interacts with a group of co-ordinate vectors, the ensuing distortion is termed anisotropic scaling. The determinant can aid in establishing the scale factors of this conversion. The determinant of a square matrix carries crucial insights about the linear alteration accomplished by the multiplication with the matrix. Particularly, the sign of the determinant mirrors the impact of the transformation on the basis of the system's orientation.

Calculating determinant is given as follows:

1. For a 1×1 matrix A, its determinant is equivalent to the single scalar present within it.

2. For larger matrices, the determinant can be calculated by securing a column, j, and then broadening using the elements within that column. As another option, it's possible to fix a row, i, and expand along that particular row. Regardless of whether you opt to fix a row or column, the end result, which is the determinant of the matrix, will remain consistent.

    with j as a fixed value ranging from 1 to d,

    $$\det(\mathbf{A}) = \sum_{i=1}^{d} (-1)^{(i+j)} a_{ij} \det\left(\mathbf{A}_{ij}\right)$$

    Or, with the fixed i,

    $$\det(\mathbf{A}) = \sum_{j=1}^{d} (-1)^{(i+j)} a_{ij} \det\left(\mathbf{A}_{ij}\right)$$

Based on the following equations, we can see that some of the cases can be easily calculated:

-   **Diagonal matrix:** For a diagonal matrix, the determinant is the product of its diagonal elements.

-   **Triangular matrix:** In the context of a triangular matrix, the determinant is found by multiplying all its diagonal elements. If all components of a matrix's row or column are 0, the determinant is also 0.

    For a 2×2 matrix of

    $$\mathbf{A} = \begin{bmatrix} a & b \\ c & d \end{bmatrix}$$

    Its determinant can be computed as $ad - bc$. If we consider a 3×3 matrix,

    $$\mathbf{A} = \begin{bmatrix} a & b & c \\ d & e & f \\ g & h & i \end{bmatrix}$$

    The determinant is calculated as follows:

    $$\det(a) = a \cdot \det[e\,f, h\,i] - d \cdot \det[b\,c, h\,i] + g \cdot \det[b\,c, e\,f]$$

    $$= a(ei - hf) - d(bi - hc) + g(bf - ec)$$

    $$= aei - ahf - dbi + dhc + gbf - gec$$

Let's now move on to eigenvalues and vectors.

Eigenvalues and eigenvectors

A vector x, belonging to a $d \times d$ matrix A, is an **eigenvector** if it satisfies the equation $Ax = \lambda x$, where λ represents the eigenvalue associated with the matrix. This relationship delineates the link between matrix A and its corresponding eigenvector x, which can be perceived as the "stretching direction" of the matrix. In the case where A is a matrix that can be diagonalized, it can be deconstructed into a $d \times d$ invertible matrix, V, and a diagonal $d \times d$ matrix, Δ, such that

$$\mathbf{A} = \mathbf{V} \, \Delta \, \mathbf{V}^{-1}$$

The columns of V encompass d eigenvectors, while the diagonal entries of Δ house the corresponding eigenvalues. The linear transformation Ax can be visually understood through a sequence of three operations. Initially, the multiplication of x by $\mathbf{V}-1$ calculates x's co-ordinates in a non-orthogonal basis associated with V's columns. Subsequently, the multiplication of $\mathbf{V}-1$ x by Δ scales these co-ordinates using the factors in Δ, aligned with the eigenvectors' directions. Finally, the multiplication with V restores the co-ordinates to the original basis, resulting in an anisotropic scaling along the d eigenvector directions.

Diagonalizable matrices signify transformations involving anisotropic scaling along d-linearly independent directions. When V's columns are orthonormal vectors, $\mathbf{V}-1$ equals its transpose, $\mathbf{V}\,T$, indicating scaling along mutually orthogonal directions. In such cases, matrix A is always diagonalizable and exhibits symmetry when V's columns are orthonormal vectors, as affirmed by the following relationship.

$$\mathbf{A}^T = \mathbf{V} \, \Delta^T \mathbf{V}^T = \mathbf{V} \, \Delta \, \mathbf{V}^T = \mathbf{A}$$

Numerical methods for finding eigenvectors

The conventional method to ascertain the eigenvectors of a $d \times d$ matrix A involves locating the d roots, $\lambda_1, \ldots, \lambda_d$ of the equation:

$$det(\mathbf{A} - \lambda \mathbf{I}) = 0$$

Some of these roots might be repeated. The subsequent step involves solving linear systems in the form $(\mathbf{A} - \lambda \mathbf{I})\mathbf{x} = 0$, typically achieved using the Gaussian elimination method. However, this method might not always be the most stable or precise, as solvers of polynomial equations can exhibit ill-conditioning and numerical instability in practical applications. Indeed, a prevalent technique for resolving high-degree polynomial equations in engineering involves constructing a companion matrix possessing the same characteristic polynomial as the original polynomial and then determining its eigenvalues.

Eigenvalue decomposition

Eigenvalue decomposition, also known as the eigen-decomposition or the diagonalization of a matrix, is a powerful mathematical tool used in linear algebra and computational mathematics. The goal of eigenvalue decomposition is to decompose a given matrix into a product of matrices that represent the eigenvectors and eigenvalues of the matrix.

The eigenvalue decomposition of matrix A is a factorization of the matrix into the product of two matrices: the matrix V and the matrix D.

V has column which are the eigenvectors of matrix A, and D is a diagonal matrix that contains the corresponding eigenvalues on its diagnol.

The eigenvalue problem is to find the non-0 vectors, v, and the scalars, λ, such that $Av = \lambda v$, where A is a square matrix, and thus v is an eigenvector of A. The scalar λ is called the eigenvalue of matrix A. The eigenvalue problem can be written in matrix form as $Av = \lambda I v$, where I is the identity matrix.

The process of determining eigenvalues is intimately linked to the characteristic equation of matrix A, which is the polynomial equation derived from $det(\mathbf{A} - \lambda \mathbf{I}) = 0$. The characteristic equation can be solved for the eigenvalues, λ, which are the roots of the equation. Once the eigenvalues are found, the eigenvectors can be found by solving the system of linear equations $(\mathbf{A} - \lambda \mathbf{I})\mathbf{v} = 0$.

One important property of eigenvalue decomposition is that it allows us to diagonalize a matrix, which means that we can transform the matrix into a diagonal form by using an appropriate eigenvectors matrix. The diagonal form of a matrix is useful because it allows us to calculate the trace and determinant of the matrix easily.

Another important property of eigenvalue decomposition is that it provides insight into the structure of the matrix. For example, the eigenvalues of a symmetric matrix are always real, and the eigenvectors are orthogonal, which means that they are perpendicular to each other. In the case of non-symmetric matrices, the eigenvalues can be complex, and the eigenvectors are not necessarily orthogonal.

The eigenvalue decomposition of a matrix has many applications in mathematics, physics, engineering, and computer science. In numerical analysis, eigenvalue decomposition is used to find the solution of linear systems, compute the eigenvalues of a matrix, and find the eigenvectors of a matrix. In physics, eigenvalue decomposition is used to analyze the stability of systems, such as the stability of an equilibrium point in a differential equation. In engineering, eigenvalue decomposition is used to study the dynamics of systems, such as the vibrations of a mechanical system.

Within the field of computer science, eigenvalue decomposition finds versatile applications across various domains, including machine learning and data analysis. In machine learning, eigenvalue decomposition plays a pivotal role in enabling **principal component analysis** (**PCA**), a technique employed for dimensionality reduction in extensive datasets. In the realm of data analysis, eigenvalue decomposition is harnessed to calculate the **singular value decomposition** (**SVD**), a potent tool for dissecting and understanding complex datasets.

Singular value decomposition

The problem of minimizing $\mathbf{x}^T \mathbf{A} \mathbf{x}$, where x is a column vector that has a unit norm, and A is a symmetric $d \times d$ data matrix, is a typical problem encountered in numerous machine learning contexts. This problem type is often found in applications such as principal component analysis, singular value decomposition, and spectral clustering, all of which involve feature engineering and dimensionality reduction. The optimization problem can be articulated as follows:

Minimize

$$\mathbf{x}^T \mathbf{A} \mathbf{x}$$

Subject to

$$||\mathbf{x}||^2 = 1$$

We can solve the optimization problem as a maximization or minimization form. Imposing the constraint that vector x must be a unit vector significantly changes the nature of the optimization problem. In contrast to the prior section, the positive semi-definiteness of matrix A is no longer crucial for determining the solution. Even when A is indefinite, the constraint on the norm of vector x ensures a well-defined solution, preventing the involvement of vectors with unbounded magnitudes or trivial solutions, such as the 0 vector. **Value singular decomposition** (SVD) is a mathematical technique that takes a rectangular matrix, A, and decomposes it into three matrices: U, S, and $\mathbf{V}^T$. Matrix A is defined as an $n \times p$ matrix. The theorem of SVD states that A can be represented as the product of three matrices: $\mathbf{U}_{nxn} \mathbf{S}_{nxp} \mathbf{V}_{pxp}$, where $\mathbf{U}^T\mathbf{U} = \mathbf{I}_{nxn}$, and $\mathbf{V}^T\mathbf{V} = \mathbf{I}_{pxp}$, and U and V are orthogonal matrices.

The U matrix's columns are known as the left singular vectors, while the rows of the transpose of the V matrix $\mathbf{V}\ T$ are the right singular vectors. The S matrix, with singular values, is a diagonal matrix of the same size as A. SVD decomposes the original data into a co-ordinate system where the defining vectors are orthonormal (both orthogonal and normal). SVD computation involves identifying the eigenvalues and eigenvectors of matrices $\mathbf{A}\mathbf{A}^T$ and $\mathbf{A}^T\mathbf{A}$. Matrix V's columns consist of eigenvectors from $\mathbf{A}^T\mathbf{A}$, and matrix U's columns consist of eigenvectors from $\mathbf{A}\mathbf{A}^T$. Singular values in the S matrix are derived from the square roots of eigenvalues from either $\mathbf{A}\mathbf{A}^T$ or $\mathbf{A}^T\mathbf{A}$, organized in decreasing order. These singular values are real numbers. If A is a real matrix, U and V will also be real.

To illustrate the calculation of SVD, an example is provided. Consider a 4×2 matrix. The eigenvalues of the matrix can be found by computing $\mathbf{A}\mathbf{A}^T$ and $\mathbf{A}^T\mathbf{A}$ and then determining the eigenvectors of these matrices. U's columns are formed by the eigenvectors of $\mathbf{A}\mathbf{A}^T$, and V's columns are formed by the eigenvectors of $\mathbf{A}^T\mathbf{A}$. The S matrix comprises the square root of eigenvalues from either $\mathbf{A}\mathbf{A}^T$ or $\mathbf{A}^T\mathbf{A}$. Eigenvalues are found by solving the characteristic equation in the given example $|\mathbf{W} - \lambda\mathbf{I}| = 0$, where W is the matrix, I is the unit matrix, and λ is the eigenvalue. The eigenvectors are then found by solving the set of equations derived from the eigenvalue equations. The final matrices U, S, and $\mathbf{V}^T$ are then obtained by combining the eigenvectors and singular values.

It should be noted that the singular values are in descending order, with $\lambda_1 > \lambda_2 > \dots$

Let's now move on to basic probability for machine learning.

Basic probability for machine learning

Probability provides information about the likelihood of an event occurring. In this field, there are several key terms that are important to understand:

- **Trial or experiment**: An action that results in a certain outcome with a certain likelihood
- **Sample space**: This encompasses all potential outcomes of a given experiment
- **Event**: This denotes a non-empty portion of the sample space

Therefore, in technical terms, probability is a measure of the likelihood of an event occurring when an experiment is conducted.

In this very simple case, the probability of event A with one outcome is equal to the chance of event A divided by the chance of all possible events. For example, in flipping a fair coin, there are two outcomes with the same chance: heads and tails. The chance of having heads will be $1/(1+1) = \frac{1}{2}$.

In order to calculate the probability, given an event, A, with n outcomes and a sample space, S, the probability of event A is calculated as

$$P(A) = \sum_{i=1}^{n} P(E_i)$$

where $E1, \ldots, En$ represents the outcomes in A. Assuming all results of the experiment have equal probability, and the selection of one does not influence the selection of others in subsequent rounds (meaning they are statistically independent), then

$$P(A) = \frac{No.\ of\ outcomes\ in\ A}{No.\ of\ outcomes\ in\ S}$$

Hence, the value of probability ranges from 0 to 1, with the sample space embodying the complete set of potential outcomes, denoted as $P(S) = 1$.

Statistically independent

In the realm of statistics, two events are defined as independent if the occurrence of one event doesn't influence the likelihood of the other event's occurrence. To put it formally, events A and B are independent precisely when $P(A\ and\ B) = P(A)P(B)$, where $P(A)$ and $P(B)$ are the respective probabilities of events A and B happening.

Consider this example to clarify the concept of statistical independence: imagine we possess two coins, one fair (an equal chance of turning up heads or tails) and the other biased (showing a head is more likely than a tail). If we flip the fair coin and the biased coin, these two events are statistically independent because the outcome of one coin flip doesn't alter the probability of the other coin turning up heads or tails. Specifically, the likelihood of both coins showing heads is the product of the individual probabilities: $(1/2) * (3/4) = 3/8$.

Statistical independence is a pivotal concept in statistics and probability theory, frequently leveraged in machine learning to outline the connections between variables within a dataset. By comprehending these relationships, machine learning algorithms can better spot patterns and deliver more precise predictions. We will describe the relationship between different types of events in the following:

- **Complementary event**: The complementary event to A, signified as A', encompasses the probability of all potential outcomes in the sample space not included in A. It's critical to understand that A and A' are statistically independent:

$$P(A') = 1 - P(A)$$

- **Union and intersection**: The complementary event to A, signified as A', encompasses the probability of all potential outcomes in the sample space not included in A. It's critical to understand that A and A' are statistically independent.

- **Mutually exclusive**: When two events have no shared outcomes, they are viewed as mutually exclusive. In other words, if A and B are mutually exclusive events, then $P(A \cap B) = 0$. This conclusion can be drawn from the addition rule of probability, as A and B are disjointed events:

$$P(A \cup B) = P(A) + P(B)$$

- **Independent**: Two events are deemed independent when the occurrence of one doesn't impact the occurrence of the other. If A and B are two independent events, then

$$P(A \cap B) = P(A) \cdot P(B)$$

Next, we are going to describe the discrete random variable, its distribution, and how to use it to calculate the probabilities.

Discrete random variables and their distribution

A discrete random variable refers to a variable that can assume a finite or countably infinite number of potential outcomes. Examples of such variables might be the count of heads resulting from a coin toss, the tally of cars crossing a toll booth within a specific time span, or the number of blonde-haired students in a classroom.

The probability distribution of a discrete random variable assigns a certain likelihood to each potential outcome the variable could adopt. For instance, in the case of a coin toss, the probability distribution assigns a 0.5 probability to both *0* and *1*, representing tails and heads, respectively. For the car toll booth scenario, the distribution could be assigning a probability of *0.1* to no cars passing, *0.3* to one car, *0.4* to two cars, *0.15* to three cars, and *0.05* to four or more cars.

A graphical representation of the probability distribution of a discrete random variable can be achieved through a **probability mass function (PMF)**, which correlates each possible outcome of the variable to its likelihood of occurrence. This function is usually represented as a bar chart or histogram, with each bar signifying the probability of a specific value.

The PMF is bound by two key principles:

- It must be non-negative across all potential values of the random variable

- The total sum of probabilities for all possible outcomes should equate to 1

The expected value of a discrete random variable offers an insight into its central tendency, computed as the probability-weighted average of its possible outcomes. This expected value is signified as *E[X]*, with X representing the random variable.

Probability density function

The **probability density function** (PDF) is a tool used to describe the distribution of a continuous random variable. It can be used to calculate the probability of a value falling within a specific range. In simpler terms, it helps determine the chances of a continuous variable, X, having a value within the interval $[a, b]$, or in statistical terms,

$$P (A < X < B)$$

For continuous variables, the probability of a single value occurring is always 0, which is in contrast to discrete variables that can assign non-0 probabilities to distinct values. PDFs provide a way to estimate the likelihood of a value falling within a given range instead of a single value.

For example, you can use a PDF to find the chances of the next IQ score measured falling between *100* and *120*.

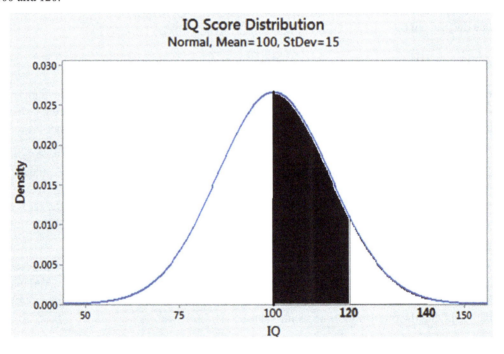

Figure 2.2 – Probability density function for IQ from 100–120

To ascertain the distribution of a discrete random variable, one can either provide its PMF or **cumulative distribution function** (**CDF**). For continuous random variables, we primarily utilize the CDF, as it is well established. However, the PMF is not suitable for these types of variables because *P(X=x)* equals *0* for all x in the set of real numbers, given that X can assume any real value between a and b. Therefore, we typically define the PDF instead. The PDF resembles the concept of mass density in physics, signifying the concentration of probability. Its unit is the probability per unit length. To get a grasp of the PDF, let's analyze a continuous random variable, X, and establish the function $fX(x)$ as follows:

$$f_X(x) = \lim_{\Delta \to 0^+} \frac{P(x < X \le (x + \Delta))}{\Delta}$$

If the limit exists.

The function $f_X(x)$ provides the probability density at a given point, x. This is equivalent to the limit of the ratio of the probability of the interval $(x, x + \Delta]$ to the length of the interval as that length approaches 0.

Let's contemplate a continuous random variable, X, possessing an absolutely continuous CDF, denoted as $F_X(x)$. If $F_X(x)$ is differentiable at x, the function $f_X(x)$ is referred to as the PDF of X:

$$f_X(x) = \lim_{\Delta \to 0^+} \frac{F_X(x + \Delta) - F_X(x)}{\Delta} = \frac{dF_X(x)}{dx} = F'_X(x)$$

Assuming $F_X(x)$ is differentiable at x.

For example, let's consider a continuous uniform random variable, X, with uniform $U(a, b)$ distribution. Its CDF is given by:

$$f_X(x) = \frac{1}{b-a} \; if \, a < x < b$$

which is 0 for any x outside the bounds.

By using integration, the CDF can be obtained from the PDF:

$$F_X(x) = \int_{-\infty}^{x} f_X(u) du$$

Additionally, we have

$$P(a < X \le b) = F_X(b) - F_X(a) = \int_{a}^{b} f_X(u) du$$

So, if we integrate over the entire real line, we will get 1:

$$\int_{-\infty}^{\infty} f_X(u) du = 1$$

Explicitly, when integrating the PDF across the entire real number line, the result should equal 1. This signifies that the area beneath the PDF curve must equate to 1, or $P(S) = 1$, which remains true for the uniform distribution. The PDF signifies the density of probability; thus, it must be non-negative and can exceed 1.

Consider a continuous random variable, X, with PDF represented as $fX(x)$. The ensuing properties are applicable:

$$f_X(x) \ge 0, \text{ for all real x}$$
$$\int_{-\infty}^{\infty} f_X(u) du = 1$$

Next, we'll move on to cover maximum likelihood.

Maximum likelihood estimation

Maximum likelihood is a statistical approach, that is used to estimate the parameters of a probability distribution. The objective is to identify the parameter values that maximize the likelihood of observing the data, essentially determining the parameters most likely to have generated the data.

Suppose we have a random sample, $X = \{X_1, \ldots, X_n\}$, from a population with a probability distribution $f(x|\theta)$, where θ is a vector of parameters. The likelihood of observing the sample, X, given the parameters, θ, is defined as the product of the individual probabilities of observing each data point:

$$L(\theta \mid X) = f(X \mid \theta)$$

In case of having independent and identically distributed observations, the likelihood function can be expressed as the product of the univariate density functions, each evaluated at the corresponding observation:

$$L(\theta|X) = f(X_1|\theta)f(X_2|\theta)\ldots f(X_n|\theta)$$

The **maximum likelihood estimate** (**MLE**) is the parameter vector value that offers the maximum value for the likelihood function across the parameter space.

In many cases, it's more convenient to employ the natural logarithm of the likelihood function, referred to as the **log-likelihood**. The peak of the log-likelihood happens at the identical parameter vector value as the likelihood function's maximum, and the conditions required for a maximum (or minimum) are acquired by equating the log-likelihood derivatives with respect to each parameter to 0. If the log-likelihood is differentiable with respect to the parameters, these conditions result in a set of equations that can be solved numerically to derive the MLE. One common use case or scenario where MLE significantly impacts ML model performance is in linear regression. When building a linear regression model, MLE is often used to estimate the coefficients that define the relationship between input features and the target variable. MLE helps find the values for the coefficients that maximize the likelihood of observing the given data under the assumed linear regression model, improving the accuracy of the predictions.

The MLEs of the parameters, θ, are the values that maximize the likelihood function. In other words, the MLEs are the values of θ that make the observed data, X, most probable.

To find the MLEs, we typically take the natural logarithm of the likelihood function, as it is often easier to work with the logarithm of a product than with the product itself:

$$\ln L(\theta|X) = \ln f(X_1|\theta) + \ln f(X_2|\theta) + \ldots + \ln f(X_n|\theta)$$

The MLEs are determined by equating the partial derivatives of the log-likelihood function with respect to each parameter to *0* and then solving these equations for the parameters:

$$\partial \ln L(\theta|X)/\partial \theta_1 = 0$$

$$\partial \ln L(\theta|X)/\partial \theta_2 = 0$$

$$\ldots$$

$$\partial \ln L(\theta|X)/\partial \theta_k = 0$$

where *k* is the number of parameters in *θ*. The goal of a maximum likelihood estimator is to find *θ* such that

$$\theta(x) = \underset{\theta}{argmax} L(\theta|x)$$

Once the MLEs have been found, they can be used to make predictions about the population based on the sample data. Maximum likelihood is widely used in many fields, including psychology, economics, engineering, and biology. It serves as a potent tool for comprehending the connections among variables and for predicting outcomes based on observed data. For example, building a word predictor using maximum likelihood estimation.

Next, we introduce the problem of word autocompletion, also known as **word prediction**, which is a feature in where an application predicts the next word a user is typing. The aim of word prediction is to save time and make typing easier by predicting what the user is likely to type next based on their previous inputs and other contextual factors. Word prediction can be found in various forms in many applications, including search engines, text editors, and mobile device keyboards, and is designed to save time and increase the accuracy of inputs.

Given a group of words that the user typed, how would we suggest the next word?

If the words were **The United States of**, then it would be trivial to assume that the next word would be **America**. However, what about finding the next word for **How are**? One could suggest several next words.

There usually isn't just one clear next word. Thus, we'd want to suggest the most likely word or perhaps even the most likely words. In that case, we would be interested in suggesting a probabilistic representation of the possible next words and picking the next word as the one that is most probable.

The maximum likelihood estimator provides us with that precise capability. It can tell us which word is most probable given the previous words that the user typed.

In order to calculate the MLE, we need to calculate the probability function of all word combinations. We can do that by processing large texts and counting how many times each combination of words exists.

Consider reviewing a large cohort of text that has the following occurrences:

	"you"	"they"	"those"	"the"	Any other word
"how are …"	16	14	0	100	10
not "how are…"	200	100	300	1,000	30,000

Table 2.1 – Sample of n-grams occurrences in a document

For instance, there are 16 occurrences in the text where the sequence "how are you" appears. There are 140 sequences that have a length of three that start with the words "how are." That is calculated as:

16 + 14 + 0 + 100 + 10 = 140

There are 216 sequences that have a length of three and that end with the word "you". That is calculated as:

16 + 200 = 216

Now, let's suggest a formula for the most likely next word.

Based on the common maximum likelihood estimation for the probablistic variable W_3, the formula would be to find a value for W_3 which maximizes:

$$P(W_3 | W_1, W_2)$$

However, this common formula has a few characteristics that wouldn't be advantagous to our application.

Consider the next formula which has specific advantages that are necessary for our use case. It is the maximum likelihood formula for parametric estimation, meaning, estimating deterministic parameters. It suggests finding a value for W_3 which maximizes:

$$P(W_1, W_2 | W_3)$$

W_3 is by no means a deterministic parameter, however, this formula suits our use case as it reduces common word bias emphasizing contextual fit, and adjusts for word specificity, thus enhancing the relevance of our predictions. We will elaborate more on these traits in the conclusion of this exercise.

Let's enhance this formula so to make it easier to calculate:

$$P(W_1, W_2 | W_3) = \frac{P(W_1, W_2, W_3)}{P(W_3)}$$

In our case, W_1 is "how" and W_2 is "are."

There are five candidates for the next word; let's calculate the probability for each of them:

- P("how", "are" | "you") = 16 / (200 + 16) = 16/216 = 2/27
- P("how", "are" | "they") = 14 / (100 +14) = 14/114 = 7/57

- P("how", "are" | "those") = 0 / 300 = 0

- P("how", "are" | "the") = 100 / (1000 + 100) = 100/1100 = 1/11

- P("how", "are" | any other word) = 10 / (30,000 + 10) = 10/30010 = 1/3001

Out of all the options, the highest value of probability is 7/57 and it is achieved when "they" is the next word.

Note that the intuition behind this maximum likelihood estimator is having the suggested next word make the words that the user typed most likely. One could wonder, why not take the word that is most probable given the first two words, meaning, the orginal maximum likelihood formula for probabilistic variables? From the table, we see that given the words "how are," the most frequent third word is "the," with a probability of 100/140. However, this approach wouldn't take into account the fact that the word "the" is extremely prevalent altogether, as it is most frequently used in the text in general. Thus, its high frequency isn't due to its relationship to the first two words; it is because it is simply a very common word in general. The maximum likelyhood formula we chose takes that into account.

Bayesian estimation

Bayesian estimation is a statistical approach that involves updating our beliefs or probabilities about a quantity of interest based on new data. The term "Bayesian" refers to Thomas Bayes, an 18th-century statistician who first developed the concept of Bayesian probability.

In Bayesian estimation, we start with prior beliefs about the quantity of interest, which are expressed as a probability distribution. These prior beliefs are updated as we collect new data. The updated beliefs are represented as a posterior distribution. The Bayesian framework provides a systematic way of updating prior beliefs with new data, taking into account the degree of uncertainty in both the prior beliefs and the new data.

The posterior distribution is calculated using Bayes' theorem, which is the fundamental equation of Bayesian estimation. Bayes' theorem states that

$$P(\Theta|X) = \frac{P(X|\Theta)P(\Theta)}{P(X)}$$

where Θ is the quantity of interest, X is the new data, $P(\Theta|X)$ is the posterior distribution, $P(X|\Theta)$ is the likelihood of the data given the parameter value, $P(\Theta)$ is the prior distribution, and $P(X)$ is the marginal likelihood or evidence.

The marginal likelihood is calculated as follows:

$$P(X) = \int P(X|\Theta) \cdot P(\Theta)d\Theta$$

where the integral is taken over the entire space of Θ. The marginal likelihood is often used as a normalizing constant, ensuring that the posterior distribution integrates to 1.

In Bayesian estimation, the choice of prior distribution is important, as it reflects our beliefs about the quantity of interest before collecting any data. The prior distribution can be chosen based on prior knowledge or previous studies. If no prior knowledge is available, a non-informative prior can be used, such as a uniform distribution.

Once the posterior distribution is calculated, it can be used to make predictions about the quantity of interest. As an example, the posterior distribution's mean can serve as a point estimate, whereas the posterior distribution itself can be employed to establish credible intervals. These intervals represent the probable range within which the true value of the target quantity resides.

Summary

This chapter was about linear algebra and probability for ML, and it covers the fundamental mathematical concepts that are essential to understanding many machine learning algorithms. The chapter began with a review of linear algebra, covering topics such as matrix multiplication, determinants, eigenvectors, and eigenvalues. It then moved on to discuss probability theory, introducing the basic concepts of random variables and probability distributions. We also covered key concepts in statistical inference, such as maximum likelihood estimation and Bayesian inference.

In the next chapter, we will cover the fundamentals of machine learning for NLP, including topics such as data exploration, feature engineering, selection methods, and model training and validation.

Further reading

Please find the additional reading content as follows:

- **Householder reflection matrix**: A Householder reflection matrix, or Householder matrix, is a type of linear transformation utilized in numerical linear algebra due to its computational effectiveness and numerical stability. This matrix is used to perform reflections of a given vector about a plane or hyperplane, transforming the vector so that it only has non-0 components in one specific dimension. The **Householder matrix (H)** is defined by

$$\mathbf{H} = \mathbf{I} - 2\,\mathbf{u}\,\mathbf{u}^{T}$$

Here, I is the identity matrix, and u is a unit vector defining the reflection plane.

The main purpose of Householder transformations is to perform QR factorization and to reduce matrices to a tridiagonal or Hessenberg form. The properties of being symmetric and orthogonal make the Householder matrix computationally efficient and numerically stable.

- **Diagonalizable**: A matrix is said to be diagonalizable if it can be written in the form **D** = **P**⁻¹**AP**, where A is the original matrix, D is a diagonal matrix, and P is a matrix for which the columns are the eigenvectors of A. Diagonalization simplifies many calculations in linear algebra, as computations with diagonal matrices are often more straightforward. For a matrix to be diagonalizable, it must have enough distinct eigenvectors to form a basis for its space, which is usually the case when all of its eigenvalues are distinct.

- **Invertible**: An invertible matrix, also known as a non-singular matrix or a non-degenerate matrix, is a square matrix that has an inverse. If a matrix, A, is invertible, there exists another matrix, often denoted as $\mathbf{A}^{-1}$, such that when they are multiplied together, they yield the identity matrix. In other words, $\mathbf{A}\mathbf{A}^{-1} = \mathbf{A}^{-1}\mathbf{A} = \mathbf{I}$, where I is the identity matrix. The identity matrix is a special square matrix with *1*s on its main diagonal and *0*s everywhere else. The existence of an inverse heavily depends on the determinant of the matrix—a matrix is invertible if and only if its determinant is not 0. Invertible matrices are crucial in numerous areas of math, including solving systems of linear equations, matrix factorization, and many applications in engineering and physics.

- **Gaussian elimination method**: Gaussian elimination is a fundamental algorithm in linear algebra for solving systems of linear equations. It accomplishes this by transforming the system to an equivalent one in which the equations are simpler to solve. This method uses a sequence of operations to modify the system of equations, with the objective of creating a row-echelon or reduced row-echelon form. Here's a simplified step-by-step process of Gaussian elimination: First, swap the rows to move any rows with a leading coefficient (the first non-*0* number from the left, also called the pivot) so as to have *1* at the top. Then, multiply or divide any rows by a scalar to create a leading coefficient of *1* if not already present. Finally, add or subtract rows to create *0*s below and above the pivot. Once the matrix is in row-echelon form (all *0* rows are at the bottom, and each leading coefficient is to the right of the leading coefficient of the row above it), we can use back substitution to find the variables. If we further simplify the matrix to a reduced row-echelon form (each leading coefficient is the only non-*0* entry in its column), the solutions can be read directly from the matrix. Gaussian elimination can also be used to find the rank of a matrix, calculate the determinant, and carry out matrix inversion if the system is square and has a unique solution.

- **Trace**: The trace of a square matrix is the sum of its diagonal elements. It's denoted as *Tr(A)* or *trace(A)*, where A is a square matrix. For example, if

$$\mathbf{A} = \begin{bmatrix} a & b \\ c & d \end{bmatrix}$$
$$Tr(A) = a + d.$$

References

- Alter O, Brown PO, Botstein D. (2000) *Singular value decomposition for genome-wide expression data processing and modeling.* Proc Natl Acad Sci U S A, 97, 10101-6.

- Golub, G.H., and Van Loan, C.F. (1989) *Matrix Computations*, 2nd ed. (Baltimore: Johns Hopkins University Press).

- Greenberg, M. (2001) *Differential equations & Linear algebra* (Upper Saddle River, N.J. : Prentice Hall).

- Strang, G. (1998) *Introduction to linear algebra* (Wellesley, MA : Wellesley-Cambridge Press).

- Lax, Peter D. *Linear algebra and its applications.* Vol. 78. John Wiley & Sons, 2007.

- Dangeti, Pratap. *Statistics for machine learning.* Packt Publishing Ltd, 2017.

- DasGupta, Anirban. *Probability for statistics and machine learning: fundamentals and advanced topics.* New York: Springer, 2011.

3
Unleashing Machine Learning Potentials in Natural Language Processing

In this chapter, we will delve into the fundamentals of **Machine Learning** (**ML**) and preprocessing techniques that are essential for **natural language processing** (**NLP**) tasks. ML is a powerful tool for building models that can learn from data, and NLP is one of the most exciting and challenging applications of ML.

By the end of this chapter, you will have gained a comprehensive understanding of data exploration, preprocessing, and data split, know how to deal with imbalanced data techniques, and learned about some of the common ML models required for successful ML, particularly in the context of NLP.

The following topics will be covered in this chapter:

- Data exploration
- Common ML models
- Model underfitting and overfitting
- Splitting data
- Hyperparameter tuning
- Ensemble models
- Handling imbalanced data
- Dealing with correlated data

Technical requirements

Prior knowledge of programming languages, particularly Python, is assumed in this chapter and subsequent chapters of this book. It is also expected that you have already gone through previous chapters to become acquainted with the necessary linear algebra and statistics concepts that will be discussed in detail.

Data exploration

When working in a methodological environment, datasets are often well known and preprocessed, such as Kaggle datasets. However, in real-world business environments, one important task is to define the dataset from all possible sources of data, explore the gathered data to find the best method for preprocessing it, and ultimately decide on the ML and natural language models that fit the problem and the underlying data best. This process requires careful consideration and analysis of the data, as well as a thorough understanding of the business problem at hand.

In NLP, the data can be quite complex, as it often includes text and speech data that can be unstructured and difficult to analyze. This complexity makes preprocessing an essential step in preparing the data for ML models. The first step of any NLP or ML solution starts with exploring the data to learn more about it, which helps us decide on our path to tackle the problem.

Once the data has been preprocessed, the next step is to explore it to gain a better understanding of its characteristics and structure. Data exploration is an iterative process that involves visualizing and analyzing the data, looking for patterns and relationships, and identifying potential issues or outliers. This process can help us to determine which features are most important for our ML models and identify any potential biases or data quality issues. To streamline data and enhance analysis through ML models, preprocessing methods such as tokenization, stemming, and lemmatization can be employed. In this chapter, we will provide an overview of general preprocessing techniques for ML problems. In the following chapter, we will delve into preprocessing techniques specific to text processing. It is important to note that employing effective preprocessing techniques can significantly enhance the performance and accuracy of ML models, making them more robust and reliable.

Finally, once the data has been preprocessed and explored, we can start building our ML models. There is no single magical solution that works for all ML problems, so it's important to carefully consider which models are best suited for the data and the problem at hand. Different types of NLP models exist, encompassing rule-based, statistical, and deep learning models. Each model type possesses unique strengths and weaknesses, underscoring the importance of selecting the most fitting one for the specific problem and dataset at hand.

Data exploration is an important and initial step in the ML workflow that involves analyzing and understanding the data before building a ML model. The goal of data exploration is to gain insights about the data, identify patterns, detect anomalies, and prepare the data for modeling. Data exploration helps in choosing the right ML algorithm and determining the best set of features to use.

Here are some common techniques that are used in data exploration:

- **Data visualization**: Data visualization involves depicting data through graphical or pictorial formats. It enables visual exploration of data, providing insights into its distribution, patterns, and relationships. Widely employed techniques in data visualization encompass scatter plots, bar charts, heatmaps, box plots, and correlation matrices.

- **Data cleaning**: Data cleaning is a step of preprocessing where we identify the errors, inconsistencies, and missing values and correct them. It affects the final results of the model since ML models are sensitive to errors in the data. Removing duplicates and filling in missing values are some of the common data cleaning techniques.

- **Feature engineering**: Feature engineering plays a crucial role in optimizing the effectiveness of machine learning models by crafting new features from existing data. This process involves not only identifying pertinent features but also transforming the existing ones and introducing novel features. Various feature engineering techniques, including scaling, normalization, dimensionality reduction, and feature selection, contribute to refining the overall performance of the models.

- **Statistical analysis**: Statistical analysis utilizes a range of statistical techniques to scrutinize data, revealing valuable insights into its inherent properties. Essential statistical methods include hypothesis testing, regression analysis, and time series analysis, all of which contribute to a comprehensive understanding of the data's characteristics.

- **Domain knowledge**: Leveraging domain knowledge entails applying a pre-existing understanding of the data domain to extract insights and make informed decisions. This knowledge proves valuable in recognizing pertinent features, interpreting results, and choosing the most suitable ML algorithm for the task at hand.

We will explore each of these techniques in the following subsections.

Data visualization

Data visualization is a crucial component of machine learning as it allows us to understand and explore complex datasets more easily. It involves creating visual representations of data using charts, graphs, and other types of visual aids. By visually presenting data, we can discern patterns, trends, and relationships that might not be readily evident when examining the raw data alone.

For NLP tasks, data visualization can help us gain insights into the linguistic patterns and structures in text data. For example, we can create word clouds to visualize the frequency of words in a corpus or use heatmaps to display the co-occurrence of words or phrases. We can also use scatter plots and line graphs to visualize changes in sentiment or topic over time.

One common type of visualization for ML is the scatter plot, which is used to display the relationship between two variables. By plotting the values of two variables on the X and Y axes, we can identify any patterns or trends that exist between them. Scatter plots are particularly useful for identifying clusters or groups of data points that share similar characteristics.

Another type of visualization that's frequently employed in ML is the histogram, a tool that illustrates the distribution of a single variable. By grouping data into bins and portraying the frequency of data points in each bin, we can pinpoint the range of values that predominate in the dataset. Histograms prove useful for detecting outliers or anomalies, and they aid in recognizing areas where the data may exhibit skewness or bias.

In addition to these basic visualizations, ML practitioners often use more advanced techniques, such as dimensionality reduction and network visualizations. Dimensionality reduction techniques, such as **principal component analysis (PCA)** and **t-distributed stochastic neighbor embedding (t-SNE)**, are commonly used for dimensional reduction and to visualize or analyze the data more easily. Network visualizations, on the other hand, are used to display complex relationships between entities, such as the co-occurrence of words or the connections between social media users.

Data cleaning

Data cleaning, alternatively termed data cleansing or data scrubbing, involves recognizing and rectifying or eliminating errors, inconsistencies, and inaccuracies within a dataset. This crucial phase in data preparation for ML significantly influences the accuracy and performance of a model, relying on the quality of the data used for training. Numerous prevalent techniques are employed in data cleaning. Let's take a closer look.

Handling missing values

Missing data is a common problem that occurs in many machine learning projects. Dealing with missing data is important because ML models cannot handle missing data and will either produce errors or provide inaccurate results.

There are several methods for dealing with missing data in ML projects:

- **Dropping rows**: Addressing missing data can involve a straightforward approach of discarding rows that contain such values. Nevertheless, exercising caution is paramount when employing this method as excessive row removal may result in the loss of valuable data, impacting the overall accuracy of the model. We usually use this method when we have a few rows in our dataset, and we have a few rows with missing values. In this case, removing a few rows can be a good and easy approach to training our model while the final performance will not be affected significantly.

- **Dropping columns**: Another approach is to drop the columns that contain missing values. This method can be effective if the missing values are concentrated in a few columns and if those columns are not important for the analysis. However, dropping important columns can lead to a loss of valuable information. It is better to perform some sort of correlation analysis to see the correlation of the values in these columns with the target class or value before dropping these columns.

- **Mean/median/mode imputation**: Mean, median, and mode imputation entail substituting missing values with the mean, median, or mode derived from the non-missing values within the corresponding column. This method is easy to implement and can be effective when the missing values are few and randomly distributed. However, it can also introduce bias and affect the variability of the data.

- **Regression imputation**: Regression imputation involves predicting the missing values based on the values of other variables in the dataset. This method can be effective when the missing values are related to other variables in the dataset, but it requires a regression model to be built for each column with missing values.

- **Multiple imputation**: Multiple imputation encompasses generating multiple imputed datasets through statistical models, followed by amalgamating the outcomes to produce a conclusive dataset. This approach proves efficacious, particularly when dealing with non-randomly distributed missing values and a substantial number of gaps in the dataset.

- **K-nearest neighbor imputation**: K-nearest neighbor imputation entails identifying the k-nearest data points to the missing value and utilizing their values to impute the absent value. This method can be effective when the missing values are clustered together in the dataset. In this approach, we can find the most similar records to the dataset to the record that has the missing value, and then use the mean of the values of those records for that specific record as the missed value.

In essence, selecting a method to handle missing data hinges on factors such as the nature and extent of the missing data, analysis objectives, and resource availability. It is crucial to thoughtfully assess the pros and cons of each method and opt for the most suitable approach tailored to the specific project.

Removing duplicates

Eliminating duplicates is a prevalent preprocessing measure that's employed to cleanse datasets by detecting and removing identical records. The occurrence of duplicate records may be attributed to factors such as data entry errors, system glitches, or data merging processes. The presence of duplicates can skew models and yield inaccurate insights. Hence, it is imperative to recognize and eliminate duplicate records to uphold the accuracy and dependability of the dataset.

There are different methods for removing duplicates in a dataset. The most common method is to compare all the rows of the dataset to identify duplicate records. If two or more rows have the same values in all the columns, they are considered duplicates. In some cases, it may be necessary to compare only a subset of columns if certain columns are more prone to duplicates.

Another method is to use a unique identifier column to identify duplicates. A unique identifier column is a column that contains unique values for each record, such as an ID number or a combination of unique columns. By comparing the unique identifier column, it is possible to identify and remove duplicate records from the dataset.

After identifying the duplicate records, the next step is to decide which records to keep and which ones to remove. One approach is to keep the first occurrence of a duplicate record and remove all subsequent occurrences. Another approach is to keep the record with the most complete information, or the record with the most recent timestamp.

It's crucial to recognize that the removal of duplicates might lead to a reduction in dataset size, potentially affecting the performance of ML models. Consequently, assessing the impact of duplicate removal on both the dataset and the ML model is essential. In some cases, it may be necessary to keep duplicate records if they contain important information that cannot be obtained from other records.

Standardizing and transforming data

Standardizing and transforming data is a critical step in preparing data for ML tasks. This process involves scaling and normalizing the numerical features of the dataset to make them easier to interpret and compare. The main objective of standardizing and transforming data is to enhance the accuracy and performance of a ML model by mitigating the influence of features with diverse scales and ranges. A widely used method for standardizing data is referred to as "standardization" or "Z-score normalization." This technique involves transforming each feature such that it has a mean of zero and a standard deviation of one. The formula for standardization is shown in the following equation:

$$x' = (x - mean(x)) / std(x)$$

Here, x represents the feature, $mean(x)$ denotes the mean of the feature, $std(x)$ indicates the standard deviation of the feature, and x' represents the new value assigned to the feature. By standardizing the data in this way, the range of each feature is adjusted to be centered around zero, which makes it easier to compare features and prevents features with large values from dominating the analysis.

Another technique for transforming data is "min-max scaling." This method rescales the data to a consistent range of values, commonly ranging between 0 and 1. The formula for min-max scaling is shown here:

$$x' = (x - min(x)) / (max(x) - min(x))$$

In this equation, x represents the feature, $min(x)$ signifies the minimum value of the feature, and $max(x)$ denotes the maximum value of the feature. Min-max scaling proves beneficial when the precise distribution of the data is not crucial, but there is a need to standardize the data for meaningful comparisons across different features.

Transforming data can also involve changing the distribution of the data. A frequently applied transformation is the log transformation, which is employed to alleviate the influence of outliers and skewness within the data. This transformation involves taking the logarithm of the feature values, which can help to normalize the distribution and reduce the influence of extreme values.

Overall, standardizing and transforming data constitute a pivotal stage in the data preprocessing workflow for ML endeavors. Through scaling and normalizing features, we can enhance the accuracy and performance of the ML model, rendering the data more interpretable and conducive to meaningful comparisons.

Handling outliers

Outliers are data points that markedly deviate from the rest of the observations in a dataset. Their occurrence may stem from factors such as measurement errors, data corruption, or authentic extreme values. The presence of outliers can wield a substantial influence on the outcomes of ML models, introducing distortion to the data and disrupting the relationships between variables. Therefore, handling outliers is an important step in preprocessing data for ML.

There are several methods for handling outliers:

- **Removing outliers**: One straightforward approach involves eliminating observations identified as outliers from the dataset. Nevertheless, exercising caution is paramount when adopting this method as excessive removal of observations may result in the loss of valuable information and potentially introduce bias to the analysis results.

- **Transforming data**: Applying mathematical functions such as logarithms or square roots to transform the data can mitigate the influence of outliers. For instance, taking the logarithm of a variable can alleviate the impact of extreme values, given the slower rate of increase in the logarithmic scale compared to the original values.

- **Winsorizing**: Winsorizing is a technique that entails substituting extreme values with the nearest highest or lowest value in the dataset. Employing this method aids in maintaining the sample size and overall distribution of the data.

- **Imputing values**: Imputation involves replacing missing or extreme values with estimated values derived from the remaining observations in the dataset. For instance, substituting extreme values with the median or mean of the remaining observations is a common imputation technique.

- **Using robust statistical methods**: Robust statistical methods exhibit lower sensitivity to outliers, leading to more accurate results even in the presence of such extreme values. For instance, opting for the median instead of the mean can effectively diminish the influence of outliers on the final results.

It's crucial to emphasize that selecting an outlier-handling method should be tailored to the unique characteristics of the data and the specific problem at hand. Generally, employing a combination of methods is advisable to address outliers comprehensively, and assessing the impact of each method on the results is essential. Moreover, documenting the steps taken to manage outliers is important for reproducibility and to provide clarity on the decision-making process.

Correcting errors

Rectifying errors during preprocessing stands as a vital stage in readying data for ML. Errors may manifest due to diverse reasons such as data entry blunders, measurement discrepancies, sensor inaccuracies, or transmission glitches. Correcting errors in data holds paramount significance in guaranteeing that ML models are trained on dependable and precise data, consequently enhancing the accuracy and reliability of predictions.

Several techniques exist to rectify errors in data. Here are some widely utilized methods:

- **Manual inspection**: An approach to rectify errors in data involves a manual inspection of the dataset, wherein errors are corrected by hand. This method is frequently employed, particularly when dealing with relatively small and manageable datasets.

- **Statistical methods**: Statistical methods prove effective in identifying and rectifying errors in data. For instance, when the data adheres to a recognized distribution, statistical techniques such as the Z-score can be employed to detect outliers, which can then be either removed or replaced.

- **ML methods**: Utilizing ML algorithms facilitates the detection and correction of errors in data. For instance, clustering algorithms prove valuable in pinpointing data points that markedly deviate from the broader dataset. Subsequently, these identified data points can undergo further examination and correction.

- **Domain knowledge**: Leveraging domain knowledge is instrumental in pinpointing errors within data. For instance, when collecting data from sensors, it becomes feasible to identify and rectify errors by considering the anticipated range of values that the sensor is capable of producing.

- **Imputation**: Imputation serves as a method to populate missing values in the data. This can be accomplished through various means, including statistical methods such as mean or median imputation, as well as ML algorithms such as k-nearest neighbor imputation.

Choosing a technique hinges on factors such as the nature of the data, the dataset's size, and the resources at your disposal.

Feature selection

Feature selection involves choosing the most pertinent features from a dataset for constructing a ML model. The objective is to decrease the number of features without substantially compromising the model's accuracy, resulting in enhanced performance, quicker training, and a more straightforward interpretation of the model.

Several approaches to feature selection exist. Let's take a look.

Filter methods

These techniques employ statistical methods to rank features according to their correlation with the target variable. Common methods encompass chi-squared, mutual information, and correlation coefficients. Features are subsequently chosen based on a predefined threshold.

Chi-squared

The chi-squared test is a widely employed statistical method in ML for feature selection that's particularly effective for categorical variables. This test gauges the dependence between two random variables, providing a P-value that signifies the likelihood of obtaining a result as extreme as or more extreme than the actual observations.

In hypothesis testing, the chi-squared test assesses whether the collected data aligns with the expected data. A small chi-squared test statistic indicates a robust match, while a large statistic implies a weak match. A P-value less than or equal to 0.05 leads to the rejection of the null hypothesis, considering it highly improbable. Conversely, a P-value greater than 0.05 results in accepting or "failing to reject" the null hypothesis. When the P-value hovers around 0.05, further scrutiny of the hypothesis is warranted.

In feature selection, the chi-squared test evaluates the relationship between each feature and the target variable in the dataset. It determines significance based on whether a statistically significant difference exists between the observed and expected frequencies of the feature, assuming independence between the feature and target. Features with a high chi-squared score exhibit a stronger dependence on the target variable, making them more informative for classification or regression tasks. The formula for calculating the chi-squared is presented in the following equation:

$$X^2 = \Sigma \frac{(O_i - E_i)^2}{E_i}$$

In this equation, O_i represents the observed value and E_i represents the expected value. The computation involves finding the difference between the observed frequency and the expected frequency, squaring the result, and then dividing by the expected frequency. The summation of these values across all categories of the feature yields the overall chi-squared statistic for that feature.

The degrees of freedom for the test relies on the number of categories in the feature and the number of categories in the target variable.

An exemplary application of chi-squared feature selection lies in text classification, particularly in scenarios where the presence or absence of specific words in a document serves as features. The chi-squared test helps identify words strongly associated with a particular class or category of documents, subsequently enabling their use as features in a ML model. In categorical data, especially where the relationship between features and the target variable is non-linear, chi-squared proves to be a valuable method for feature selection. However, its suitability diminishes for continuous or highly correlated features, where alternative feature selection methods may be more fitting.

Mutual information

Mutual information acts as a metric to gauge the interdependence of two random variables. In the context of feature selection, it quantifies the information a feature provides about the target variable. The core methodology entails calculating the mutual information between each feature and the target variable, ultimately selecting features with the highest mutual information scores.

Mathematically, the mutual information between two discrete random variables, X and Y, can be defined as follows:

$$I(X;Y) = \sum_{x \in X}\sum_{y \in Y} P(x,y)\log\left(\frac{P(x,y)}{P(x)P(y)}\right)$$

In the given equation, $p(x, y)$ represents the joint probability mass function of X and Y, while $p(x)$ and $p(y)$ denote the marginal probability mass functions of X and Y, respectively.

In the context of feature selection, mutual information calculation involves treating the feature as X and the target variable as Y. By computing the mutual information score for each feature, we can then select features with the highest scores.

To estimate the probability mass functions needed for calculating mutual information, histogram-based methods can be employed. This involves dividing the range of each variable into a fixed number of bins and estimating the probability mass functions based on the frequencies of observations in each bin. Alternatively, kernel density estimation can be utilized to estimate the probability density functions, and mutual information can then be computed based on the estimated densities.

In practical applications, mutual information is often employed alongside other feature selection methods, such as chi-squared or correlation-based methods, to enhance the overall performance of the feature selection process.

Correlation coefficients

Correlation coefficients serve as indicators of the strength and direction of the linear relationship between two variables. In the realm of feature selection, these coefficients prove useful in identifying features highly correlated with the target variable, thus serving as potentially valuable predictors.

The prevalent correlation coefficient employed for feature selection is the Pearson correlation coefficient, also referred to as Pearson's r. Pearson's r measures the linear relationship between two continuous variables, ranging from -1 (indicating a perfect negative correlation) to 1 (indicating a perfect positive correlation), with 0 denoting no correlation. Its calculation involves dividing the covariance between the two variables by the product of their standard deviations, as depicted in the following equation:

$$r = \frac{cov(X, Y)}{std(X) \cdot std(Y)}$$

In the given equation, X and Y represent the two variables of interest, $cov()$ denotes the covariance function, and $std()$ represents the standard deviation function.

Utilizing Pearson's r for feature selection involves computing the correlation between each feature and the target variable. Features with the highest absolute correlation coefficients are then selected. A high absolute correlation coefficient signifies a strong correlation with the target variable, whether positive or negative. The interpretation of Pearson correlation values and their degree of correlation is outlined in *Table 3.1*:

Pearson Correlation Value	Degree of Correlation
± 1	Perfect
± 0.50 - ± 1	High degree
± 0.30 - ± 0.49	Moderate degree
< +0.29	Low degree
0	No correlation

Table 3 .1 – Pearson correlation values and their degree of correlation

It's worth noting that Pearson's r is only appropriate for identifying linear relationships between variables. If the relationship is nonlinear, or if one or both of the variables are categorical, other correlation coefficients such as Spearman's ρ or Kendall's τ may be more appropriate. Additionally, it is important to be cautious when interpreting correlation coefficients as a high correlation does not necessarily imply causation.

Wrapper methods

These techniques delve into subsets of features through iterative model training and testing. Widely known methods encompass forward selection, backward elimination, and recursive feature elimination. While computationally demanding, these methods have the potential to significantly enhance model accuracy.

A concrete illustration of a wrapper method is **recursive feature elimination** (RFE). Functioning as a backward elimination approach, RFE systematically removes the least important feature until a predetermined number of features remains. During each iteration, a machine learning model is trained on the existing features, and the least important feature is pruned based on its feature importance score. This sequential process persists until the specified number of features is attained. The feature importance score can be extracted from diverse methods, including coefficient values from linear models or feature importance scores derived from decision trees. RFE is a computationally expensive method, but it can be useful when the number of features is very large and there is a need to reduce the feature space. An alternative approach is to have feature selection during the training process, something that's done via embedding methods.

Embedded methods

These methods select features during the training process of the model. Popular methods include LASSO and ridge regression, decision trees, and random forests.

LASSO

LASSO, an acronym for **Least Absolute Shrinkage and Selection Operator**, serves as a linear regression technique that's commonly employed for feature selection in machine learning. Its mechanism involves introducing a penalty term to the standard regression loss function. This penalty encourages the model to reduce the coefficients of less important features to zero, effectively eliminating them from the model.

The LASSO method proves especially valuable when grappling with high-dimensional data, where the number of features far exceeds the number of samples. In such scenarios, discerning the most crucial features for predicting the target variable can be challenging. LASSO comes to the fore by automatically identifying the most relevant features while simultaneously shrinking the coefficients of others.

The LASSO method works by finding the solution for the following optimization problem, which is a minimization problem:

$$\min_{w} \|\mathbf{y} - \mathbf{Xw}\|_2^2 + \lambda \|\mathbf{w}\|_1$$

In the given equation, vector y represents the target variable, X denotes the feature matrix, w signifies the vector of regression coefficients, λ is a hyperparameter dictating the intensity of the penalty term, and $\|w\|_1$ stands for the ℓ_1 norm of the coefficients (that is, the sum of their absolute values).

The inclusion of the ℓ_1 penalty term in the objective function prompts the model to precisely zero out certain coefficients, essentially eliminating the associated features from the model. The degree of penalty strength is governed by the λ hyperparameter, which can be fine-tuned through the use of cross-validation.

LASSO has several advantages over other feature selection methods, such as its ability to handle correlated features and its ability to perform feature selection and regression simultaneously. However, LASSO has some limitations, such as its tendency to select only one feature from a group of correlated features, and its performance may deteriorate if the number of features is much larger than the number of samples.

Consider the application of LASSO for feature selection in predicting house prices. Imagine a dataset encompassing details about houses – such as the number of bedrooms, lot size, construction year, and so on – alongside their respective sale prices. Employing LASSO, we can pinpoint the most crucial features to predict the sale price while concurrently fitting a linear regression model to the dataset. The outcome is a model that's ready to forecast the sale price of a new house based on its features.

Ridge regression

Ridge regression, a linear regression method applicable to feature selection, closely resembles ordinary least squares regression but introduces a penalty term to the cost function to counter overfitting.

In ridge regression, the cost function undergoes modification with the inclusion of a penalty term directly proportional to the square of the coefficients' magnitude. This penalty term is regulated by a hyperparameter, often denoted as λ or α dictating the regularization strength. When α is set to zero, ridge regression reverts to ordinary least squares regression.

The penalty term's impact manifests in shrinking the coefficients' magnitude toward zero. This proves beneficial in mitigating overfitting, discouraging the model from excessively relying on any single feature. In effect, the penalty term acts as a form of feature selection by reducing the importance of less relevant features.

The equation for the ridge regression loss function is as follows:

$$\min_{\mathbf{w}} \|\mathbf{y} - \mathbf{Xw}\|_2^2 + \alpha \|\mathbf{w}\|_2$$

Here, we have the following:

- N is the number of samples in the training set.
- y is the column vector of target values of size N.
- X is the design matrix of input features.
- w is the vector of regression coefficients to be estimated.
- α is the regularization parameter that controls the strength of the penalty term. It is a hyperparameter that needs to be tuned.

The first term in the loss function measures the mean squared error between the predicted values and the true values. The second term is the ℓ_2 penalty term that shrinks the coefficients toward zero. The ridge regression algorithm finds the values of the regression coefficients that minimize this loss function. By tuning the regularization parameter, α, we can control the bias-variance trade-off of the model, with higher alpha values leading to more regularization and lower overfitting.

Ridge regression can be used for feature selection by examining the magnitudes of the coefficients produced by the model. Features with coefficients that are close to zero or smaller are considered less important and can be dropped from the model. The value of α can be tuned using cross-validation to find the optimal balance between model complexity and accuracy.

One of the main advantages of ridge regression is its ability to handle multicollinearity, which occurs when there are strong correlations between the independent variables. In such cases, ordinary least squares regression can produce unstable and unreliable coefficient estimates, but ridge regression can help stabilize the estimates and improve the overall performance of the model.

Choosing LASSO or ridge regression

Ridge regression and LASSO are both regularization techniques that are used in linear regression to prevent overfitting of the model by penalizing the model's coefficients. While both methods seek to prevent overfitting, they differ in their approach to how the coefficients are penalized.

Ridge regression adds a penalty term to the **sum of squared errors** (**SSE**) that is proportional to the square of the magnitude of the coefficients. The penalty term is controlled by a regularization parameter (α), which determines the amount of shrinkage applied to the coefficients. This penalty term shrinks the values of the coefficients toward zero but does not set them exactly to zero. Therefore, ridge regression can be used to reduce the impact of irrelevant features in a model, but it will not eliminate them completely.

On the other hand, LASSO also adds a penalty term to the SSE, but the penalty term is proportional to the absolute value of the coefficients. Like ridge, LASSO also has a regularization parameter (λ) that determines the amount of shrinkage applied to the coefficients. However, LASSO has a unique property of setting some of the coefficients exactly to zero when the regularization parameter is sufficiently high. Therefore, LASSO can be used for feature selection as it can eliminate irrelevant features and set their corresponding coefficients to zero.

In general, if the dataset has many features and a small number of them are expected to be important, LASSO regression is a better choice as it will set the coefficients of irrelevant features to zero, leading to a simpler and more interpretable model. On the other hand, if most of the features in the dataset are expected to be relevant, ridge regression is a better choice as it will shrink the coefficients toward zero but not set them exactly to zero, preserving all the features in the model.

However, it is important to note that the optimal choice between ridge and LASSO depends on the specific problem and dataset, and it is often recommended to try both and compare their performance using cross-validation techniques.

Dimensionality reduction techniques

These methods transform the features into a lower-dimensional space while retaining as much information as possible. Popular methods include PCA, **linear discriminant analysis** (**LDA**), and t-SNE.

PCA

PCA is a widely used technique in machine learning for reducing the dimensionality of large datasets while retaining most of the important information. The basic idea of PCA is to transform a set of correlated variables into a set of uncorrelated variables known as principal components.

The goal of PCA is to identify the directions of maximum variance in the data and project the data in these directions, reducing the dimensionality of the data. The principal components are sorted in order of the amount of variance they explain, with the first principal component explaining the most variance in the data.

The PCA algorithm involves the following steps:

1. **Standardize the data**: PCA requires the data to be standardized – that is, each feature must have zero mean and unit variance.

2. **Compute the covariance matrix**: The covariance matrix is a square matrix that measures the linear relationships between pairs of features in the data.

3. **Compute the eigenvectors and eigenvalues of the covariance matrix**: The eigenvectors represent the primary directions of the highest variance within the dataset, while the eigenvalues quantify the extent of variance elucidated by each eigenvector.

4. **Select the number of principal components**: The number of principal components to retain can be determined by analyzing the eigenvalues and selecting the top k eigenvectors that explain the most variance.

5. **Project the data onto the selected principal components**: The original data is projected onto the selected principal components, resulting in a lower-dimensional representation of the data.

PCA can be used for feature selection by selecting the top k principal components that explain the most variance in the data. This can be useful for reducing the dimensionality of high-dimensional datasets and improving the performance of machine learning models. However, it's important to note that PCA may not always lead to improved performance, especially if the data is already low-dimensional or if the features are not highly correlated. It's also important to consider the interpretability of the selected principal components as they may not always correspond to meaningful features in the data.

LDA

LDA is a dimensionality reduction technique that's used for feature selection in machine learning. It is often used in classification tasks to reduce the number of features by transforming them into a lower-dimensional space while retaining as much class-discriminatory information as possible.

In LDA, the goal is to find a linear combination of the original features that maximizes the separation between classes. The input to LDA is a dataset of labeled examples, where each example is a feature vector with a corresponding class label. The output of LDA is a set of linear combinations of the original features, which can be used as new features in a machine learning model.

To perform LDA, the first step is to compute the mean and covariance matrix of each class. The overall mean and covariance matrix are then calculated from the class means and covariance matrices. The goal is to project the data onto a lower-dimensional space while still retaining the class information. This is achieved by finding the eigenvectors and eigenvalues of the covariance matrix, sorting them in descending order of the eigenvalues, and selecting the top k eigenvectors that correspond to the k largest eigenvalues. The selected eigenvectors form the basis for the new feature space.

The LDA algorithm can be summarized in the following steps:

1. Compute the mean vector of each class.

2. Compute the covariance matrix of each class.

3. Compute the overall mean vector and overall covariance matrix.

4. Compute the between-class scatter matrix.

5. Compute the within-class scatter matrix.

6. Compute the eigenvectors and eigenvalues of the matrix using the following equation:

$$\mathbf{S}_w^{-1} * \mathbf{S}_b$$

Here, $\mathbf{S}_w$ is the within-class scatter matrix and $\mathbf{S}_b$ is the between-class scatter matrix.

7. Select the top k eigenvectors with the highest eigenvalues as the new feature space.

LDA is particularly useful when the number of features is large and the number of examples is small. It can be used in a variety of applications, including image recognition, speech recognition, and NLP. However, it assumes that the classes are normally distributed and that the class covariance matrices are equal, which may not always be the case in practice.

t-SNE

t-SNE is a dimensionality reduction technique that's used for visualizing high-dimensional data in a low-dimensional space, often used for feature selection. It was developed by Laurens van der Maaten and Geoffrey Hinton in 2008.

The basic idea behind t-SNE is to preserve the pairwise similarities of data points in a low-dimensional space, as opposed to preserving the distances between them. In other words, it tries to retain the local structure of the data while discarding the global structure. This can be useful in situations where the high-dimensional data is difficult to visualize, but there may be meaningful patterns and relationships among the data points.

t-SNE starts by calculating the pairwise similarity between each pair of data points in the high-dimensional space. The similarity is usually measured using a Gaussian kernel, which gives higher weights to nearby points and lower weights to distant points. The similarity matrix is then converted into a probability distribution using a softmax function. This distribution is used to create a low-dimensional space, typically 2D or 3D.

In the low-dimensional space, t-SNE again calculates the pairwise similarities between each pair of data points, but this time using a student's t-distribution instead of a Gaussian distribution. The t-distribution has heavier tails than the Gaussian distribution, which helps to better preserve the local structure of the data. t-SNE then adjusts the position of the points in the low-dimensional space to minimize the difference between the pairwise similarities in the high-dimensional space and the pairwise similarities in the low-dimensional space.

t-SNE is a powerful technique for visualizing high-dimensional data by reducing it to a low-dimensional space. However, it is not typically used for feature selection as its primary purpose is to create visualizations of complex datasets.

Instead, t-SNE can be used to help identify clusters of data points that share similar features, which may be useful in identifying groups of features that are important for a particular task. For example, suppose you have a dataset of customer demographics and purchase history, and you want to identify groups of customers that are similar based on their purchasing behavior. You could use t-SNE to reduce the high-dimensional feature space to two dimensions, and then plot the resulting data points on a scatter plot. By examining the plot, you might be able to identify clusters of customers with similar purchasing behavior, which could then inform your feature selection process. Here's a sample t-SNE for the MNIST dataset:

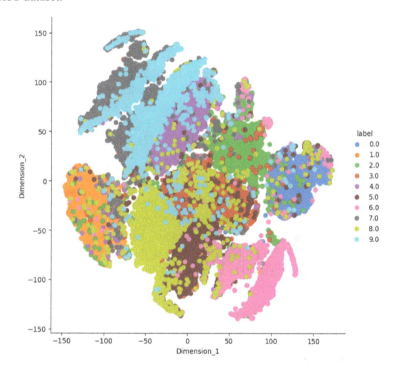

Figure 3.1 – t-SNE on the MNIST dataset

It's worth noting that t-SNE is primarily a visualization tool and should not be used as the sole method for feature selection. Instead, it can be used in conjunction with other techniques, such as LDA or PCA, to gain a more complete understanding of the underlying structure of your data.

The choice of feature selection method depends on the nature of the data, the size of the dataset, the complexity of the model, and the computational resources available. It is important to carefully evaluate the performance of the model after feature selection to ensure that important information has not been lost. Another important process is feature engineering, which is about transforming or selecting features for the machine learning models.

Feature engineering

Feature engineering is the process of selecting, transforming, and extracting features from raw data to improve the performance of machine learning models. Features are the individual measurable properties or characteristics of the data that can be used to make predictions or classifications.

One common technique in feature engineering is feature selection, which involves selecting a subset of relevant features from the original dataset to improve the model's accuracy and reduce its complexity. This can be done through statistical methods such as correlation analysis or feature importance ranking using decision trees or random forests.

Another technique in feature engineering is feature extraction, which involves transforming the raw data into a new set of features that may be more useful for the model. The primary distinction between feature selection and feature engineering lies in their approaches: while feature selection retains a subset of the original features without modifying the selected features, feature engineering algorithms reconfigure and transform the data into a new feature space. Feature engineering can be done through techniques such as dimensionality reduction, PCA, or t-SNE. Feature selection and extraction were explained in detail in the previous subsection (3-1-3).

Feature scaling is another important technique in feature engineering that involves scaling the values of features to the same range, typically between 0 and 1 or -1 and 1. This is done to prevent certain features from dominating others in the model and to ensure that the algorithm can converge quickly during training. When the features in the dataset have different scales, this can lead to issues when using certain machine learning algorithms that are sensitive to the relative magnitudes of the features. Feature scaling can help to address this problem by ensuring that all features are on a similar scale. Common methods for feature scaling include min-max scaling, Z-score scaling, and scaling by the maximum absolute value.

There are several common methods for feature scaling:

- **Min-max scaling**: Also known as normalization, this technique scales the values of the feature to be between a specified range, typically between 0 and 1 (for regular machine learning models, and sometimes -1 and 1 for deep learning models). The formula for min-max scaling is shown here:

$$x_{scaled} = \left(x - min\left(x\right)\right) / \left(max\left(x\right) - min\left(x\right)\right)$$

Here, x is the original feature value, $min(x)$ is the minimum value of the feature, and $max(x)$ is the maximum value of the feature.

- **Standardization**: This technique transforms the feature values to have a mean of 0 and a standard deviation of 1. Standardization is less affected by outliers in the data than min-max scaling. The formula for standardization is shown here:

$$x_{scaled} = (x - mean(x)) / std(x)$$

Here, x is the original feature value, $mean(x)$ is the mean of the feature, and $std(x)$ is the standard deviation of the feature.

- **Robust scaling**: This technique is similar to standardization but uses the median and **interquartile range (IQR)** instead of the mean and standard deviation. Robust scaling is useful when the data contains outliers that would significantly affect the mean and standard deviation. The formula for robust scaling is shown here:

$$x_{scaled} = (x - median(x)) / (Q3(x) - Q1(x))$$

Here, x is the original feature value, $median(x)$ is the median of the feature, $Q1(x)$ is the first quartile of the feature, and $Q3(x)$ is the third quartile of the feature.

- **Log transformation**: This technique is used when the data is highly skewed or has a long tail. By taking the logarithm of the feature values, the distribution can be made more normal or symmetric, which can improve the performance of some machine learning algorithms. The formula for log transformation is shown here:

$$x_{transformed} = log(x)$$

Here, x is the original feature value.

- **Power transformation**: This technique is similar to log transformation but allows for a broader range of transformations. The most common power transformation is the Box-Cox transformation, which raises the feature values to a power that is determined using maximum likelihood estimation. The formula for the Box-Cox transformation is shown here:

$$x_{transformed} = \frac{x^\lambda - 1}{\lambda}$$

Here, x is the original feature value, and λ is the power parameter that is estimated using maximum likelihood.

These are some of the most common methods for feature scaling in machine learning. The choice of method depends on the distribution of the data, the machine learning algorithm being used, and the specific requirements of the problem.

One final technique in feature engineering is feature construction, which involves creating new features by combining or transforming existing ones. This can be done through techniques such as polynomial expansion, logarithmic transformation, or interaction terms.

Polynomial expansion

Polynomial expansion is a feature construction technique that involves creating new features by taking polynomial combinations of existing features. This technique is commonly used in machine learning to model nonlinear relationships between features and the target variable.

The idea behind polynomial expansion is to create new features by raising the existing features to different powers and taking their products. For example, suppose we have a single feature, x. We can create new features by taking the square of x (x^2). We can also create higher-order polynomial features by taking x to even higher powers, such as x^3, x^4, and so on. In general, we can create polynomial features of degree d by taking all possible combinations of products and powers of the original features up to degree d.

In addition to creating polynomial features from a single feature, we can also create polynomial features from multiple features. For example, suppose we have two features, x_1 and x_2. We can create new polynomial features by taking their products ($x_1 x_2$) and raising them to different powers (x_1^2, x_2^2, and so on). Again, we can create polynomial features of any degree by taking all possible combinations of products and powers of the original features.

One important consideration when using polynomial expansion is that it can quickly lead to a large number of features, especially for high degrees of polynomials. This can make the resulting model more complex and harder to interpret, and can also lead to overfitting if the number of features is not properly controlled. To address this issue, it is common to use regularization techniques or feature selection methods to select a subset of the most informative polynomial features.

Overall, polynomial expansion is a powerful feature construction technique that can help capture complex nonlinear relationships between features and the target variable. However, it should be used with caution and with appropriate regularization or feature selection to avoid overfitting and maintain model interpretability.

For example, in a regression problem, you might have a dataset with a single feature, say x, and you want to fit a model that can capture the relationship between x and the target variable, y. However, the relationship between x and y may not be linear, and a simple linear model may not be sufficient. In this case, polynomial expansion can be used to create additional features that capture the non-linear relationship between x and y.

To illustrate, let's say you have a dataset with a single feature, x, and a target variable, y, and you want to fit a polynomial regression model. The goal is to find a function, $f(x)$, that minimizes the difference between the predicted and actual values of y.

Polynomial expansion can be used to create additional features based on x, such as x^2, x^3, and so on. This can be done using libraries such as `scikit-learn`, which has a `PolynomialFeatures` function that can automatically generate polynomial features of a specified degree.

By adding these polynomial features, the model becomes more expressive and can capture the non-linear relationship between x and y. However, it's important to be careful not to overfit the data as adding too many polynomial features can lead to a model that is overly complex and performs poorly on new, unseen data.

Logarithmic transformation

Logarithmic transformation is a common feature engineering technique that's used in data preprocessing. The goal of logarithmic transformation is to make data less skewed and more symmetric by applying a logarithmic function to the features. This technique can be particularly useful for features that are skewed, such as those with a long tail of high values.

The logarithmic transformation is defined as an equation taking the natural logarithm of the data:

$$y = log(x)$$

Here, y is the transformed data and x is the original data. The logarithmic function maps the original data to a new space, where the relationship between the values is preserved but the scale is compressed. The logarithmic transformation is particularly useful for features with large ranges or that are distributed exponentially, such as the prices of products or the incomes of individuals.

One of the benefits of the logarithmic transformation is that it can help normalize data and make it more suitable for certain machine learning algorithms that assume normally distributed data. Additionally, logarithmic transformation can reduce the impact of outliers on the data, which can help improve the performance of some models.

It's important to note that the logarithmic transformation is not appropriate for all types of data. For example, if the data includes zero or negative values, the logarithmic transformation cannot be applied directly. In these cases, a modified logarithmic transformation, such as adding a constant before taking the logarithm, may be used. Overall, logarithmic transformation is a useful technique for feature engineering that can help improve the performance of machine learning models, especially when dealing with skewed or exponentially distributed data.

In summary, feature engineering is a critical step in the machine learning pipeline as it can significantly impact the performance and interpretability of the resulting models. Effective feature engineering requires domain knowledge, creativity, and an iterative process of testing and refining different techniques until the optimal set of features is identified.

Interaction terms

In feature construction, interaction terms refer to creating new features by combining two or more existing features in a dataset through multiplication, division, or other mathematical operations. These new features capture the interaction or relationship between the original features, and they can help improve the accuracy of machine learning models.

For example, in a dataset of real estate prices, you might have features such as the number of bedrooms, the number of bathrooms, and the square footage of the property. By themselves, these features provide some information about the price of the property, but they do not capture any interaction effects between the features. However, by creating an interaction term between the number of bedrooms and the square footage, you can capture the idea that larger properties with more bedrooms tend to be more expensive than smaller ones with the same number of bedrooms.

In practice, interaction terms are created by multiplying or dividing two or more features together. For example, if we have two features, x and y, we can create an interaction term by multiplying them together: xy. We can also create interaction terms by dividing one feature by another: x/y.

When creating interaction terms, it is important to consider which features to combine and how to combine them. Here are some common techniques:

- **Domain knowledge**: Use domain knowledge or expert intuition to identify which features are likely to interact and how they might interact.

- **Pairwise combinations**: Create interaction terms by pairwise combining all pairs of features in the dataset. This can be computationally expensive, but it can help identify potential interaction effects.

- **PCA**: Use PCA to identify the most important combinations of features, and create interaction terms based on these combinations.

Overall, interaction terms are a powerful tool in feature construction that can help capture complex relationships between features and improve the accuracy of machine learning models. However, it is important to be careful when creating interaction terms as too many or poorly chosen terms can lead to overfitting or decreased model interpretability.

Common machine learning models

Here, we will explain some of the most common machine learning models, as well as their advantages and disadvantages. Knowing this information will help you pick the best model for the problem and be able to improve the implemented model.

Linear regression

Linear regression is a type of supervised learning algorithm that's used to model the relationship between a dependent variable and one or more independent variables. It assumes a linear relationship between the input features and the output. The goal of linear regression is to find the best-fit line that predicts the value of the dependent variable based on the independent variables.

The equation for a simple linear regression with one independent variable (also called a **simple linear equation**) is as follows:

$$y = mx + b$$

Here, we have the following:

- y is the dependent variable (the variable we want to predict)
- x is the independent variable (the input variable)
- m is the slope of the line (how much y changes when x changes)
- b is the y-intercept (where the line intercepts the Y-axis when $x = 0$)

The goal of linear regression is to find the values of m and b that minimize the difference between the predicted values and the actual values of the dependent variable. This difference is typically measured using a cost function, such as mean squared error or mean absolute error.

Multiple linear regression is an extension of simple linear regression, where there are multiple independent variables. The equation for multiple linear regression is shown here:

$$y = b_0 + b_1 x_1 + b_2 x_2 + ... + b_n x_n$$

Here we have the following:

- y is the dependent variable
- $x_1, x_2, ..., x_n$ are the independent variables
- b_0 is the y-intercept (when all the independent variables are equal to 0)
- $b_1, b_2, ..., b_n$ are the coefficients (how much y changes when each independent variable changes)

Similar to simple linear regression, the goal of multiple linear regression is to find the values of b_0 , $b_1, b_2, ..., b_n$ that minimize the difference between the predicted values and the actual values of the dependent variable.

The advantages of linear regression are as follows:

- It's simple and easy to understand
- It can be used to model a wide range of relationships between the dependent and independent variables
- It's computationally efficient, making it fast and suitable for large datasets
- It provides interpretable results, allowing for the analysis of the impact of each independent variable on the dependent variable

The disadvantages of linear regression are as follows:

- It assumes a linear relationship between the input features and the output, which may not always be the case in real-world data
- It may not capture complex non-linear relationships between the input features and the output

- It's sensitive to outliers and influential observations, which can affect the accuracy of the model

- It assumes that the errors are normally distributed with constant variance, which may not always hold true in practice

Logistic regression

Logistic regression is a popular machine learning algorithm that's used for classification problems. Unlike linear regression, which is used for predicting continuous values, logistic regression is used for predicting discrete outcomes, typically binary outcomes (0 or 1).

The goal of logistic regression is to estimate the probability of a certain outcome based on one or more input variables. The output of logistic regression is a probability score, which can be converted into a binary class label by applying a threshold value. The threshold value can be adjusted to balance between precision and recall based on the specific requirements of the problem.

The logistic regression model assumes that the relationship between the input variables and the output variable is linear in the logit (log odds) space. The logit function is defined as follows:

$$logit(p) = log(p \, / \, (1 - p))$$

Here, p is the probability of the positive outcome (that is, the probability of the event occurring).

The logistic regression model can be represented mathematically as follows:

$$logit(p) = \beta_0 + \beta_1 \, x_1 + \beta_2 \, x_2 + \dots + \beta_n \, x_n$$

Here, $\beta_0, \beta_1, \beta_2, \dots, \beta_n$ are the coefficients of the model, $x_1, x_2, \dots, x_n$ are the input variables, and $logit(p)$ is the logit function of the probability of a positive outcome.

The logistic regression model is trained using a dataset of labeled examples, where each example consists of a set of input variables and a binary label indicating whether the positive outcome occurred or not. The coefficients of the model are estimated using maximum likelihood estimation, which seeks to find the values of the coefficients that maximize the likelihood of the observed data.

The advantages of logistic regression are as follows:

- **Interpretable**: The coefficients of the model can be interpreted as the change in the log odds of the positive outcome associated with a unit change in the corresponding input variable, making it easy to understand the impact of each input variable on the predicted probability of the positive outcome

- **Computationally efficient**: Logistic regression is a simple algorithm that can be trained quickly on large datasets

- **Works well with small datasets**: Logistic regression can be effective even with a small number of observations, provided that the input variables are relevant to the prediction task

The disadvantages of logistic regression are as follows:

- **Assumes linearity**: Logistic regression assumes a linear relationship between the input variables and the logit of the probability of the positive outcome, which may not always be the case in real-world datasets

- **May suffer from overfitting**: If the number of input variables is large compared to the number of observations, the model may suffer from overfitting, leading to poor generalization performance on new data

- **Not suitable for non-linear problems**: Logistic regression is a linear algorithm and is not suitable for problems where the relationship between the input variables and the output variable is non-linear

Decision trees

Decision trees are a type of supervised learning algorithm used for classification and regression analysis. A decision tree consists of a series of nodes that represent decision points, each of which has one or more branches that lead to other decision points or a final prediction.

In a classification problem, each leaf node of the tree represents a class label, while in a regression problem, each leaf node represents a numerical value. The process of building a decision tree involves choosing a sequence of attributes that best splits the data into subsets that are more homogenous concerning the target variable. This process is typically repeated recursively for each subset until a stopping criterion is met, such as a minimum number of instances in each subset or a maximum depth of the tree.

The equations for decision trees involve calculating the information gain (or another splitting criterion, such as Gini impurity or entropy) for each potential split at each decision point. The attribute with the highest information gain is selected as the split criterion for that node. The conceptual formula for information gain is shown here:

Information gain = entropy(parent) − [weighted average of entropies of patent's children]

Here, *entropy* is a measure of the impurity or randomness of a system. In the context of decision trees, entropy is used to measure the impurity of a node in the tree.

The *entropy* of a node is calculated as follows:

$$Entropy = \sum_{i=1}^{c} - p_i \log_2 p_i$$

Here, c is the number of classes and p_i is the proportion of the samples that belong to class i in the node.

The entropy of a node ranges from 0 to 1, with 0 indicating a pure node (that is, all samples belong to the same class) and 1 indicating a node that is evenly split between all classes.

In a decision tree, the entropy of a node is used to determine the splitting criterion for the tree. The idea is to split the node into two or more child nodes such that the entropy of the child nodes is lower than the entropy of the parent node. The split with the lowest entropy is chosen as the best split.

Please note that the choice of the next node in the decision tree differs based on the underlying algorithm – for example, CART, ID3, or C4.5. What we explained here was CART, which uses Gini impurity and entropy to split the data.

The advantage of using entropy as a splitting criterion is that it can handle both binary and multi-class classification problems. It is also relatively computationally efficient compared to other splitting criteria. However, one disadvantage of using entropy is that it tends to create biased trees in favor of attributes with many categories.

Here are some of the advantages of decision trees:

- Easy to understand and interpret, even for non-experts
- Can handle both categorical and numerical data
- Can handle missing data and outliers
- Can be used for feature selection
- Can be combined with other models in ensemble methods, such as random forests

Here are some of the disadvantages of decision trees:

- Can be prone to overfitting, especially if the tree is too deep or complex
- Can be sensitive to small changes in the data or the way the tree is built
- Can be biased toward features with many categories or high cardinality
- Can have problems with rare events or imbalanced datasets

Random forest

Random forest is an ensemble learning method that's versatile and can perform classification and regression tasks. It operates by generating multiple decision trees during training, predicting the target class for classification based on the majority of the trees, and the predicted value based on the mean prediction by trees for regression tasks. The algorithm for constructing a random forest can be summarized in the following steps:

1. **Bootstrap sampling**: Randomly select a subset of the data with replacement to create a new dataset that's the same size as the original dataset.

2. **Feature selection**: Randomly select a subset of the features (columns) for each split when building a decision tree. This helps to create diversity in the trees and reduce overfitting.

3. **Tree building**: Construct a decision tree for each bootstrap sample and feature subset. The decision tree is constructed recursively by splitting the data based on the selected features until a stopping criterion is met (for example, maximum depth or minimum number of samples in a leaf node).

4. **Ensemble learning**: Combine the predictions of all decision trees to make a final prediction. For classification, the class that receives the most votes from the decision trees is the final prediction. For regression, the average of the predictions from all decision trees is the final prediction.

The random forest algorithm can be expressed mathematically as follows.

Given a dataset, D, with N samples and M features, we create T decision trees $\{ Tree_1, Tree_2, ..., Tree_T\}$ by applying the preceding steps. Each decision tree is constructed using a bootstrap sample of the data, D', with size N' ($N' <= N$) and a subset of the features, F', with size m ($m <= M$). For each split in the decision tree, we randomly select k ($k < m$) features from F' and choose the best feature to split the data based on an impurity measure (for example, Gini index or entropy). The decision tree is built until a stopping criterion is met (for example, the maximum depth or minimum number of samples in a leaf node).

The final prediction, $\hat{y}$, for a new sample, x, is obtained by aggregating the predictions from all decision trees.

For classification, $\hat{y}$ is the class that receives the most votes from all decision trees:

$$\hat{y} = argmax_j \sum_i I\left(y_{i,j} = 1\right)$$

Here, $y_{i,j}$ is the prediction of the j-th decision tree for the i-th sample, and $I()$ is the indicator function that returns 1 if the condition is true and 0 otherwise.

For regression, $\hat{y}$ is the average of the predictions from all decision trees:

$$\hat{y} = \left(1/T\right) \sum_{i=1}^{T} y_i$$

Here, y_i is the prediction of the i-th decision tree for the new sample, x.

In summary, random forest is a powerful machine learning algorithm that can handle high-dimensional and noisy datasets. It works by constructing multiple decision trees using bootstrap samples of the data and feature subsets, and then aggregating the predictions of all decision trees to make a final prediction. The algorithm is scalable, easy to use, and provides a measure of feature importance, making it a popular choice for many machine learning applications.

The advantages of random forests are as follows:

*   **Robustness**: Random forest is a very robust algorithm that can handle a variety of input data types, including numerical, categorical, and ordinal data

*   **Feature selection**: Random forest can rank the importance of features, allowing users to identify the most important features for classification or regression tasks

- **Overfitting**: Random forest has a built-in mechanism for reducing overfitting, called bagging, which helps to generalize well on new data

- **Scalability**: Random forest can handle large datasets with a high number of features, making it a good choice for big data applications

- **Outliers**: Random forest is robust to the presence of outliers as it is based on decision trees, which can handle outliers effectively

The disadvantages of random forests are as follows:

- **Interpretability**: Random forest models can be difficult to interpret as they are based on an ensemble of decision trees

- **Training time**: The training time of a random forest can be longer than other simpler algorithms, especially when the number of trees in the ensemble is large

- **Memory usage**: Random forest requires more memory than some other algorithms as it has to store the decision trees in memory

- **Bias**: Random forest can suffer from bias if the data is imbalanced or if the target variable has a high cardinality

- **Overfitting**: Although random forest is designed to prevent overfitting, it is still possible to overfit the model if the hyperparameters are not properly tuned

Overall, random forest is a powerful machine learning algorithm that has many advantages, but it is important to carefully consider its limitations before applying it to a particular problem.

Support vector machines (SVMs)

SVMs are considered robust supervised learning algorithms that can perform both classification and regression tasks. They excel in scenarios with intricate decision boundaries, surpassing the limitations of linear models. At their core, SVMs aim to identify a hyperplane within a multi-dimensional space that maximally segregates the classes. This hyperplane is positioned to maximize the distance between itself and the closest points from each class, known as support vectors. Here's how SVMs work for a binary classification problem. Given a set of training data, $\{(x_1, y_1), (x_2, y_2), ..., (x_n, y_n)\}$, where x_i is a d-dimensional feature vector and y_i is the binary class label (+1 or -1), the goal of an SVM is to find a hyperplane that separates the two classes with the largest margin. The margin is defined as the distance between the hyperplane and the closest data points from each class:

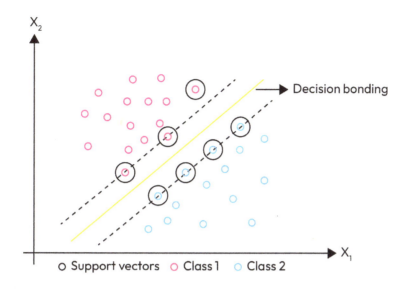

Figure 3.2 – SVM margins

The hyperplane is defined by a weight vector, w, and a bias term, b, such that for any new data point, x, the predicted class label, y, is given by the following equation:

$$y = sign(\mathbf{w}^T\mathbf{x}+b)$$

Here, *sign* is the sign function, which returns +1 if the argument is positive and -1 otherwise.

The objective function of an SVM is to minimize the classification error subject to the constraint that the margin is maximized. This can be formulated as an optimization problem:

$$minimize\ 1/2\ \|\mathbf{w}\|^2$$

$$subject\ to\ y_i\left(\mathbf{w}^T\mathbf{x}_i + b\right) \geq 1\ for\ i = 1,2,...,n$$

Here, $\|\mathbf{w}\|^2$ is the squared Euclidean norm of the weight vector, w. The constraints ensure that all data points are correctly classified and that the margin is maximized.

Here are some of the advantages of SVMs:

- Effective in high-dimensional spaces, which is useful when the number of features is large
- Can be used for both classification and regression tasks
- Works well with both linearly separable and non-linearly separable data
- Can handle outliers well due to the use of the margin concept
- Has a regularization parameter that allows you to control overfitting

Here are some of the disadvantages of SVMs:

- Can be sensitive to the choice of kernel function, which can greatly affect the performance of the model

- Computationally intensive for large datasets

- It can be difficult to interpret the results of an SVM model

- Requires careful tuning of parameters to achieve good performance

Neural networks and transformers

Neural networks and transformers are both powerful machine learning models that are used for a variety of tasks, such as image classification, NLP, and speech recognition.

Neural networks

Neural networks draw inspiration from the structure and functioning of the human brain. They represent a category of machine learning models that are proficient in various tasks such as classification, regression, and more. Comprising multiple layers of interconnected nodes known as neurons, these networks adeptly process and manipulate data. The output of each layer is fed into the next layer, creating a hierarchy of feature representations. The input to the first layer is the raw data, and the output of the final layer is the prediction. A simple neural network for detecting the gender of a person based on their height and weight is shown in *Figure 3.3*:

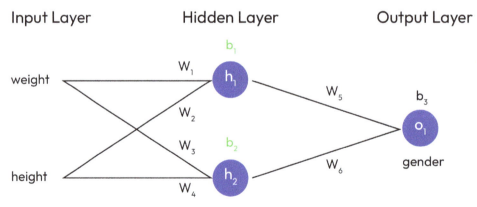

Figure 3.3 – Simple neural network

The operation of a single neuron in a neural network can be represented by the following equation:

$$y = f\left(\sum_{i=1}^{n} w_i x_i + b \right)$$

Here, x_i is the input values, w_i is the weights of the connections between the neurons, b is the bias term, and f is the activation function. The activation function applies a non-linear transformation to the weighted sum of the inputs and bias term.

Training a neural network involves adjusting the weights and biases of the neurons to minimize a loss function. This is typically done using an optimization algorithm such as stochastic gradient descent.

The advantages of neural networks include their ability to learn complex non-linear relationships between input and output data, their ability to automatically extract meaningful features from raw data, and their scalability to large datasets.

The disadvantages of neural networks include their high computational and memory requirements, their sensitivity to hyperparameter tuning, and the difficulty of interpreting their internal representations.

Transformers

Transformers are a type of neural network architecture that is particularly well suited to sequential data such as text or speech. They were introduced in the context of NLP and have since been applied to a wide range of tasks.

The core component of a transformer is the self-attention mechanism, which allows the model to attend to different parts of the input sequence when computing the output. The self-attention mechanism is based on a dot product between a query vector, a set of key vectors, and a set of value vectors. The resulting attention weights are used to weight the values, which are then combined to produce the output.

The self-attention operation can be represented by the following equations:

$$Q = X W_Q$$

$$K = X W_K$$

$$V = X W_V$$

$$A\left(Q, K, V\right) = softmax\left(\frac{QK^T}{\sqrt{d_K}}\right) V$$

Here, X is the input sequence, W_Q, W_K, and W_V are learned projection matrices for the query, key, and value vectors, respectively, d_K is the dimensionality of the key vectors, and W_Q is a learned projection matrix that maps the output of the attention mechanism to the final output.

The advantages of transformers include their ability to handle variable-length input sequences, their ability to capture long-range dependencies in the data, and their state-of-the-art performance on many NLP tasks.

The disadvantages of transformers include their high computational and memory requirements, their sensitivity to hyperparameter tuning, and their difficulty in handling tasks that require explicit modeling of sequential dynamics.

These are just a few of the most popular machine learning models. The choice of model depends on the problem at hand, the size and quality of the data, and the desired outcome. Now that we have explored the most common machine learning models, we will explain model underfitting and overfitting, which happens during the training process.

Model underfitting and overfitting

In machine learning, the ultimate goal is to build a model that can generalize well on unseen data. However, sometimes, a model can fail to achieve this goal due to either underfitting or overfitting.

Underfitting occurs when a model is too simple to capture the underlying patterns in the data. In other words, the model can't learn the relationship between the features and the target variable properly. This can result in poor performance on both the training and testing data. For example, in *Figure 3.4*, we can see that the model is underfitted, and it cannot present the data very well. This is not what we like in machine learning models, and we usually like to see a precise model, as shown in *Figure 3.5*:

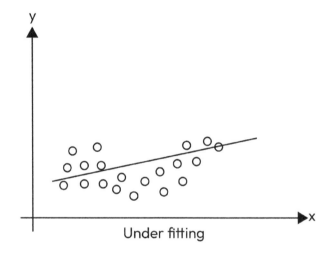

Figure 3.4 – The machine learning model underfitting on the training data

Underfitting happens when the model is not trained well, or the model complexity is not enough to catch the underlying pattern in the data. To solve this problem, we can use more complex models, and continue the training process:

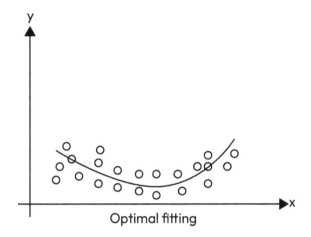

Figure 3.5 – Optimal fitting of the machine learning model on the training data

Optimal fitting happens when the model captures the pattern in the data pretty well but does not overfit every single sample. This helps the model work better on unseen data:

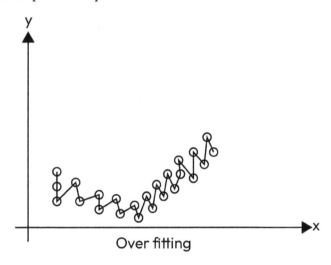

Figure 3.6 – Overfitting the model on the training data

On the other hand, overfitting occurs when a model is too complex and fits the training data too closely, which can lead to poor generalization on new, unseen data, as shown in *Figure 3.6*. This happens when the model learns the noise or random fluctuations in the training data, rather than the underlying patterns. In other words, the model becomes too specialized for the training data and does not perform well on the testing data. As shown in the preceding figure, the model is overfitted, and the model tried to predict every single sample very precisely. The problem with this model is that it does not learn the general pattern, and learns the pattern of each individual sample, which makes it work poorly when facing new, unseen records.

A useful way to understand the trade-off between underfitting and overfitting is through the bias-variance trade-off. Bias refers to the difference between the predicted values of the model and the actual values in the training data. A high bias means that the model is not complex enough to capture the underlying patterns in the data and underfits the data (*Figure 3.7*). An underfit model has poor performance on both the training and testing data:

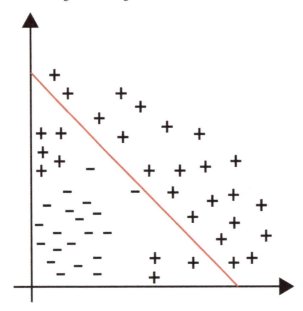

Figure 3.7 – High bias

Variance, on the other hand, refers to the sensitivity of the model to small fluctuations in the training data. A high variance means that the model is overly complex and overfits the data, which leads to poor generalization performance on new data. An overfit model has good performance on the training data but poor performance on the testing data:

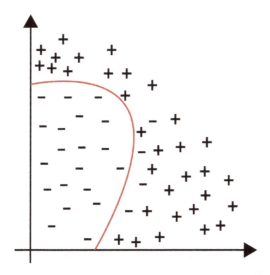

Figure 3.8 – Just right (not high bias, not high variance)

To strike a balance between bias and variance, we need to choose a model that is neither too simple nor too complex. As mentioned previously, this is often referred to as the bias-variance trade-off (*Figure 3.8*). A model with a high bias and low variance can be improved by increasing the complexity of the model, while a model with a high variance and low bias can be improved by decreasing the complexity of the model:

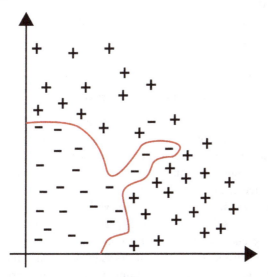

Figure 3.9 – High variance

There are several methods to reduce bias and variance in a model. One common approach is regularization, which adds a penalty term to the loss function to control the complexity of the model. Another approach is to use ensembles, which combine multiple models to improve the overall performance by reducing the variance. Cross-validation can also be used to evaluate the model's performance and tune its hyperparameters to find the optimal balance between bias and variance.

Overall, understanding bias and variance is crucial in machine learning as it helps us to choose an appropriate model and identify the sources of error in the model.

Bias refers to the error that is introduced by approximating a real-world problem with a simplified model. Variance, on the other hand, refers to the error that is introduced by the model's sensitivity to small fluctuations in the training data.

When a model has high bias and low variance, it is underfitting. This means that the model is not capturing the complexity of the problem and is making overly simplistic assumptions. When a model has low bias and high variance, it is overfitting. This means that the model is too sensitive to the training data and is fitting the noise instead of the underlying patterns.

To overcome underfitting, we can try increasing the complexity of the model, adding more features, or using a more sophisticated algorithm. To prevent overfitting, several methods can be used:

- **Cross-validation**: Assessing the performance of machine learning models is essential. Cross-validation serves as a method for assessing the effectiveness of a machine learning model. It entails training the model on one portion of the data and testing it on another. By employing distinct subsets for training and evaluation, cross-validation mitigates the risk of overfitting. Further elaboration on this technique will be provided in the subsequent section on data splitting.

- **Regularization**: Regularization is a technique that's used to add a penalty term to the loss function during training, which helps to reduce the complexity of the model and prevent overfitting. There are different types of regularization, including L1 regularization (LASSO), L2 regularization (ridge), and elastic net regularization.

- **Early stopping**: Early stopping is a technique that's used to stop the training process when the performance of the model on the validation data starts to degrade. This helps to prevent overfitting by stopping the model from continuing to learn from the training data when it has already reached its maximum performance. This technique is usually used in iterative algorithms such as deep learning methods, where the model is being trained for multiple iterations (epochs). To use early stopping, we usually train the model while evaluating the model performance on the training and validation subsets. The model's performance usually improves on the training set with more training, but since the model has not seen the validation set, the validation error usually decreases initially and at some point, starts increasing again. This point is where the model starts overfitting. By visualizing the training and validation error of the model during training, we can identify and stop the model at this point (*Figure 3.10*):

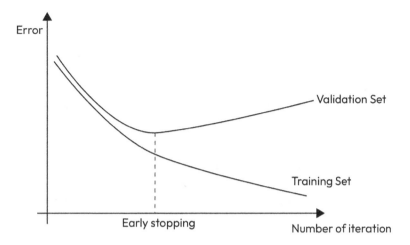

Figure 3.10 – Early stopping

- **Dropout**: Dropout is a technique in deep learning models that is used to randomly drop out some neurons during training, which helps to prevent the model from relying too heavily on a small subset of features or neurons and overfitting the training data. By dropping the weight of neurons in the model during the process, we make the model learn the general pattern and prevent it from memorizing the training data (overfitting).

- **Data augmentation**: Data augmentation is a method that we can use to artificially expand the training data size by applying transformations, such as rotation, scaling, and flipping, to the existing dataset, which helps us to extend our training data. This strategy aids in mitigating overfitting by offering the model a more diverse set of examples to learn from.

- **Ensemble methods**: Ensemble methods are techniques that are used to combine multiple models to improve their performance and prevent overfitting. This can be done by using techniques such as bagging, boosting, or stacking.

By using these techniques, it is possible to prevent overfitting and build models that generalize well to new, unseen data. In practice, it is important to monitor both the training and testing performance of the model and make adjustments accordingly to achieve the best possible generalization performance. We will explain how to split our data into training and testing in the next section.

Splitting data

When developing a machine learning model, it's important to split the data into training, validation, and test sets; this is called data splitting. This is done to evaluate the performance of the model on new, unseen data and to prevent overfitting.

The most common method for splitting the data is the train-test split, which splits the data into two sets: the training set, which is used to train the model, and the test set, which is used to evaluate the performance of the model. The data is randomly divided into two sets, with a typical split being 80% of the data for training and 20% for testing. Using this approach the model will be trained using the majority of the data (training data) and then tested on the remaining data (test set). Using this approach, we can ensure that the model's performance is based on new, unseen data.

Most of the time in machine learning model development, we have a set of hyperparameters for our model that we like to tune (we will explain hyperparameter tuning in the next subsection). In this case, we like to make sure that the performance that we get on the test set is reliable and not just by chance based on a set of hyperparameters. In this case, based on the size of our training data, we can divide the data into 60%, 20%, and 20% (or 70%, 15%, and 15%) for training, validation, and testing. In this case, we train the model on the training data and select the set of hyperparameters that give us the best performance on the validation set. We then report the actual model performance on the test set, which has not been seen or used before during model training or hyperparameter selection.

A more advanced method for splitting the data, especially when the size of our training data is limited, is k-fold cross-validation. In this method, the data is split into k equally sized "folds," and the model is trained and tested k times, with each fold being used as the test set once and the remaining folds used as the training set. The results of each fold are then averaged to get an overall measure of the model's performance. K-fold cross-validation is useful for small datasets where the train-test split may result in a large variance in performance evaluation. In this case, we report the average, minimum, and maximum performance of the model on each of the k folds, as shown in *Figure 3.11*.

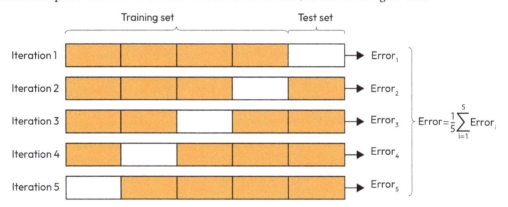

Figure 3.11 – K-fold cross-validation

Another variant of k-fold cross-validation is stratified k-fold cross-validation, which ensures that the distribution of the target variable is consistent across all folds. This is useful when dealing with imbalanced datasets, where the number of instances of one class is much smaller than the others.

Time series data requires special attention when splitting. In this case, we typically use a method called time series cross-validation, which preserves the temporal order of the data. In this method, the data is split into multiple segments, with each segment representing a fixed time interval. The model is then trained on the past data and tested on the future data. This helps to evaluate the performance of the model in real-world scenarios. You can see an example of how to split the data in a time series problem in *Figure 3.12*:

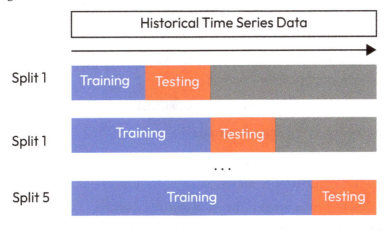

Figure 3.12 – Time series data splitting

In all cases, it's important to ensure that the split is done randomly but with the same random seed each time to ensure the reproducibility of the results. It's also important to ensure that the split is representative of the underlying data – that is, the distribution of the target variable should be consistent across all sets. Once we have split the data into different subsets for training and testing our model, we can try to find the best set of hyperparameters for our model. This process is called hyperparameter tuning and will be explained next.

Hyperparameter tuning

Hyperparameter tuning is an important step in the machine learning process that involves selecting the best set of hyperparameters for a given model. Hyperparameters are values that are set before the training process begins and can have a significant impact on the model's performance. Examples of hyperparameters include learning rate, regularization strength, number of hidden layers in a neural network, and many others.

The process of hyperparameter tuning involves selecting the best combination of hyperparameters that results in the optimal performance of the model. This is typically done by searching through a predefined set of hyperparameters and evaluating their performance on a validation set.

There are several methods for hyperparameter tuning, including grid search, random search, and Bayesian optimization. Grid search involves creating a grid of all possible hyperparameter combinations and evaluating each one on a validation set to determine the optimal set of hyperparameters. Random search, on the other hand, randomly samples hyperparameters from a predefined distribution and evaluates their performance on a validation set.

Random search and **grid search** are methods that are used to search the search space, entirely or randomly, without considering previous hyperparameter results. Thus, these methods are inefficient. An alternative Bayesian optimization method has been proposed that iteratively computes the posterior distribution of the function and considers past evaluations to find the best hyperparameters. Using this approach, we can find the best set of hyperparameters with less iterations.

Bayesian optimization utilizes past evaluations to probabilistically map hyperparameters to objective function scores, as demonstrated in the following equation:

$$P(score|hyperparameters)$$

Here are the steps Bayesian optimization undertakes:

1. It develops a surrogate probabilistic model for the objective function.
2. It identifies the optimal hyperparameters based on the surrogate.
3. It utilizes these hyperparameters in the actual objective function.
4. It updates the surrogate model to integrate the latest results.
5. It reiterates *steps 2* to *4* until it reaches the maximum iteration count or time limit.

Sequential model-based optimization (**SMBO**) methods are a formalization of Bayesian optimization, with trials run one after another, trying better hyperparameters each time and updating a probability model (surrogate). SMBO methods differ in *steps 3* and *4* – specifically, how they build a surrogate of the objective function and the criteria used to select the next hyperparameters. These variants include Gaussian processes, random forest regressions, and tree-structured Parzen estimators, among others.

In low-dimensional problems with numerical hyperparameters, Bayesian optimization is considered the best available hyperparameter optimization method. However, it is restricted to problems of moderate dimension.

In addition to these methods, there are also several libraries available that automate the process of hyperparameter tuning. Examples of these libraries include scikit-learn's `GridSearchCV` and `RandomizedSearchCV`, `Keras Tuner`, and `Optuna`. These libraries allow for efficient hyperparameter tuning and can significantly improve the performance of machine learning models.

Hyperparameter optimization in machine learning can be a complex and time-consuming process. Two primary complexity challenges arise in the search process: the trial execution time and the complexity of the search space, including the number of evaluated hyperparameter combinations. In deep learning, these challenges are especially pertinent due to the extensive search space and the utilization of large training sets.

To address these issues and reduce the search space, some standard techniques may be used. For example, reducing the size of the training dataset based on statistical sampling or applying feature selection techniques can help reduce the execution time of each trial. Additionally, identifying the most important hyperparameters for optimization and using additional objective functions beyond just accuracy, such as the number of operations or optimization time, can help reduce the complexity of the search space.

By combining accuracy with visualization through a deconvolution network, researchers have achieved superior results. However, it's important to note that these techniques are not exhaustive, and the best approach may depend on the specific problem at hand.

Another common approach for improving model performance is to use multiple models in parallel; these are called ensemble models. They are very useful in dealing with machine learning problems.

Ensemble models

Ensemble modeling is a technique in machine learning that combines the predictions of multiple models to improve overall performance. The idea behind ensemble models is that multiple models can be better than a single model as different models may capture different patterns in the data.

There are several types of ensemble models, all of which we'll cover in the following sections.

Bagging

Bootstrap aggregating, also known as **bagging**, is an ensemble method that combines multiple independent models trained on different subsets of the training data to reduce variance and improve model generalization.

The bagging algorithm can be summarized as follows:

1. Given a training dataset of size n, create m bootstrap samples of size n (that is, sample n instances with replacement m times).

2. Train a base model (for example, a decision tree) on each bootstrap sample independently.

3. Aggregate the predictions of all base models to obtain the ensemble prediction. This can be done by either taking the majority vote (in the case of classification) or the average (in the case of regression).

The bagging algorithm is particularly effective when the base models are unstable (that is, have high variance), such as decision trees, and when the training dataset is small.

The equation for aggregating the predictions of the base models depends on the type of problem (classification or regression). For classification, the ensemble prediction is obtained by taking the majority vote:

$$Y_{ensemble} = argmax_j \sum_{i=1}^{m} I\left(y_{ij} = j\right)$$

Here, y_{ij} is the predicted class of the i_{th} base model for the j_{th} instance and $I()$ is the indicator function (equal to 1 if x is true, and 0 otherwise).

For regression, the ensemble prediction is obtained by taking the average score:

$$Y_{ensemble} = \sum_{i=1}^{m} y_i$$

Here, y_i is the predicted value of the i_{th} base model.

The advantages of bagging are as follows:

- Improved model generalization by reducing variance and overfitting
- Ability to handle high-dimensional datasets with complex relationships
- Can be used with a variety of base models

The disadvantages of bagging are as follows:

- Increased model complexity and computation time due to the use of multiple base models
- It can sometimes lead to overfitting if the base models are too complex or the dataset is too small
- It does not work well when the base models are highly correlated or biased

Boosting

Boosting is another popular ensemble learning technique that aims to improve the performance of weak classifiers by combining them into a stronger classifier. Unlike bagging, boosting focuses on iteratively improving the accuracy of the classifier by adjusting the weights of the training examples. The basic idea behind boosting is to learn from the mistakes of the previous weak classifiers and to put more emphasis on the examples that were incorrectly classified in the previous iteration.

There are several boosting algorithms, but one of the most popular ones is AdaBoost (short for adaptive boosting). The AdaBoost algorithm works as follows:

1. First, it initializes the weights of the training examples to be equal.
2. Then, it trains a weak classifier on the training set.
3. Next, it computes the weighted error rate of the weak classifier.
4. After, it computes the importance of the weak classifier based on its weighted error rate.
5. Then, it increases the weights of the examples that were misclassified by the weak classifier.
6. Once it's done this, it normalizes the weights of the examples so that they sum up to one.
7. It repeats *steps 2* to *6* for a predetermined number of iterations or until the desired accuracy is achieved.

8. Finally, it combines the weak classifiers into a strong classifier by assigning weights to them based on their importance.

The final classifier is a weighted combination of the weak classifiers. The importance of each weak classifier is determined by its weighted error rate, which is computed as an equation:

$$ERROR_m = \frac{\sum_{i=1}^{N} w_i I(y_i - h_m(x_i))}{\sum_{i=1}^{N} w_i}$$

Here, m is the index of the weak classifier, N is the number of training examples, w_i is the weight of the i_{th} training example, y_i is the true label of the i_{th} training example, $h_m(x_i)$ is the prediction of the m_{th} weak classifier for the i_{th} training example, and $I(y_i - h_m(x_i))$ is an indicator function that returns 1 if the prediction of the weak classifier is incorrect and 0 otherwise.

The importance of the weak classifier is computed by the following equation:

$$\alpha_m = \ln \frac{1 - error_m}{error_m}$$

The weights of the examples are updated based on their importance:

$$w_i = w_i^{\alpha_m I(y_i - h_m(x_i))}$$

The final classifier is then obtained by combining the weak classifiers:

$$H_x = sign\left(\sum_{m=1}^{M} \alpha_m h_m(x)\right)$$

Here, M is the total number of weak classifiers, $h_m(x)$ is the prediction of the m-th weak classifier, and `sign()` is a function that returns +1 if its argument is positive and -1 otherwise.

Let's look at some of the advantages of boosting:

- Boosting can improve the accuracy of weak classifiers and can lead to a significant improvement in performance

- Boosting is relatively easy to implement and can be applied to a wide range of classification problems

- Boosting can handle noisy data and reduce the risk of overfitting

Here are some of the disadvantages of boosting:

- Boosting can be sensitive to outliers and can overfit to noisy data

- Boosting can be computationally expensive, especially when dealing with large datasets

- Boosting can be difficult to interpret as it involves combining multiple weak classifiers

Stacking

Stacking is another popular ensemble learning technique that combines the predictions of multiple base models by training a higher-level model on their predictions. The idea behind stacking is to leverage the strengths of different base models to achieve better predictive performance.

Here's how stacking works:

1. Divide the training data into two parts: the first part is used to train the base models, while the second part is used to create a new dataset of predictions from the base models.

2. Train multiple base models on the first part of the training data.

3. Use the trained base models to make predictions on the second part of the training data to create a new dataset of predictions.

4. Train a higher-level model (also known as a metamodel or blender) on the new dataset of predictions.

5. Use the trained higher-level model to make predictions on the test data.

The higher-level model is typically a simple model such as a linear regression, logistic regression, or a decision tree. The idea is to use the predictions of the base models as input features for the higher-level model. This way, the higher-level model learns to combine the predictions of the base models to make more accurate predictions.

Random forests

One of the most commonly known ensemble models is random forest, where the model combines the predictions of multiple decision trees and outputs the predictions. This is usually more accurate and prone to overfitting. We elaborated on Random Forest earlier in this chapter.

Gradient boosting

Gradient boosting is another ensemble model that can be used for classification and regression tasks. It works by getting a weak classifier (such as a simple tree), and in each step tries to improve this weak classifier to build a better model. The main idea here is that the model tries to focus on its mistakes in each step and improve itself by fitting the model by correcting the errors made in previous trees.

During each iteration, the algorithm computes the negative gradient of the loss function concerning the predicted values, followed by fitting a decision tree to these negative gradient values. The predictions of the new tree are then combined with the predictions of the previous trees, using a learning rate parameter that controls the contribution of each tree to the final prediction.

The overall prediction of the gradient boosting model is obtained by summing up the predictions of all the trees, which are weighted by their respective learning rates.

Let's take a look at the equation for the gradient boosting algorithm.

First, we initialize the model with a constant value:

$$F_0\left(x\right) = argmin_c \sum_{i=1}^{N} L\left(y_i, c\right)$$

Here, c is a constant, y_i is the true label of the *i-th* sample, N is the number of samples, and L is the loss function, which is used to measure the error between the predicted and true labels.

At each iteration, m, the algorithm fits a decision tree to the negative gradient values of the loss function concerning the predicted values, $r_m = -\nabla L(y, F(x))$. The decision tree predicts the negative gradient values, which are then used to update the predictions of the model via the following equation:

$$F_m(x) = F_{m-1}(x) + \eta\, h_m(x)$$

Here, $F_{m-1}(x)$ is the prediction of the model at the previous iteration, η is the learning rate, and $h_m(x)$ is the prediction of the decision tree at the current iteration.

The final prediction of the model is obtained by combining the predictions of all the trees:

$$F\left(x\right) = \sum_{m=1}^{M} \eta_m\, h_m(x)$$

Here, M is the total number of trees in the model and η_m and $h_m(x)$ are the learning rate and prediction of the *m-th* tree, respectively.

Let's look at some of the advantages of gradient boosting:

- High prediction accuracy
- Handles both regression and classification problems
- Can handle missing data and outliers
- Can be used with various loss functions
- Can handle high-dimensional data

Now, let's look at some of the disadvantages:

- Sensitive to overfitting, especially when the number of trees is large
- Computationally expensive and time-consuming to train, especially for large datasets
- Requires careful tuning of hyperparameters, such as the number of trees, the learning rate, and the maximum depth of the trees

With that, we have reviewed the ensemble models that can help us improve our model performance. However, sometimes, our dataset has some features that we need to consider before we apply machine learning models. One common case is when we have an imbalanced dataset.

Handling imbalanced data

In most real-world problems, our data is imbalanced, which means that the distribution of records from different classes (such as patients with and without cancer) is different. Handling imbalanced datasets is an important task in machine learning as it is common to have datasets with uneven class distribution. In such cases, the minority class is often under-represented, which can cause poor model performance and biased predictions. The reason behind this is that machine learning methods are trying to optimize their fitness function to minimize the error in the training set. Now, let's say that we have 99% of the data from the positive class and 1% from the negative class. In this case, if the model predicts all records as positive, the error will be 1%; however, this model is not useful for us. That's why, if we have an imbalanced dataset, we need to use various methods to handle imbalanced data. In general, we can have three categories of methods to handle imbalanced datasets:

- **Undersampling**: A very simple method that comes to mind is to use fewer training records from the majority class. This method works, but we need to consider that by using less training data, we are feeding less information to the model causes to have a less robust training and final model.

- **Resampling**: Resampling methods involve modifying the original dataset to create a balanced distribution. This can be achieved by either oversampling the minority class (creating more samples of the minority class) or undersampling the majority class (removing samples from the majority class). Oversampling techniques include **random oversampling**, **Synthetic Minority Oversampling Technique** (**SMOTE**), and **Adaptive Synthetic Sampling** (**ADASYN**). Undersampling techniques include **random undersampling**, **Tomek links**, and **cluster centroids**.

- **Handling imbalanced datasets in machine learning models**: Such as modifying cost function, or modified batching in deep learning models.

SMOTE

SMOTE is a widely used algorithm for handling imbalanced datasets in machine learning. It is a synthetic data generation technique that creates new, synthetic samples in the minority class by interpolating between existing samples. SMOTE works by identifying the k-nearest neighbors of a minority class sample and then generating new samples along the line segments that connect these neighbors.

Here are the steps of the SMOTE algorithm:

1. Select a minority class sample, x.

2. Choose one of its k-nearest neighbors, x'.

3. Generate a synthetic sample by interpolating between x and x'. To do this, choose a random number, r, between 0 and 1, and then calculate the synthetic sample, as follows:

$$new\ sample\ =\ x + r\ (x' - x)$$

This creates a new sample that is somewhere between x and x', but not the same as either one.

4. Repeat *steps 1* to *3* until the desired number of synthetic samples has been generated.

Here are the advantages and disadvantages of SMOTE:

- It helps to address the problem of class imbalance by creating synthetic samples in the minority class.
- SMOTE can be combined with other techniques, such as random undersampling or Tomek links, to further improve the balance of the dataset.
- SMOTE can be applied to both categorical and numerical data.
- SMOTE can sometimes create synthetic samples that are unrealistic or noisy, leading to overfitting.
- SMOTE can sometimes cause the decision boundary to be too sensitive to the minority class, leading to poor performance of the majority class.
- SMOTE can be computationally expensive for large datasets.

Here is an example of SMOTE in action. Suppose we have a dataset with two classes: the majority class (class 0) has 900 samples, and the minority class (class 1) has 100 samples. We want to use SMOTE to generate synthetic samples for the minority class:

1. We select a minority class sample, x.
2. We choose one of its k-nearest neighbors, x'.
3. We generate a synthetic sample by interpolating between x and x' using a random number, r:

$$new\ sample = x + r\left(x' - x\right)$$

For example, suppose x is $(1, 2)$, x' is $(3, 4)$, and r is 0.5. In this case, the new sample is as follows:

$$nesample = (1, 2) + 0.5\left((3, 4) - (1, 2)\right) = (2, 3)$$

4. We repeat *steps 1* to *3* until we have generated the desired number of synthetic samples. For example, suppose we want to generate 100 synthetic samples. We repeat *steps 1* to *3* for each of the 100 minority class samples and then combine the original minority class samples with the synthetic samples to create a balanced dataset with 200 samples in each class.

The NearMiss algorithm

The `NearMiss` algorithm is a technique for balancing class distribution by undersampling (removing) the records from the major class. When two classes have records that are very close to each other, eliminating some of the records from the majority class increases the distance between the two classes, which helps the classification process. To avoid information loss problems in the majority of undersampling methods, near-miss methods are widely used.

The working of nearest-neighbor methods is based on the following steps:

1. Find the distances between all records from the major class and minor class. Our goal is to undersample the records from the major class.

2. Choose n records from the major class that are closest to the minor class.

3. If there are k records in the minor class, the nearest method will return kn records from the major class.

There are three variations of applying the `NearMiss` algorithm that we can use to find the n closest records in the major class:

- We can select the records of the major class for which the average distances to the k-closest records of the minor class are the smallest.

- We can select the records of the major class for which the average distances to the k-farthest records of the minor class are the smallest.

- We can implement two steps. In the first step, for each record from the minor class, their M nearest neighbors will be stored. Then, the records from the major class are selected such that the average distance to the N nearest neighbors is the largest.

Cost-sensitive learning

Cost-sensitive learning is a method that's used to train machine learning models on imbalanced datasets. In imbalanced datasets, the number of examples in one class (usually the minority class) is much lower than in the other class (usually the majority class). Cost-sensitive learning involves assigning misclassification costs to the model that differ based on the class being predicted, which can help the model focus more on correctly classifying the minority class.

Let's assume we have a binary classification problem with two classes, positive and negative. In cost-sensitive learning, we assign different costs to different types of errors. For example, we may assign a higher cost to misclassifying a positive example as negative because in an imbalanced dataset, the positive class is the minority class, and misclassifying positive examples can have a greater impact on the performance of the model.

We can assign costs in the form of a confusion matrix:

	Predicted Positive	Predicted Negative
Actual Positive	TP_cost	FN_cost
Actual Negative	FP_cost	TN_cost

Table 3.2 – Confusion matrix costs

Here, `TP_cost`, `FN_cost`, `FP_cost`, and `TN_cost` are the costs associated with true positives, false negatives, false positives, and true negatives, respectively.

To incorporate the cost matrix into the training process, we can modify the standard loss function that the model optimizes during training. One common cost-sensitive loss function is the weighted cross-entropy loss, which is defined as follows:

$$loss = -\left(w_{pos}\, y\, log(\hat{y}) + w_{neg} \left(1 - y\right) log\left(1 - \hat{y}\right) \right)$$

Here, y is the true label (either 0 or 1), $\hat{y}$ is the predicted probability of the positive class, and w_{pos} and w_{neg} are weights that are assigned to the positive and negative classes, respectively.

The weights, w_{pos} and w_{neg}, can be determined by the costs assigned in the confusion matrix. For example, if we assign a higher cost to false negatives (that is, misclassifying a positive example as negative), we may set w_{pos} to a higher value than w_{neg}.

Cost-sensitive learning can also be used with other types of models, such as decision trees and SVMs. The concept of assigning costs to different types of errors can be applied in various ways to improve the performance of a model on imbalanced datasets. However, it's important to carefully select the appropriate cost matrix and loss function based on the specific characteristics of the dataset and the problem being solved:

- **Ensemble techniques**: Ensemble techniques combine multiple models to improve predictive performance. In imbalanced datasets, an ensemble of models can be trained on different subsets of the dataset, ensuring that each model is trained on both the minority and majority classes. Examples of ensemble techniques for imbalanced datasets include bagging and boosting.

- **Anomaly detection**: Anomaly detection techniques can be used to identify the minority class as an anomaly in the dataset. These techniques aim to identify rare events that are significantly different from the majority class. The identified samples can then be used to train the model on the minority class.

Data augmentation

The idea behind data augmentation is to generate new examples by applying transformations to the original ones, while still retaining the label. These transformations can include rotation, translation, scaling, flipping, and adding noise, among others. This can be particularly useful for imbalanced datasets, where the number of examples in one class is much smaller than in the other.

In the context of imbalanced datasets, data augmentation can be used to create new examples of the minority class, effectively balancing the dataset. This can be done by applying the same set of transformations to the minority class examples, creating a new set of examples that are still representative of the minority class but are slightly different from the original ones.

The equations that are involved in data augmentation are relatively simple as they are based on applying transformation functions to the original examples. For example, to rotate an image by a certain angle, we can use a rotation matrix:

$$x' = x \, cos(\theta) - y \, sin(\theta)$$

$$y' = x \, sin(\theta) + y \, cos(\theta)$$

Here, x and y are the original coordinates of a pixel in the image, x' and y' are the new coordinates after rotation, and θ is the angle of rotation.

Similarly, to apply translation, we can simply shift the image by a certain number of pixels:

$$x' = x + dx$$

$$y' = y + dy$$

Here, dx and dy are the horizontal and vertical shifts, respectively.

Data augmentation can be a powerful technique for addressing imbalanced datasets as it can create new examples that are representative of the minority class, while still preserving the label information. However, it is important to be careful when applying data augmentation as it can also introduce noise and artifacts in the data, and can lead to overfitting if not done properly.

In conclusion, handling imbalanced datasets is an important aspect of machine learning. There are several techniques available to handle imbalanced datasets, each with its advantages and disadvantages. The choice of technique depends on the dataset, the problem, and the available resources. Besides having imbalanced data, in the case of working on time series data, we might face correlated data. We'll take a closer look at this next.

Dealing with correlated data

Dealing with correlated time series data in machine learning models can be challenging as traditional techniques such as random sampling can introduce biases and overlook dependencies between data points. Here are some approaches that can help:

- **Time series cross-validation**: Time series data is often dependent on past values and it's important to preserve this relationship during model training and evaluation. Time series cross-validation involves splitting the data into multiple folds, with each fold consisting of a continuous block of time. This approach ensures that the model is trained on past data and evaluated on future data, which better simulates how the model will perform in real-world scenarios.

- **Feature engineering**: Correlated time series data can be difficult to model with traditional machine learning algorithms. Feature engineering can help transform the data into a more suitable format. Examples of feature engineering for time series data include creating lags or differences in the time series, aggregating data into time buckets or windows, and creating rolling statistics such as moving averages.

- **Time series-specific models**: There are several models specifically designed for time series data, such as **AutoRegressive Integrated Moving Average (ARIMA)**, **Seasonal ARIMA (SARIMA)**, **Prophet**, and **Long Short-Term Memory (LSTM)** networks. These models are designed to capture the dependencies and patterns in time series data and may outperform traditional machine learning models.

- **Time series preprocessing techniques**: Time series data can be preprocessed to remove correlations and make the data more suitable for machine learning models. Techniques such as differencing, detrending, and normalization can help remove trends and seasonal components from the data, which can help reduce correlations.

- **Dimensionality reduction techniques**: Correlated time series data can have a high dimensionality, which can make modeling difficult. Dimensionality reduction techniques such as PCA or autoencoders can help reduce the number of variables in the data while preserving the most important information.

In general, it's important to approach time series data with techniques that preserve the temporal dependencies and patterns in the data. This can require specialized modeling techniques and preprocessing steps.

Summary

In this chapter, we learned about various concepts related to machine learning, starting with data exploration and preprocessing techniques. We then explored various machine learning models, such as logistic regression, decision trees, support vector machines, and random forests, along with their strengths and weaknesses. We also discussed the importance of splitting data into training and test sets, as well as techniques for handling imbalanced datasets.

The chapter also covered the concepts of model bias, variance, underfitting, and overfitting, and how to diagnose and address these issues. We also explored ensemble methods such as bagging, boosting, and stacking, which can improve model performance by combining the predictions of multiple models.

Finally, we learned about the limitations and challenges of machine learning, including the need for large amounts of high-quality data, the risk of bias and unfairness, and the difficulty of interpreting complex models. Despite these challenges, machine learning offers powerful tools for solving a wide range of problems and has the potential to transform many industries and fields.

In the next chapter, we will discuss text preprocessing, which is required for text to be used by machine learning models.

References

- Shahriari, B., Swersky, K., Wang, Z., Adams, R.P., de Freitas, N.: *Taking the human out of the loop: A review of Bayesian optimization. Proceedings of the IEEE 104(1), 148–175 (2016). DOI 10.1109/JPROC.2015.2494218.*

4

Streamlining Text Preprocessing Techniques for Optimal NLP Performance

Text preprocessing stands as a vital initial step in the realm of **natural language processing** (**NLP**). It encompasses converting raw, unrefined text data into a format that machine learning algorithms can readily comprehend. To extract meaningful insights from textual data, it is essential to clean, normalize, and transform the data into a more structured form. This chapter provides an overview of the most commonly used text preprocessing techniques, including tokenization, stemming, lemmatization, stop word removal, and **part-of-speech** (**POS**) tagging, along with their advantages and limitations.

Effective text preprocessing is essential for various NLP tasks, including sentiment analysis, language translation, and information retrieval. By applying these techniques, raw text data can be transformed into a structured and normalized format that can be easily analyzed using statistical and machine learning methods. However, selecting the appropriate preprocessing techniques can be challenging since the optimal methods depend on the specific task and dataset at hand. Therefore, it is important to carefully evaluate and compare different text preprocessing techniques to determine the most effective approach for a given application.

The following topics will be covered in this chapter:

- Lowercasing in NLP
- Removing special characters and punctuations
- Removing stop words
- Named entity recognition (NER)
- POS tagging
- Explaining the preprocessing pipeline

Technical requirements

To follow along with the examples and exercises in this chapter on text preprocessing, you will need a working knowledge of a programming language such as Python, as well as some familiarity with NLP concepts. You will also need to have certain libraries installed, such as **Natural Language Toolkit (NLTK)**, **spaCy**, and **scikit-learn**. These libraries provide powerful tools for text preprocessing and feature extraction. It is recommended that you have access to a **Jupyter Notebook** environment or another interactive coding environment to facilitate experimentation and exploration. Additionally, having a sample dataset to work with can help you understand the various techniques and their effects on text data.

Text normalization is the process of transforming text into a standard form to ensure consistency and reduce variations. Different techniques are used for normalizing text, including lowercasing, removing special characters, spell checking, and stemming or lemmatization. We will explain these steps in detail, and how to use them, with code examples.

Lowercasing in NLP

Lowercasing is a common text preprocessing technique that's used in NLP to standardize text and reduce the complexity of vocabulary. In this technique, all the text is converted into lowercase characters.

The main purpose of lowercasing is to make the text uniform and avoid any discrepancies that may arise from capitalization. By converting all the text into lowercase, the machine learning algorithms can treat the same words that are capitalized and non-capitalized as the same, reducing the overall vocabulary size and making the text easier to process.

Lowercasing is particularly useful for tasks such as text classification, sentiment analysis, and language modeling, where the meaning of the text is not affected by the capitalization of the words. However, it may not be suitable for certain tasks, such as NER, where capitalization can be an important feature.

Removing special characters and punctuation

Removing special characters and punctuation is an important step in text preprocessing. Special characters and punctuation marks do not add much meaning to the text and can cause issues for machine learning models if they are not removed. One way to perform this task is by using regular expressions, such as the following:

```
re.sub(r"[^a-zA-Z0-9]+", "", string)
```

This will remove non-characters and numbers from our input string. Sometimes, there may be special characters that we would want to replace with a whitespace. Take a look at the following examples:

- president-elect
- body-type

In these two examples, we would want to replace the "-" with whitespace, as follows:

- President elect
- Body type

Next, we'll cover stop word removal.

Stop word removal

Stop words are words that do not contribute much to the meaning of a sentence or piece of text, and therefore can be safely removed without us losing much information. Examples of stop words include "a," "an," "the," "and," "in," "at," "on," "to," "for," "is," "are," and so on.

Stop word removal is a common text preprocessing step that is performed before any text analysis tasks, such as **sentiment analysis**, **topic modeling**, or **information retrieval**. The goal is to reduce the size of the vocabulary and the dimensionality of the feature space, which can improve the efficiency and effectiveness of subsequent analysis steps.

The process of stop word removal involves identifying a list of stop words (usually predefined or learned from a corpus), tokenizing the input text into words or tokens, and then removing any words that match the stop word list. The resulting text consists of only the important words that carry the meaning of the text.

Stop word removal can be performed using various programming languages, tools, and libraries. For example, NLTK, which is a popular Python library for NLP, provides a list of stop words for various languages, as well as a method for removing stop words from text.

Here's an example of stop word removal:

This is a sample sentence demonstrating stop word filtration.

After performing stop word removal, we get the following output:

Sample sentence demonstrating stop word filtration

This chapter contains Python code dedicated to this. You can refer to it for each of the actions that are described in this chapter.

As we can see, the stop words "This," "is," and "a," have been removed from the original sentence, leaving only the important words.

Spell checking and correction

Spell checking and correction involves correcting misspelled words in the text. This is important because misspelled words can cause inconsistencies in the data and affect the accuracy of algorithms. For example, take a look at the following sentence:

I am going to the bakkery

This would be transformed into the following:

I am going to the bakery

Let's move on to lemmatization.

Lemmatization

Lemmatization is a text normalization approach that aims to simplify a word to its base or dictionary form, referred to as a lemma. The primary objective of lemmatization is to aggregate various forms of the same word, facilitating their analysis as a unified term.

For example, consider the following sentence:

Three cats were chasing the mice in the fields, while one cat watched one mouse.

In the context of this sentence, "cat" and "cats" are two different forms of the same word, and "mouse" and "mice" are also two different forms of the same word. Lemmatization would reduce these words to their base forms:

the cat be chasing the mouse in the field, while one cat watched one mouse.

In this case, "cat" and "cats" have both been reduced to their base form of "cat," and "mouse" and "mice" have both been reduced to their base form of "mouse." This allows for better analysis of the text since the occurrences of "cat" and "mouse" are now treated as the same term, regardless of their inflectional variations.

Lemmatization is different from stemming, which involves reducing a word to a common stem that may not necessarily be a word in its own right. For example, the stem of "cats" and "cat" would both be "cat." The lemma of "cats" and "cat" would be "cat" as well.

Lemmatization can be performed using various NLP libraries and tools, such as NLTK, spaCy, and Stanford CoreNLP.

Stemming

Stemming involves reducing words to their fundamental or root form, referred to as the "stem." This process is commonly used in NLP to prepare text for analysis, retrieval, or storage. Stemming algorithms work by cutting off the ends or suffixes of words, leaving only the stem.

The goal of stemming is to convert all inflected or derived forms of a word into a common base form. For example, the stem of the word "running" is "run," and the stem of the word "runs" is also "run."

One commonly used stemming algorithm is the Porter stemming algorithm. This algorithm is based on a series of rules that identify suffixes and remove them from words to obtain the stem. For example, the Porter algorithm would convert the word "leaping" into "leap" by removing the "ing" suffix.

Let's look at an example sentence to see stemming in action:

They are running and leaping across the walls

Here's the stemmed text (using the Porter algorithm):

They are run and leap across the wall

As you can see, the words "running" and "leaping" have been converted into their base forms of "run" and "leap," respectively, and the suffix "s" has been removed from "walls."

Stemming can be useful for text analysis tasks such as information retrieval or sentiment analysis as it reduces the number of unique words in a document or corpus and can help to group similar words. However, stemming can also introduce errors as it can sometimes produce stems that are not actual words or produce stems that are not the intended base form of the word. For example, the stemmer might produce "walk" as the stem for both "walked" and "walking," even though "walk" and "walked" have different meanings. Therefore, it's important to evaluate the results of stemming to ensure that it is producing accurate and useful results.

NER

NER is an NLP technique that's designed to detect and categorize named entities within text, including but not limited to person's names, organization's names, locations, and more. NER's primary objective is to autonomously identify and extract information about these named entities from unstructured text data.

NER typically involves using machine learning models, such as **conditional random fields** (**CRFs**) or **recurrent neural networks** (**RNNs**), to tag words in a given sentence with their corresponding entity types. The models are trained on large annotated datasets that contain text with labeled entities. These models then use context-based rules to identify named entities in new text.

There are several categories of named entities that can be identified by NER, including the following:

- **Person**: A named individual, such as "Barack Obama"
- **Organization**: A named company, institution, or organization, such as "Google"
- **Location**: A named place, such as "New York City"
- **Date**: A named date or time, such as "January 1, 2023"
- **Product**: A named product or brand, such as "iPhone"

Here's an example of how NER works. Take a look at the following sentence:

Apple Inc. is a technology company headquartered in Cupertino, California.

Here, NER would identify "Apple Inc." as an organization and "Cupertino, California" as a location. The output of an NER system could be a structured representation of the sentence, as shown here:

```
{"organization": "Apple Inc.",
 "location": "Cupertino, California"}
```

NER has many applications in various fields, including **information retrieval**, **question-answering**, **sentiment analysis**, and more. It can be used to automatically extract structured information from unstructured text data, which can be further analyzed or used for downstream tasks.

There are different approaches and tools to perform NER, but the general steps when performing NER are as follows:

1. **Data collection**: The first step is to collect the data that will be used for NER. This data can be in the form of unstructured text, such as articles, social media posts, or web pages.

2. **Preprocessing**: The next step is to preprocess the data, which involves various steps such as tokenization, stop word removal, stemming or lemmatization, and normalization.

3. **Labeling**: After preprocessing, the next step is to label the data with named entity tags. There are different tagging schemes, but one of the most commonly used is the **Inside-Outside-Beginning (IOB)** tagging scheme. In this scheme, each word in the text is labeled as either **B** (**beginning of a named entity**), I (**inside of a named entity**), or **O** (**outside of a named entity**).

4. **Training**: Once the data has been labeled, the next step is to train a machine learning model to recognize named entities in new, unseen text. Different types of models can be used for NER, such as rule-based systems, statistical models, and deep learning models.

5. **Evaluation**: After training the model, it is important to evaluate its performance on a test dataset. This can help identify any issues with the model, such as overfitting, underfitting, or bias.

6. **Deployment**: Finally, the trained model can be deployed to perform NER on new, unseen text. This can be done in real time or in batch mode, depending on the application's requirements.

Here's an example of how NER can be performed:

Original text:

Apple is negotiating to buy a Chinese start-up this year.

Preprocessed text:

apple negotiating buy Chinese start-up year

Tagged text:

B-ORG   O   O   B-LOC   O   O

In this example, the named entities "Apple" and "Chinese" are identified as an organization (B-ORG) and a location (B-LOC), respectively. "this year" is not recognized as a named entity in this example, but it would be if a more complex tagging scheme is used or if the model is trained on data that would promote that.

Several libraries can be used for NER, depending on the programming language and specific needs of the project. Let's take a look at some commonly used libraries:

- **spaCy:** **spaCy** is a widely used open source library designed for various NLP tasks, including NER. Offering pre-trained models across multiple languages, the library additionally empowers users to undertake model training for distinct domains tailored to their specific needs.

- **NLTK:** This is another widely used library for NLP tasks, including NER. It provides several pre-trained models and also allows users to train their models.

- **Stanford Named Entity Recognizer** (**NER**): This is a Java-based NER tool that provides pre-trained models for several languages, including English, German, and Chinese.

- **AllenNLP:** AllenNLP is a popular open source library for building and evaluating NLP models, including NER. It provides pre-trained models for several tasks, including NER, and also allows users to train their own models.

- **Flair:** Flair is a Python library for state-of-the-art NLP, including NER. It provides pre-trained models for several languages and also allows users to train their own models.

- **General Architecture for Text Engineering** (**GATE**): This is a suite of tools for NLP, including NER. It provides a graphical interface for creating and evaluating NLP models and also allows users to develop custom plugins for specific tasks.

There are many other libraries available for NER, and the choice of library will depend on factors such as the programming language, available models, and specific requirements of the project. In the next section, we will explain POS tagging and different methods to perform this task.

POS tagging

POS tagging is the practice of attributing grammatical labels, such as nouns, verbs, adjectives, and others, to individual words within a sentence. This tagging process holds significance as a foundational step in various NLP tasks, including text classification, sentiment analysis, and machine translation.

POS tagging can be performed using different approaches such as rule-based methods, statistical methods, and deep learning-based methods. In this section, we'll provide a brief overview of each approach.

Rule-based methods

Rule-based methods for POS tagging involve defining a set of rules or patterns that can be used to automatically tag words in a text with their corresponding parts of speech, such as nouns, verbs, adjectives, and so on.

The process involves defining a set of rules or patterns for identifying the different parts of speech in a sentence. For example, a rule may state that any word ending in "-ing" is a gerund (a verb acting as a noun), while another rule may state that any word preceded by an article such as "a" or "an" is likely a noun.

These rules are typically based on linguistic knowledge, such as knowledge of grammar and syntax, and are often specific to a particular language. They can also be supplemented with lexicons or dictionaries that provide additional information about the meanings and usage of words.

The process of rule-based tagging involves applying these rules to a given text and identifying the parts of speech for each word. This can be done manually but is typically automated using software tools and programming languages that support regular expressions and pattern matching.

One advantage of rule-based methods is that they can be highly accurate when the rules are well-designed and cover a wide range of linguistic phenomena. They can also be customized to specific domains or genres of text, such as scientific literature or legal documents.

However, one limitation of rule-based methods is that they may not be able to capture the full complexity and variability of natural language, and may require significant effort to develop and maintain the rules as language evolves and changes over time. They may also struggle with ambiguity, such as in cases where a word can have multiple possible parts of speech depending on the context.

Despite these limitations, rule-based methods for POS tagging remain an important approach in NLP, especially for applications that require high accuracy and precision.

Statistical methods

Statistical methods for POS tagging are based on using probabilistic models to automatically assign the most likely POS tag to each word in a sentence. These methods rely on a training corpus of tagged text, where the POS tags have already been assigned to the words, to learn the probabilities of a particular word being associated with each tag.

Two main types of statistical methods are used for POS tagging: **Hidden Markov Models** (**HMMs**) and CRFs.

HMMs serve as a category of probabilistic models that are extensively applied in handling sequential data, including text. In the context of POS tagging, HMMs represent the probability distribution of a sequence of POS tags concerning a sequence of words. HMMs assume that the likelihood of a POS tag at a specific position within a sentence is contingent solely upon the preceding tag in the sequence. Furthermore, they presume that the likelihood of a particular word, given its tag, remains independent of other words within the sentence. To identify the most probable sequence of POS tags for a given sentence, HMMs employ the Viterbi algorithm.

CRFs are another type of probabilistic model that is commonly used for sequence labeling tasks, including POS tagging. CRFs differ from HMMs in that they model the conditional probability of the output sequence (that is, the POS tags) given the input sequence (that is, the words), rather than the joint probability of the output and input sequences. This allows CRFs to capture more complex dependencies between the input and output sequences than HMMs. CRFs use an iterative algorithm, such as gradient descent or L-BFGS, to learn the optimal set of weights for the model.

Let's look at the advantages of statistical methods:

- Statistical methods can capture the context of a word and the relationships between words in a sentence, leading to more accurate tagging results

- These methods can handle unseen words and sentences that are not present in the training data

- Statistical methods can be trained on large datasets, allowing them to capture more variations and patterns in the language

Now, let's look at the disadvantages:

- These methods require a large amount of annotated data for training, which can be time-consuming and expensive to create

- Statistical methods can be sensitive to the quality of the training data and may perform poorly if the data is noisy or biased

- Statistical models are typically black boxes, making it difficult to interpret the decisions made by the model

Deep learning-based methods

Deep learning-based methods for POS tagging involve training a neural network model to predict the POS tags for each word in a given sentence. These methods can learn complex patterns and relationships in the text data to accurately tag words with their appropriate parts of speech.

One of the most popular deep learning-based methods for POS tagging is using an RNN with LSTM cells. LSTM-based models can process sequences of words and capture dependencies between them. The input to the model is a sequence of word embeddings, which are vector representations of words in a high-dimensional space. These embeddings are learned during the training process.

The LSTM-based model is comprised of three main layers: an input layer, an LSTM layer, and an output layer. The structure involves taking word embeddings as input into the input layer. Subsequently, the LSTM layer processes the sequence of these embeddings, aiming to grasp the interdependencies inherent within them. Ultimately, the output layer is responsible for predicting the POS tag for each word within the input sequence. Another popular deep learning-based method for POS tagging is using a transformer-based model, such as **Bidirectional Encoder Representations from Transformers (BERT)**. BERT is a language model that comes pre-trained and employs a transformer-based architecture to acquire a profound understanding of contextual relationships among words within a sentence. It undergoes training with vast quantities of text data and can be fine-tuned to excel in diverse NLP tasks, one of which is POS tagging.

To use BERT for POS tagging, the input sentence must be tokenized, and each token must be assigned an initial POS tag. The token embeddings are then fed into the pre-trained BERT model, which outputs contextualized embeddings for each token. These embeddings are passed through a feedforward neural network to predict the final POS tag for each token.

Deep learning approaches for POS tagging have demonstrated leading-edge performance across numerous benchmark datasets. Nonetheless, their effectiveness demands substantial training data and computational resources, and the training process can be time-consuming. Moreover, they may suffer from a lack of interpretability, which makes it difficult to understand how the model is making its predictions.

Several libraries are available for performing POS tagging in various programming languages, including Python, Java, and C++. Some popular NLP libraries that provide POS tagging functionality include NLTK, spaCy, Stanford CoreNLP, and Apache OpenNLP.

Here is an example of POS tagging using the NLTK library in Python:

```
import nltk
input_sentence = "The young white cat jumps over the lazy dog"
processed_tokens = nltk.word_tokenize(input_sentence)
tags = nltk.pos_tag(processed_tokens)
print(tags)
```

The output is as follows:

```
[('The', 'DT'), (young, 'JJ'), (white, 'NN'), ('cat', 'NN'), ('jumps',
'VBZ'), ('over', 'IN'), ('the', 'DT'), ('lazy', 'JJ'), ('dog', 'NN')]
```

In this example, the `nltk.pos_tag()` function is used to tag the words in the sentence. The function returns a list of tuples where each tuple contains a word and its POS tag. The POS tags that have been used here are based on the **Penn Treebank tagset**.

Regular expressions

A regular expression is a type of text pattern that has various applications in modern programming languages and software. They are useful for validating whether an input conforms to a particular text pattern, locating text within a larger text body that matches the pattern, replacing text that matches the pattern with alternative text or rearranging parts of the matched text, and dividing a block of text into a list of subtexts, but can cause unintended consequences if used incorrectly.

In computer science and mathematics, the term **regular expression** is derived from the concept of "regularity" in mathematical expressions.

A regular expression, often referred to as regex or regexp, is a series of characters that constitutes a search pattern. Regular expressions are used to match and manipulate text, typically in the context of text processing, search algorithms, and NLP.

A regular expression comprises a mix of characters and metacharacters, which collectively establish a pattern to search for within a text string. The simplest form of a regular expression is a mere sequence of characters that must be matched precisely. For example, the regular expression "hello" would match any string that contains the characters "hello" in sequence.

Metacharacters are unique characters within regular expressions that possess pre-defined meanings. For instance, the "." (dot) metacharacter is employed to match any individual character, whereas the "*" (asterisk) metacharacter is used to match zero or more instances of the preceding characters or group. Regular expressions can be used for a wide range of text-processing tasks. Let's take a closer look.

Validating input

Regular expressions can be used to validate input by matching it against a pattern. For example, you can use a regular expression to validate an email address or a phone number.

Text manipulation

Text manipulation using regular expressions involves using pattern-matching techniques to find and manipulate text strings in a document or dataset. Regular expressions are powerful tools for working with text data, allowing for complex search and replace operations, text extraction, and formatting.

Some common text manipulation tasks that can be accomplished with regular expressions are as follows:

- **Search and replace**: Using regular expressions to search for specific patterns or character sequences in a document and replace them with other text or formatting

- **Data extraction**: Regular expressions can be used for data extraction from text by defining patterns that match specific data formats

Here are the general steps for using regular expressions for data extraction:

1. **Define a regular expression pattern**: The first step is to define a regular expression pattern that matches the data you want to extract. For example, if you want to extract all phone numbers from a text document, you can define a pattern that matches the format of a phone number.

2. **Compile the regular expression pattern**: After establishing the regular expression pattern, the next step involves compiling it into a regular expression object, which can then be utilized for matching purposes.

3. **Search for the pattern in the text**: Once you have compiled the regular expression object, you can use it to search for the pattern in the text. You can search for the pattern in a single string or a larger block of text.

4. **Extract the matched data**: After you have searched for the pattern in the text, you can extract the data that matches that pattern. You can extract all occurrences of the matched data or only the first occurrence.

Here's an example of how to extract all email addresses from a string using regular expressions in Python:

```
import re
text = "John's email is john@example.com and Jane's email is jane@
example.com"
# Pattern for email addresses:
```

```
pattern = r'\b[A-Za-z0-9._%+-]+@[A-Za-z0-9.-]+\.[A-Z|a-z]{2,}\b'
regex = re.compile(pattern)
# Search for all occurrences of the pattern in the text:
matches = regex.findall(text)
print(matches)
```

Here's the output:

```
['john@example.com', 'jane@example.com']
```

Next, we'll cover text cleaning.

Text cleaning

Text cleaning means using regular expressions to clean and standardize text data, thereby removing unwanted characters, whitespace, or other formatting.

Here are some common text-cleaning techniques that use regular expressions:

- **Removing special characters**: Regular expressions can be used to match and remove specific characters such as punctuation marks, brackets, and other special symbols. For example, the [^a-zA-Z0-9] regular expression will match any non-alphanumeric character.

- **Removing stop words**: Stop words are common words such as "the," "and," and "but" that are often removed from text to focus on the most meaningful words. Regular expressions can be used to match and remove these words from text.

- **Removing HTML tags**: If you're working with text that has been scraped from a website, you may need to remove HTML tags before analyzing the text. Regular expressions can be used to match and remove HTML tags.

- **Converting text into lowercase**: Regular expressions can be used to convert all text into lowercase or uppercase, which can make it easier to compare and analyze.

- **Normalizing text**: Normalization involves transforming text into a standard format. Regular expressions can be used to perform tasks such as stemming and lemmatization, which involves reducing words to their root form.

By using regular expressions for text cleaning, you can remove noise and irrelevant information from text, making it easier to analyze and extract meaningful insights.

Parsing

Parsing involves analyzing a text string to discern its grammatical structure according to a specified grammar. Regular expressions serve as potent instruments for text parsing, especially when dealing with uncomplicated and regular grammatical patterns.

To parse text using regular expressions, you need to define a grammar for the language you want to parse. The grammar should specify the possible components of a sentence, such as nouns, verbs, adjectives, and so on, as well as the rules that dictate how these components can be combined to form valid sentences.

Once you have defined the grammar, you can use regular expressions to identify the individual components of a sentence and the relationships between them. For example, you can use regular expressions to match all the nouns in a sentence or to identify the subject and object of a verb.

One common approach to parsing with regular expressions is to define a set of patterns that correspond to the different parts of speech and sentence structures in your grammar. For example, you might define a pattern for matching nouns, a pattern for matching verbs, and a pattern for matching sentences that consist of a subject followed by a verb and an object.

To use these patterns for parsing, you would apply them to a text string using a regular expression engine, which would match the patterns to the appropriate parts of the string. The output of the parsing process would be a parse tree or other data structure that represents the grammatical structure of the sentence.

One limitation of regular expression parsing is that it is generally not suitable for handling more complex or ambiguous grammar. For example, it can be difficult to handle cases where a word could be either a noun or a verb depending on the context, or where the structure of a sentence is ambiguous.

We can also use regular expressions to break a larger text document into smaller chunks or tokens based on specific patterns or delimiters.

To use regular expressions for text manipulation, you typically need to define a pattern that matches the text you want to find or manipulate. This pattern can include special characters and syntax to define the specific sequence of characters, numbers, or other elements that make up the text string.

For example, the regular expression pattern $\d{3}-\d{2}-\d{4}$ might be used to search for and extract Social Security numbers in a larger text document. This pattern matches a sequence of three digits, followed by a dash, then two more digits, another dash, and four final digits followed by a non-digit, which together represent the standard format for a Social Security number in the USA.

Once you have defined your regular expression pattern, you can use it with various text manipulation tools and programming languages, such as grep, sed, awk, Perl, Python, and many others, to perform complex text manipulation tasks.

Some programming languages, such as Perl and Python, have built-in support for regular expressions. Other programming languages, such as Java and C++, require you to use a library or API to work with regular expressions.

While regular expressions are powerful tools for text processing, they can also be complex and difficult to understand. It's important to be familiar with the syntax and behavior of regular expressions to use them effectively in your code.

Tokenization

Tokenization is a process in NLP that involves breaking down a piece of text or a sentence into individual words or terms, known as tokens. The tokenization process can be applied to various forms of data, such as textual documents, social media posts, web pages, and more.

The tokenization process is an important initial step in many NLP tasks as it transforms unstructured text data into a structured format that can be analyzed using machine learning algorithms or other techniques. These tokens can be used to perform various operations in the text, such as counting word frequencies, identifying the most common phrases, and so on.

There are different methods of tokenization:

- **Word tokenization**: This method splits a piece of text into individual words or tokens using whitespace, punctuation, and other characters as delimiters. For example, take a look at the following sentence:

  The nimble white cat jumps over the sleepy dog

  This can be tokenized into the following list of words:

  ["The", "nimble", "white", "cat", "jumps", "over", "the", "sleepy", "dog"]

- **Sentence tokenization**: This method splits a piece of text into individual sentences by using punctuation marks such as periods, exclamation marks, and question marks as delimiters. For example, take a look at the following paragraph:

  This is the first sentence.

  This is the second sentence.

  This is the third sentence.

  This can be tokenized into the following list of sentences:

  ["This is the first sentence.",

  "This is the second sentence.",

  "This is the third sentence."]

- **Regular expression tokenization**: This method uses regular expressions to define the tokenization rules. Regular expressions can be used to match patterns in the text, such as email addresses, URLs, or phone numbers, and extract them as individual tokens.

Tokenization is an important step in NLP and is used in many applications, such as sentiment analysis, document classification, machine translation, and more.

Tokenization is also an important step in language models. For example, in BERT, which is a well-known language model, a tokenizer is a sub-word tokenizer, meaning it breaks down words into smaller sub-word units called tokens. It uses **WordPiece** tokenization, which is a data-driven approach that builds a large vocabulary of sub-words based on the corpus of text being trained on.

Using a tokenizer is an important step in language models as well. For example, BERT utilizes a WordPiece tokenizer, which employs the technique of dividing words into either their full forms or smaller components known as word pieces. This means that a single word can be represented by several tokens. It employs a data-driven approach that builds a large vocabulary of sub-words based on the corpus of text being trained on. These sub-word units are represented as embeddings that are used as input to the BERT model.

One of the key features of the BERT tokenizer is that it can handle **out-of-vocabulary** (**OOV**) words. If the tokenizer encounters a word that is not in its vocabulary, it will break the word down into sub-words and represent the word as a combination of its sub-word embeddings. We will explain BERT and its tokenizer in more detail later in this book. The benefit of using a tokenizer in language models is that we can limit the number of inputs to the size of our dictionary rather than all possible inputs. For example, BERT has a 30,000-word vocabulary size, which helps us limit the size of the deep learning language model. Using a bigger tokenizer will increase the size of the model. In the next section, we will explain how to use the methods that were covered in this chapter in a complete preprocessing pipeline.

Explaining the preprocessing pipeline

We will explain a complete preprocessing pipeline that has been provided by the authors to you, the reader. Please refer to notebook: Ch4_Preprocessing_pipeline.ipynb.

As shown in the following code, the input is a formatted text with encoded tags, similar to what we can extract from HTML web pages:

```
"<SUBJECT LINE> Employees details<END><BODY TEXT>Attached are 2
files,\n1st one is pairoll, 2nd is healtcare!<END>"
```

Let's take a look at the effect of applying each step to the text:

1. Decode/remove encoding:

    Employees details. Attached are 2 files, 1st one is pairoll, 2nd is healtcare!

2. Lowercasing:

    employees details. attached are 2 files, 1st one is pairoll, 2nd is healtcare!

3. Digits to words:

    employees details. attached are two files, first one is pairoll, second is healtcare!

4. Remove punctuation and other special characters:

    employees details attached are two files first one is pairoll second is healtcare

5. Spelling corrections:

    employees details attached are two files first one is payroll second is healthcare

6. Remove stop words:

    employees details attached two files first one payroll second healthcare

7. Stemming:

    employe detail attach two file first one payrol second healthcar

8. Lemmatizing:

    employe detail attach two file first one payrol second healthcar

With that, we've learned about different preprocessing methods. Next, we'll review a piece of code for performing NER and POS.

Code for NER and POS

Please refer to notebook: Ch4_NER_and_POS.ipynb.

For this example, we used the spaCy library for Python to perform these tasks. Here our input is:

```
The companies that would be releasing their quarterly reports tomorrow
are Microsoft, 4pm, Google, 4pm, and AT&T, 6pm.
```

Here's the output for NER:

The companies that would be releasing their quarterly DATE reports tomorrow DATE are Microsoft ORG , 4pm TIME , Google ORG , 4pm TIME , and AT&T ORG , 6pm TIME .

As you can see, using NER, we were able to detect parts of the sentence that are related to company names (ORG) or dates.

Figure 4.1 shows an example of performing POS tagging:

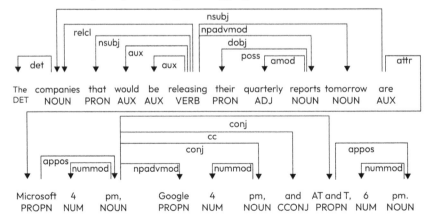

Figure 4.1 – POS tagging using spaCy

Here's the output:

```
[['companies', 'NOUN'],
 ['releasing', 'VERB'],
 ['quarterly', 'ADJ'],
 ['reports', 'NOUN'],
 ['tomorrow', 'NOUN'],
 ['Microsoft', 'PROPN'],
 ['pm', 'NOUN'],
 ['Google', 'PROPN'],
 ['pm', 'NOUN'],
 ['AT&T', 'PROPN'],
 ['pm', 'NOUN']]
```

The preceding code examples exemplify the various aspects of preprocessing, which processes raw text and transforms it into a form that suits the downstream model so that it suits the purpose of the overall design.

Summary

In this chapter, we covered a range of techniques and methods for text preprocessing, including normalization, tokenization, stop word removal, POS tagging, and more. We explored different approaches to these techniques, such as rule-based methods, statistical methods, and deep learning-based methods. We also discussed the advantages and disadvantages of each method and provided examples and code snippets to illustrate their use.

At this point, you should have a solid understanding of the importance of text preprocessing and the various techniques and methods available for cleaning and preparing text data for analysis. You should be able to implement these techniques using popular libraries and frameworks in Python and understand the trade-offs between different approaches. Furthermore, you should have a better understanding of how to process text data to achieve better results in NLP tasks such as sentiment analysis, topic modeling, and text classification.

In the next chapter, we will explain text classification, and different methods for performing this task.

Empowering Text Classification: Leveraging Traditional Machine Learning Techniques

In this chapter, we'll delve into the fascinating world of text classification, a foundational task in **natural language processing** (**NLP**) and **machine learning** (**ML**) that deals with categorizing text documents into predefined classes. As the volume of digital text data continues to grow exponentially, the ability to accurately and efficiently classify text has become increasingly important for a wide range of applications, such as sentiment analysis, spam detection, and document organization. This chapter provides a comprehensive overview of the key concepts, methodologies, and techniques that are employed in text classification, catering to readers from diverse backgrounds and skill levels.

We'll begin by exploring the various types of text classification tasks and their unique characteristics, offering insights into the challenges and opportunities each type presents. Next, we'll introduce the concept of **N-grams** and discuss how they can be utilized as features for text classification, capturing not only individual words but also the local context and word sequences within the text. We'll then examine the widely used **term frequency-inverse document frequency** (**TF-IDF**) method, which assigns weights to words based on their frequency in a document and across the entire corpus, showcasing its effectiveness in distinguishing relevant words for classification tasks.

Following that, we'll delve into the powerful **Word2Vec** algorithm and its application in text classification. We'll discuss how **Word2Vec** creates dense vector representations of words that capture semantic meaning and relationships, and how these embeddings can be used as features to improve classification performance. Furthermore, we'll cover popular architectures such as **continuous bag-of-words** (**CBOW**) and Skip-Gram, providing a deeper understanding of their inner workings.

Lastly, we'll explore the concept of topic modeling, a technique for discovering hidden thematic structures within a collection of documents. We'll examine popular algorithms such as **latent Dirichlet allocation** (**LDA**) and describe how topic modeling can be applied to text classification, enabling the discovery of semantic relationships between documents and improving classification performance.

Throughout this chapter, we aim to provide a thorough understanding of the underlying concepts and techniques that are employed in text classification, equipping you with the knowledge and skills needed to successfully tackle real-world text classification problems.

The following topics will be covered in this chapter:

- Types of text classification
- Text classification based on N-grams
- Text classification based on TF-IDF
- Word2Vec and its application in text classification
- Topic modeling
- Reviewing our use case – ML system design for NLP classification in a Jupyter notebook

Technical requirements

To effectively read and understand this chapter, it is essential to have a solid foundation in various technical areas. A strong grasp of fundamental concepts in NLP, ML, and linear algebra is crucial. Familiarity with text preprocessing techniques, such as tokenization, stop word removal, and stemming or lemmatization, is necessary to comprehend the data preparation stage.

Additionally, understanding basic ML algorithms, such as logistic regression and **support vector machines (SVMs)**, is crucial for implementing text classification models. Finally, being comfortable with evaluation metrics such as accuracy, precision, recall, and F1 score, along with concepts such as overfitting, underfitting, and hyperparameter tuning, will enable a deeper appreciation of the challenges and best practices in text classification.

Types of text classification

Text classification is an NLP task where ML algorithms assign predefined categories or labels to text based on its content. It involves training a model on a labeled dataset to enable it to accurately predict the category of unseen or new text inputs. Text classification methods can be categorized into three main types – **supervised learning**, **unsupervised learning**, and **semi-supervised learning**:

- **Supervised learning**: This type of text classification involves training a model on labeled data, where each data point is associated with a target label or category. The model then uses this labeled data to learn the patterns and relationships between the input text and the target labels. Examples of supervised learning algorithms for text classification include naive bayes, SVMs, and neural networks such as **convolutional neural networks (CNNs)** and **recurrent neural networks (RNNs)**.

- **Unsupervised learning**: This type of text classification involves clustering or grouping text documents into categories or topics without any prior knowledge of the categories or labels. Unsupervised learning is useful when there is no labeled data available or when the number of categories or topics is not known. Examples of unsupervised learning algorithms for text classification include K-means clustering, LDA, and **hierarchical Dirichlet process (HDP)**.

- **Semi-supervised learning**: This type of text classification combines both supervised and unsupervised learning approaches. It involves using a small amount of labeled data to train a model and then using the model to classify the remaining unlabeled data. The model then uses the unlabeled data to improve its classification performance. Semi-supervised learning is useful when labeled data is scarce or expensive to obtain. Examples of semi-supervised learning algorithms for text classification include **self-training**, **co-training**, and **multi-view learning**.

Each of these text classification types has its strengths and weaknesses and is suitable for different types of applications. Understanding these types can help in choosing the appropriate approach for a given problem. In the following subsections, we'll explain each of these methods in detail.

Supervised learning

Supervised learning is a type of ML where an algorithm learns from labeled data to predict the label of new, unseen data.

In the context of text classification, supervised learning involves training a model on a labeled dataset, where each document or text sample is labeled with the corresponding category or class. The model then uses this training data to learn patterns and relationships between the text features and their associated labels:

1. In a supervised text classification task, the first step is to obtain a labeled dataset, where each text sample is annotated with its corresponding category or class.

   A labeled dataset is assumed to possess the highest level of reliability. Often, it is derived by having subject matter experts manually review the text and assign the appropriate class to each item. In other scenarios, there may be automated methods for deriving the labels. For instance, in cybersecurity, you may collect historical data and then assign labels, which may collect the outcome that followed each item – that is, whether the action was legitimate or not. Since such historical data exists in most domains, that too can serve as a reliable labeled set.

2. The next step is to preprocess the text data to prepare it for modeling. This may include steps such as tokenization, stemming or lemmatization, removing stop words, and other text preprocessing techniques.

3. After preprocessing, the text data is transformed into numerical features, often using techniques such as bag-of-words or TF-IDF encoding.

4. Then, a supervised learning algorithm such as logistic regression, SVM, or a neural network is trained on the labeled dataset using these numerical features.

Once the model has been trained, it can be used to predict the category or class of new, unseen text data based on the learned patterns and relationships between the text features and their associated labels.

Supervised learning algorithms are commonly used for text classification tasks. Let's look at some common supervised learning algorithms that are used for text classification.

Naive Bayes

Naive Bayes is a probabilistic algorithm that is commonly used for text classification. It is based on Bayes' theorem, which states that the probability of a hypothesis (in this case, a document belonging to a particular class), given some observed evidence (in this case, the words in the document), is proportional to the probability of the evidence given the hypothesis times the prior probability of the hypothesis. Naive Bayes assumes that the features (words) are independent of each other given the class label, which is where the "naive" part of the name comes from.

Logistic regression

Logistic regression is a statistical method that is used for binary classification problems (that is, problems where there are only two possible classes). It models the probability of the document belonging to a particular class using a logistic function, which maps any real-valued input to a value between 0 and 1.

SVM

SVM is a powerful classification algorithm that is used in a variety of applications, including text classification. SVM works by finding the hyperplane that best separates the data into different classes. In text classification, the features are typically the words in the document, and the hyperplane is used to divide the space of all possible documents into different regions corresponding to different classes.

All of these algorithms can be trained using labeled data, where the class labels are known for each document in the training set. Once trained, the model can be used to predict the class label of new, unlabeled documents. The performance of the model is typically evaluated using metrics such as accuracy, precision, recall, and F1 score.

Unsupervised learning

Unsupervised learning is a type of ML where the data is not labeled and the algorithm is left to find patterns and structures on its own. In the context of text classification, unsupervised learning methods can be used when there is no labeled data available or when the goal is to discover hidden patterns in the text data.

One common unsupervised learning method for text classification is **clustering**. Clustering algorithms group similar documents together based on their content, without any prior knowledge of what each document is about. Clustering can be used to identify topics in a collection of documents or to group similar documents together for further analysis.

Another popular unsupervised learning algorithm for text classification is **LDA**. LDA is a probabilistic generative model that assumes that each document in a corpus is a mixture of topics, and each topic is a probability distribution over words. LDA can be used to discover the underlying topics in a collection of documents, even when the topics are not explicitly labeled.

Finally, word embeddings are a popular unsupervised learning technique used for text classification. Word embeddings are dense vector representations of words that capture their semantic meaning based on the context in which they appear. They can be used to identify similar words and to find relationships between words, which can be useful for tasks such as text similarity and recommendation systems. Common word embedding models include Word2Vec and GloVe.

Word2Vec is a popular algorithm that's used to generate word embeddings, which are vector representations of words in a high-dimensional space. The algorithm was developed by a team of researchers at Google, led by Tomas Mikolov, in 2013. The main idea behind Word2Vec is that words that appear in similar contexts tend to have similar meanings.

The algorithm takes in a large corpus of text as input and generates a vector representation for each word in the vocabulary. The vectors are typically high-dimensional (for example, 100 or 300 dimensions) and can be used to perform various NLP tasks, such as sentiment analysis, text classification, and machine translation.

Two main architectures are used in Word2Vec: **CBOW** and **skip-gram**. In the CBOW architecture, the algorithm tries to predict the target word given a window of context words. In the skip-gram architecture, the algorithm tries to predict the context words given a target word. The training objective is to maximize the likelihood of the target word or context words given the input.

Word2Vec has been widely adopted in the NLP community and has shown state-of-the-art performance on various benchmarks. It has also been used in many real-world applications, such as recommender systems, search engines, and chatbots.

Semi-supervised learning

Semi-supervised learning is an ML paradigm that sits between supervised and unsupervised learning. It utilizes a combination of labeled and unlabeled data for training, which is especially useful when the underlying models require labeled data which is expensive or time-consuming. This approach allows the model to leverage the information in the unlabeled data to improve its performance on the classification task.

In the context of text classification, semi-supervised learning can be beneficial when we have a limited number of labeled documents but a large corpus of unlabeled documents. The goal is to improve the performance of the classifier by leveraging the information contained in the unlabeled data.

There are several common semi-supervised learning algorithms, including label propagation and co-training. We'll discuss each of these in more detail next.

Label propagation

Label propagation is a graph-based semi-supervised learning algorithm. It builds a graph using both labeled and unlabeled data points, with each data point represented as a node and edges representing the similarity between nodes. The algorithm works by propagating the labels from the labeled nodes to the unlabeled nodes based on their similarity.

The key idea is that similar data points should have similar labels. The algorithm begins by assigning initial label probabilities to the unlabeled nodes, typically based on their similarity to labeled nodes. Then, an iterative process propagates these probabilities throughout the graph until convergence. The final label probabilities are used to classify the unlabeled data points.

Co-training

Co-training is another semi-supervised learning technique that trains multiple classifiers on different views of the data. A view is a subset of features that are sufficient for the learning task and are conditionally independent given the class label. The basic idea is to use one classifier's predictions to label some of the unlabeled data, and then use that newly labeled data to train the other classifier. This process is performed iteratively, with each classifier improving the other until a stopping criterion is met.

To apply semi-supervised learning in a specific domain, let's consider a medical domain where we want to classify scientific articles into different categories such as **cardiology**, **neurology**, and **oncology**. Suppose we have a small set of labeled articles and a large set of unlabeled articles.

A possible approach could be to use label propagation by creating a graph of articles where the nodes represent the articles and the edges represent the similarity between the articles. The similarity could be based on various factors, such as the words used, the topics covered, or the citation networks between the articles. After propagating the labels, we can classify the unlabeled articles based on the final label probabilities.

Alternatively, we could use co-training by splitting the features into two views, such as the abstract and the full text of the articles. We would train two classifiers, one for each view, and iteratively update the classifiers using the predictions made by the other classifier on the unlabeled data.

In both cases, the goal is to leverage the information in the unlabeled data to improve the performance of the classifier in the specific domain.

In this chapter, we'll elaborate on supervised text classification and topic modeling.

Sentence classification using one-hot encoding vector representation

One-hot encoded vector representation is a method of representing categorical data, such as words, as binary vectors. In the context of text classification, one-hot encoding can be used to represent text data as numerical input features for a classification model. Here's a detailed explanation of text classification using one-hot encoding vectors.

Text preprocessing

The first step is to preprocess the text data, as explained in the previous chapter. The main goal of preprocessing is to transform raw text into a more structured and consistent format that can be easily understood and processed by ML algorithms. Here are several reasons why text preprocessing is essential for one-hot encoded vector classification:

- **Noise reduction**: Raw text data often contains noise, such as typos, spelling errors, special characters, and formatting inconsistencies. Preprocessing helps to clean the text, reducing noise that may negatively impact the performance of the classification model.

- **Dimensionality reduction**: One-hot encoded vector representation has a high dimensionality as each unique word in the dataset corresponds to a separate feature. Preprocessing techniques, such as stop word removal, stemming, or lemmatization, can help reduce the size of the vocabulary, leading to a lower-dimensional feature space. This can improve the efficiency of the classification algorithm and reduce the risk of overfitting.

- **Consistent representation**: Converting all text to lowercase and applying stemming or lemmatization ensures that words with the same meaning or root form are consistently represented in the one-hot encoding vectors. This can help the classification model learn more meaningful patterns from the data as it will not treat different forms of the same word as separate features.

- **Handling irrelevant information**: Preprocessing can help remove irrelevant information, such as URLs, email addresses, or numbers, that may not contribute to the classification task. Removing such information can improve the model's ability to focus on the meaningful words and patterns in the text.

- **Improving model performance**: Preprocessed text data can lead to better performance of the classification model as the model will learn from a cleaner and more structured dataset. This can result in improved accuracy and generalization to new, unseen text data.

Once we preprocess the text, we can start extracting the words in the text. We call this task vocabulary construction.

Vocabulary construction

Construct a vocabulary containing all unique words in the preprocessed text. Assign a unique index to each word in the vocabulary.

Vocabulary construction is an essential step in preparing text data for one-hot encoded vector classification. The vocabulary is a set of all unique words (tokens) in the preprocessed text data. It serves as a basis for creating one-hot-encoded feature vectors for each document. Here's a detailed explanation of the vocabulary construction process for one-hot encoded vector classification:

1. **Create a set of unique words**: After preprocessing the text data, gather all the words from all documents and create a set of unique words. This set will represent the vocabulary. The order of

the words in the vocabulary does not matter, but it's crucial to keep track of the indices assigned to each word as they will be used to create one-hot encoded vectors later.

For example, consider that the following preprocessed dataset consists of two documents:

- **Document 1**: "apple banana orange"
- **Document 2**: "banana grape apple"

The vocabulary for this dataset would be {"apple", "banana", "orange", "grape"}.

2. **Assign indices to the words**: Once you have the set of unique words, assign a unique index to each word in the vocabulary. These indices will be used to create one-hot-encoded vectors for each document.

Using the preceding example, you might assign the following indices:

- "apple": 0
- "banana": 1
- "orange": 2
- "grape": 3

One-hot encoding

With the constructed vocabulary and assigned indices, you can now create one-hot encoded vectors for each document in the dataset. One simple approach to creating a one-hot encoded vector is to use **bag-of-words**. For each word in a document, find its corresponding index in the vocabulary and set the value at that index to 1 in the one-hot-encoded vector. If a word appears multiple times in the document, its corresponding value in the one-hot-encoded vector remains 1. All other values in the vector will be 0.

For example, using the vocabulary and indices mentioned previously, the one-hot encoded vectors for the documents would be as follows:

- **Document 1**: [1, 1, 1, 0] (apple, banana, and orange are present)
- **Document 2**: [1, 1, 0, 1] (apple, banana, and grape are present)

Once we have the corresponding values for each document, we can create a feature matrix with one-hot-encoded vectors as rows, where each row represents a document and each column represents a word from the vocabulary. This matrix will be used as input for the text classification model. For example, in the previous example, the feature vectors for two documents are as follows:

	Apple	Banana	Orange	Grape
Document 1	1	1	1	0
Document 2	1	1	0	1

Table 5.1 – Sample one-hot-encoded vector for two documents

Please note that with text preprocessing, it helps to have a smaller vocabulary and it gives us better model performance. Besides that, if needed, we can perform feature selection methods (as explained previously in this book) on the extracted feature vectors to improve our model performance.

While creating a one-hot encoded vector from words is useful, sometimes, we need to consider the existence of two words beside each other. For example, "very good" and "not good" can have different meanings. To achieve this goal, we can use N-grams.

N-grams

N-grams are a generalization of the bag-of-words model that takes into account the order of words by considering sequences of n consecutive words. An N-gram is a contiguous sequence of n items (typically words) from a given text. For example, in the sentence "The cat is on the mat," the 2-grams (bigrams) would be "The cat," "cat is," "is on," "on the," and "the mat."

Using N-grams can help capture local context and word relationships, which may improve the performance of the classifier. However, it also increases the dimensionality of the feature space, which can be computationally expensive.

Model training

Train an ML model, such as logistic regression, SVM, or neural networks, on the feature matrix to learn the relationship between the one-hot encoded text features and the target labels. The model will learn to predict the class label based on the presence or absence of specific words in the document. Once we've decided on the training process, we need to perform the following tasks:

- **Model evaluation**: Evaluate the performance of the model using appropriate evaluation metrics, such as accuracy, precision, recall, F1 score, or confusion matrix, and use techniques such as cross-validation to get a reliable estimate of the model's performance on unseen data.

- **Model application**: Apply the trained model to new, unseen text data. Preprocess and one-hot encode the new text data using the same vocabulary and use the model to predict the class labels.

One potential limitation of using one-hot encoded vectors for text classification is that they do not capture word order, context, or semantic relationships between words. This can lead to suboptimal performance, especially in more complex classification tasks. More advanced techniques, such as word embeddings (for example, Word2Vec or GloVe) or deep learning models (for example, CNNs or RNNs), can provide better representations for text data in these cases.

In summary, text classification using one-hot-encoded vectors involves preprocessing text data, constructing a vocabulary, representing text data as one-hot encoded feature vectors, training an ML model on the feature vectors, and evaluating and applying the model to new text data. The one-hot encoded vector representation is a simple but sometimes limited approach to text classification, and more advanced techniques may be necessary for complex tasks.

So far, we've learned about classifying documents using N-grams. However, this approach has a drawback. There are a considerable number of words that occur in the documents frequently and do not add value to our models. To improve the models, text classification using TF-IDF has been proposed.

Text classification using TF-IDF

One-hot encoded vector is a good approach to perform classification. However, one of its weaknesses is that it does not consider the importance of different words based on different documents. To solve this issue, using **TF-IDF** can be helpful.

TF-IDF is a numerical statistic that is used to measure the importance of a word in a document within a document collection. It helps reflect the relevance of words in a document, considering not only their frequency within the document but also their rarity across the entire document collection. The TF-IDF value of a word increases proportionally to its frequency in a document but is offset by the frequency of the word in the entire document collection.

Here's a detailed explanation of the mathematical equations involved in calculating TF-IDF:

- **Term frequency (TF)**: The TF of a word, t, in a document, d, represents the number of times the word occurs in the document, normalized by the total number of words in the document. The TF can be calculated using the following equation:

$$TF(t, d) = (\textit{Number of times word 't' appears in document 'd'}) / (\textit{Total number of words in document 'd'})$$

  The TF measures the importance of a word within a specific document.

- **Inverse document frequency (IDF)**: The IDF of a word, t, reflects the rarity of the word across the entire document collection. IDF can be calculated using the following equation:

$$IDF(t) = log \left((\textit{Total number of documents in the collection}) / (\textit{Number of documents containing word 't'}) \right)$$

The logarithm is used to dampen the effect of the IDF component. If a word appears in many documents, its IDF value will be closer to 0, and if it appears in fewer documents, its IDF value will be higher.

- **TF-IDF computation**: The TF-IDF value of a word, *t*, in a document, *d*, can be calculated by multiplying the TF of the word in the document with the IDF of the word across the document collection:

$$TF - IDF(t, d) = TF(t, d) * IDF(t)$$

The resulting TF-IDF value represents the importance of a word in a document, taking into account both its frequency within the document and its rarity across the entire document collection. High TF-IDF values indicate words that are more significant in a particular document, whereas low TF-IDF values indicate words that are either common across all documents or rare within the specific document.

Let's consider a simple example of classifying movie reviews into two categories: positive and negative. We have a small dataset with three movie reviews and their respective labels, as follows:

- **Document 1 (positive)**: "I loved the movie. The acting was great and the story was captivating."

- **Document 2 (negative)**: "The movie was boring. I did not like the story, and the acting was terrible."

- **Document 3 (positive)**: "An amazing movie with a wonderful story and brilliant acting."

Now, we will use TF-IDF to classify a new, unseen movie review:

- **Document 4 (unknown)**: "The story was interesting, and the acting was good."

Here are the steps that we need to perform to have the classifier predict the class of our document:

1. **Step 1 – preprocess the text data**: Tokenize, lowercase, remove stop words, and apply stemming or lemmatization to the words in all documents:

   - **Document 1**: "love movi act great stori captiv"

   - **Document 2**: "movi bore not like stori act terribl"

   - **Document 3**: "amaz movi wonder stori brilliant act"

   - **Document 4**: "stori interest act good"

2. **Step 2 – create the vocabulary**: Combine all unique words from the preprocessed documents:

   Vocabulary: {"love", "movi", "act", "great", "stori", "captiv", "bore", "not", "like", "terribl", "amaz", "wonder", "brilliant", "interest", "good"}

3. **Step 3 – calculate the TF and IDF values**: Compute the TF and IDF for each word in each document.

   For example, for the word "stori" in Document 4, we have the following:

   $$TF("stori", Document\ 4) = 1\ /\ 4 = 0.25$$

   $$IDF("stori") = log(4\ /\ 3) \approx 0.287$$

4. **Step 4 – compute the TF-IDF values**: Calculate the TF-IDF values for each word in each document.

   $$TF - IDF("stori", Document\ 4) = 0.25 * 0.287 \approx 0.0717$$

   Repeat this process for all words in all documents and create a feature matrix with the TF-IDF values.

5. **Step 5 – train a classifier**: Split the dataset into a training set (documents 1 to 3) and a test set (document 4). Train a classifier, such as logistic regression or SVM, using the training set's TF-IDF feature matrix and their corresponding labels (positive or negative).

6. **Step 6 – predict the class label**: Preprocess and compute the TF-IDF values for the new movie review (document 4) using the same vocabulary. Use the trained classifier to predict the class label for document 4 based on its TF-IDF feature vector.

For example, if the classifier predicts a positive label for document 4, the classification result would be as follows:

- **Document 4 (Predicted)**: "Positive"

By following these steps, you can use the TF-IDF representation to classify text documents based on the importance of words in the documents relative to the entire document collection.

In summary, the TF-IDF value is calculated using the mathematical equations for TF and IDF. It serves as a measure of the importance of a word in a document relative to the entire document collection, considering both the frequency of the word within the document and its rarity across all documents.

Text classification using Word2Vec

One of the methods to perform text classification is to convert the words into embedding vectors so that you can use those vectors for classification. Word2Vec is a well-known method to perform this task.

Word2Vec

Word2Vec is a group of neural network-based models that are used to create word embeddings, which are dense vector representations of words in a continuous vector space. These embeddings capture the semantic meaning and relationships between words based on the context in which they appear in the text. Word2Vec has two main architectures. As mentioned previously, the two main architectures that were designed to learn word embeddings are **CBOW** and **skip-gram**. Both architectures are designed to learn word embeddings by predicting words based on their surrounding context:

- **CBOW**: The CBOW architecture aims to predict the target word given its surrounding context words. It takes the average of the context word embeddings as input and predicts the target word. CBOW is faster to train and works well with smaller datasets but may be less accurate for infrequent words.

  In the CBOW model, the objective is to maximize the average log probability of observing the target word given the context words:

$$Objective_{CBow} = \frac{1}{T} \sum_{context} log\left(P\left(target \mid context \right) \right)$$

  Here, T is the total number of words in the text, and P(target | context) is the probability of observing the target word given the context words, which is calculated using the softmax function:

$$P(target \mid context) = \frac{e^{v_{target}^T \cdot v_{context}}}{\sum_i e^{v_i^T \cdot v_{context}}}$$

  Here, v_{target}^T is the output vector (word embedding) of the target word, $v_{context}$ is the average input vector (context word embedding) of the context words, and the sum in the denominator runs over all words in the vocabulary.

- **Skip-gram**: The skip-gram architecture aims to predict the surrounding context words given the target word. It takes the target word embedding as input and predicts the context words. Skip-gram works well with larger datasets and can capture the meaning of infrequent words more accurately, but it may be slower to train compared to CBOW.

  In the skip-gram model, the objective is to maximize the average log probability of observing the context words given the target word:

$$Objective_{Skip-Gram} = \frac{1}{T} \sum_{context} log(P(context \mid target))$$

  Here, T is the total number of words in the text, and P(context | target) is the probability of observing the context words given the target word, which is calculated using the softmax function:

$$P(context \mid target) = \frac{e^{v_{context}^T \cdot v_{target}}}{\sum_i e^{v_i^T \cdot v_{target}}}$$

  Here, $v_{context}^T$ is the output vector (context word embedding) of the context word, v_{target} is the input vector (word embedding) of the target word, and the sum in the denominator runs over all words in the vocabulary.

The training process for both CBOW and skip-gram involves iterating through the text and updating the input and output weight matrices using **stochastic gradient descent** (**SGD**) and backpropagation to minimize the difference between the predicted words and the actual words. The learned input weight matrix contains the word embeddings for each word in the vocabulary.

Text classification using Word2Vec

Text classification using Word2Vec involves creating word embeddings using the Word2Vec algorithm and then training an ML model to classify text based on these embeddings. The following steps outline the process in detail, including the mathematical aspects:

1. **Text preprocessing**: Clean and preprocess the text data by tokenizing, lowercasing, removing stop words, and stemming or lemmatizing the words.

2. **Train the Word2Vec model**: Train a Word2Vec model (either CBOW or Skip-Gram) on the preprocessed text data to create word embeddings. The Word2Vec algorithm learns to predict a target word based on its context (CBOW) or predict the context words based on a target word (skip-gram). The training objective is to maximize the average log probability of observing the context words given the target word:

$$Objective = \frac{1}{T} \sum_{context} \log(P(context|target))$$

Here, T is the total number of words in the text, and $P(context \mid target)$ is the probability of observing the context words given the target word, which is calculated using the softmax function:

$$P(context|target) = \frac{e^{\mathbf{v}_{context}^T \cdot \mathbf{v}_{target}}}{\sum_i e^{\mathbf{v}_i^T \cdot \mathbf{v}_{target}}}$$

Here, $\mathbf{v}_{context}^T$ is the output vector (context word embedding) of the context word, $\mathbf{v}_{target}$ is the input vector (word embedding) of the target word, and the sum in the denominator runs over all words in the vocabulary.

3. **Create document embeddings**: For each document in the dataset, calculate the document embedding by averaging the word embeddings of the words in the document:

$$Document\ Embedding = \frac{1}{N} \sum_i WordEmbedding_i$$

Here, N is the number of words in the document, and the sum runs over all words in the document. Please note that based on our experience, this approach for text classification using Word2Vec is only useful when the document's length is short. If you have longer documents or there are opposite words in the document, this approach won't perform well. An alternative solution is to use Word2Vec and CNN together to fetch the word embeddings and then feed those embeddings as input of the CNN.

4. **Model training**: Use the document embeddings as features to train an ML model, such as logistic regression, SVM, or a neural network, for text classification. The model learns to predict the class label based on the document embeddings.

5. **Model evaluation**: Evaluate the performance of the model using appropriate evaluation metrics, such as accuracy, precision, recall, F1 score, or confusion matrix, and use techniques such as cross-validation to get a reliable estimate of the model's performance on unseen data.

6. **Model application**: Apply the trained model to new, unseen text data. Preprocess and compute the document embeddings for the new text data using the same Word2Vec model and vocabulary, and use the model to predict the class labels.

In summary, text classification using Word2Vec involves creating word embeddings with the Word2Vec algorithm, averaging these embeddings to create document embeddings, and training an ML model to classify text based on these document embeddings. The Word2Vec algorithm learns word embeddings by maximizing the average log probability of observing context words given a target word, capturing the semantic relationships between words in the process.

Model evaluation

Evaluating the performance of text classification models is crucial to ensure that they meet the desired level of accuracy and generalizability. Several metrics and techniques are commonly used to evaluate text classification models, including accuracy, precision, recall, F1 score, and confusion matrix. Let's discuss each of these in more detail:

- **Accuracy**: Accuracy is the most straightforward metric for classification tasks. It measures the number of correctly classified records out of all classified records. It is defined as follows:

$$Accuracy = \frac{(True\ Positives + True\ Negatives)}{(True\ Positives + True\ Negatives + False\ Positives + False\ Negatives)}$$

  While accuracy is easy to understand, it may not be the best metric for imbalanced datasets, where the majority class can dominate the metric's value.

- **Precision**: Precision gauges the ratio of correctly identified positive instances to the total instances predicted as positive by the model. It is also referred to as **positive predictive value (PPV)**. Precision proves valuable in scenarios where the expense associated with false positives is significant. Precision is defined as follows:

$$Precision = \frac{True\ Positives}{True\ Positives + False\ Positives}$$

- **Recall**: Recall, also recognized as sensitivity or the **true positive rate (TPR)**, assesses the ratio of correctly identified positive instances among the total actual positive instances. Recall is useful when the cost of false negatives is high. Mathematically, it is defined as follows:

$$Recall = \frac{True\ Positives}{True\ Positives + False\ Positives}$$

- **F1 score**: The F1 score, derived as the harmonic mean of precision and recall, integrates both metrics into a unified value. It is an important metric in the context of imbalanced datasets as it considers both false positives and false negatives. Spanning from 0 to 1, with 1 representing the optimal outcome, the F1 score is mathematically expressed as follows:

$$F1\ Score = 2\frac{Precision \cdot Recall}{Precision + Recall}$$

When dealing with multi-class classification, we have F1 micro and F1 macro. F1 micro and F1 macro are two ways to compute the F1 score for multi-class or multi-label classification problems. They aggregate precision and recall differently, leading to different interpretations of the classifier's performance. Let's discuss each in more detail:

- **F1 macro**: F1 macro computes the F1 score for each class independently and then takes the average of those values. This approach treats each class as equally important and does not consider the class imbalance. Mathematically, F1 macro is defined as follows:

$$F1_{Macro} = \frac{1}{n} \sum_i F1_i$$

Here, n is the number of classes, and $F1_i$ is the F1 score for the i-th class.

F1 macro is particularly useful when you want to evaluate the performance of a classifier across all classes without giving more weight to the majority class. However, it may not be suitable when the class distribution is highly imbalanced as it can provide an overly optimistic estimate of the model's performance.

- **F1 micro**: F1 micro, on the other hand, aggregates the contributions of all classes to compute the F1 score. It does this by calculating the global precision and recall values across all classes and then computing the F1 score based on these global values. F1 micro takes class imbalance into account as it considers the number of instances in each class. Mathematically, F1 micro is defined as follows:

$$F1_{Micro} = 2\frac{Global\ Precision \cdot Global\ Recall}{Global\ Precision + Global\ Recall}$$

Here, global precision and global recall are calculated as follows:

$$Global\ Precision = \frac{\sum True\ Positives}{\sum True\ Positives + \sum False\ Positives}$$

$$Global\ Recall = \frac{\sum True\ Positives}{\sum True\ Positives + \sum False\ Negatives}$$

F1 micro is useful when you want to evaluate the overall performance of a classifier considering the class distribution, especially when dealing with imbalanced datasets.

In summary, F1 macro and F1 micro are two ways to compute the F1 score for multi-class or multi-label classification problems. F1 macro treats each class as equally important, regardless of the class distribution, while F1 micro takes class imbalance into account by considering the number of instances in each class. The choice between F1 macro and F1 micro depends on the specific problem and whether class imbalance is an important factor to consider.

Confusion matrix

A confusion matrix serves as a tabular representation, showcasing the count of true positive, true negative, false positive, and false negative predictions made by a classification model. This matrix offers a nuanced perspective on the model's efficacy, enabling a thorough comprehension of both its strengths and weaknesses.

For a binary classification problem, the confusion matrix is arranged as follows:

Actual/Predicted	(Predicted) Positive	(Predicted) Negative
(Actual) Positive	True Positive	False Negative
(Actual) Negative	False Positive	True Negative

Table 5.2 – Confusion matrix – general view

For multi-class classification problems, the confusion matrix is extended to include the true and predicted counts for each class. The diagonal elements represent the correctly classified instances, while the off-diagonal elements represent misclassifications.

In summary, evaluating text classification models involves using various metrics and techniques, such as accuracy, precision, recall, F1 score, and the confusion matrix. Selecting the appropriate evaluation metrics depends on the specific problem, dataset characteristics, and the trade-offs between false positives and false negatives. Evaluating a model using multiple metrics can provide a more comprehensive understanding of its performance and help guide further improvements.

Overfitting and underfitting

Overfitting and underfitting are two common issues that arise during the training of ML models, including text classification models. They both relate to how well a model generalizes to new, unseen data. This section will explain overfitting and underfitting, when they happen, and how to prevent them.

Overfitting

Overfitting arises when a model excessively tailors itself to the intricacies of the training data. In this case, the model captures noise and random fluctuations rather than discerning the fundamental patterns. Consequently, although the model may exhibit high performance on the training data, its effectiveness diminishes when applied to unseen data, such as a validation or test set.

To avoid overfitting in text classification, consider the following strategies:

- **Regularization**: Introduce regularization techniques, such as ℓ_1 or ℓ_2 regularization, which add a penalty to the loss function, discouraging overly complex models.

- **Early stopping**: In this approach, we monitor the performance of the model on the validation set, and stop the training process as soon as the performance on the validation set starts getting worse, even though the model performance on the training set is getting better. It helps us to prevent overfitting.

- **Feature selection**: Reduce the number of features used for classification by selecting the most informative features or using dimensionality reduction techniques such as PCA or LSA.

- **Ensemble methods**: Combine multiple models, such as bagging or boosting, to reduce overfitting by averaging their predictions.

- **Cross-validation**: Use k-fold cross-validation to get a more reliable estimate of model performance on unseen data and fine-tune model hyperparameters accordingly.

Next, we'll cover underfitting.

Underfitting

Underfitting happens when a model is too simple and fails to capture the underlying patterns in the data. Consequently, the model performance is low on both training and test data. The model is too simple to represent the complexity of the data and can't generalize well.

To avoid underfitting in text classification, consider the following strategies:

- **Increase model complexity**: Use a more complex model, such as a deeper neural network, to capture more intricate patterns in the data.

- **Feature engineering**: Create new, informative features that help the model better understand the underlying patterns in the text data, such as adding N-grams or using word embeddings.

- **Hyperparameter tuning**: Optimize model hyperparameters, such as the learning rate, number of layers, or number of hidden units, to improve the model's ability to learn from the data. We'll explain hyperparameter tuning and the different methods to perform this task in the next section.

- **Increase training data**: If possible, collect more labeled data for training, as more examples can help the model learn the underlying patterns better.

- **Reduce regularization**: If the model is heavily regularized, consider reducing the regularization strength, allowing the model to become more complex and better fit the data.

In summary, overfitting and underfitting are two common issues in text classification that affect a model's ability to generalize to new data. Avoiding these issues involves balancing model complexity, using appropriate features, tuning hyperparameters, employing regularization, and monitoring model performance on a validation set. By addressing overfitting and underfitting, you can improve the performance and generalizability of your text classification models.

Hyperparameter tuning

An important step in building an effective classification model is hyperparameter tuning. Hyperparameters are the model parameters that are defined before training; they will not change during training. These parameters determine the model architecture and behavior. Some of the hyperparameters that can be used are the learning rate and the number of iterations. They can significantly impact the model's performance and generalizability.

The process of hyperparameter tuning in text classification involves the following steps:

1. **Define the hyperparameters and their search space**: Identify the hyperparameters you want to optimize and specify the range of possible values for each of them. Common hyperparameters in text classification include the learning rate, number of layers, number of hidden units, dropout rate, regularization strength, and feature extraction parameters such as N-grams or vocabulary size.

2. **Choose a search strategy**: Select a method to explore the hyperparameter search space, such as grid search, random search, or Bayesian optimization. Grid search systematically evaluates all combinations of hyperparameter values, while random search samples random combinations within the search space. Bayesian optimization uses a probabilistic model to guide the search, balancing exploration and exploitation based on the model's predictions.

3. **Choose an evaluation metric and method**: Select a performance metric that best represents the goals of your text classification task, such as accuracy, precision, recall, F1 score, or area under the ROC curve. Also, choose an evaluation method, such as k-fold cross-validation, to get a reliable estimate of the model's performance on unseen data.

4. **Perform the search**: For each combination of hyperparameter values, train a model on the training data, and evaluate its performance using the chosen metric and evaluation method. Keep track of the best-performing hyperparameter combination.

5. **Select the best hyperparameters**: After the search is complete, select the hyperparameter combination that yields the best performance on the evaluation metric. Retrain the model using these hyperparameters on the entire training set.

6. **Evaluate on the test set**: Assess the performance of the final model with the optimized hyperparameters on a held-out test set to get an unbiased estimate of its generalizability.

Hyperparameter tuning affects the performance of the model by finding the optimal combination of parameters that results in the best model performance on the chosen evaluation metric. Tuning hyperparameters can help address issues such as overfitting and underfitting, balance model complexity, and improve the model's ability to generalize to new data.

Hyperparameter tuning is a crucial process in text classification that involves searching for the optimal combination of model parameters to maximize performance on a chosen evaluation metric. By carefully tuning hyperparameters, you can improve the performance and generalizability of your text classification models.

Additional topics in applied text classification

In the real world, applying text classification involves various practical considerations and challenges that arise from the nature of real-world data and problem requirements. Some common issues include dealing with imbalanced datasets, handling noisy data, and choosing appropriate evaluation metrics.

Let's discuss each of these in more detail.

Dealing with imbalanced datasets

Text classification tasks often encounter imbalanced datasets, wherein certain classes boast a notably higher number of instances compared to others. This imbalance can result in models that are skewed, excelling in predicting the majority class while faltering in accurately classifying the minority class. To handle imbalanced datasets, consider the following strategies:

- **Resampling**: You can oversample the minority class, undersample the majority class, or use a combination of both to balance the class distribution.

- **Weighted loss function**: Assign higher weights to the minority class in the loss function, making the model more sensitive to misclassifications in the minority class.

- **Ensemble methods**: Use ensemble techniques such as bagging or boosting with a focus on the minority class. For example, you can use random under-sampling with bagging or cost-sensitive boosting algorithms.

- **Evaluation metrics**: Choose evaluation metrics that are less sensitive to class imbalance, such as precision, recall, F1 score, or area under the ROC curve, instead of accuracy.

- **Handling noisy data**: Real-world text data is often noisy, containing misspellings, grammatical errors, or irrelevant information. Noisy data can negatively impact the performance of text classification models.

To handle noisy data, consider the following strategies:

- **Preprocessing**: Clean the text data by correcting misspellings, removing special characters, expanding contractions, and converting text into lowercase

- **Stopword removal**: Remove common words that do not carry much meaning, such as "the," "is," "and," and so on

- **Stemming or lemmatization**: Reduce words to their root form to minimize the impact of morphological variations

- **Feature selection**: Use techniques such as chi-square or mutual information to select the most informative features, reducing the impact of noisy or irrelevant features

Whether we're working on imbalanced data or not, we always need to evaluate our model, and choosing the right metric to evaluate our model is important. Next, we'll explain how to select the best metric to evaluate our model.

Choosing appropriate evaluation metrics

Selecting the right evaluation metrics is crucial for measuring the performance of your text classification model and guiding model improvements.

Consider the following when choosing evaluation metrics:

- **Problem requirements**: Choose metrics that align with the specific goals of your text classification task, such as minimizing false positives or false negatives

- **Class imbalance**: For imbalanced datasets, use metrics that account for class imbalance, such as precision, recall, F1 score, or area under the ROC curve, instead of accuracy

- **Multi-class or multi-label problems**: For multi-class or multi-label classification tasks, use metrics such as micro- and macro-averaged F1 scores, which aggregate precision and recall differently based on the problem's requirements

In summary, practical considerations in text classification include dealing with imbalanced datasets, handling noisy data, and choosing appropriate evaluation metrics. Addressing these issues can help improve the performance and generalizability of your text classification models and ensure that they meet the specific requirements of your problem.

Topic modeling – a particular use case of unsupervised text classification

Topic modeling is an unsupervised ML technique that's used to discover abstract topics or themes within a large collection of documents. It assumes that each document can be represented as a mixture of topics, and each topic is represented as a distribution over words. The goal of topic modeling is to find the underlying topics and their word distributions, as well as the topic proportions for each document.

There are several topic modeling algorithms, but one of the most popular and widely used is LDA. We will discuss LDA in detail, including its mathematical formulation.

LDA

LDA is a generative probabilistic model that assumes the following generative process for each document:

1. Choose the number of words in the document.
2. Choose a topic distribution (θ) for the document from a Dirichlet distribution with parameter α.
3. For each word in the document, do the following:

    I.   Choose a topic (z) from the topic distribution (θ).

    II. Choose a word (w) from the word distribution of the chosen topic (φ), which is a distribution over words for that topic, drawn from a Dirichlet distribution with parameter β.

The generative process is a theoretical model used by LDA to reverse-engineer the original documents from presumed topics.

LDA aims to find the topic-word distributions (φ) and document-topic distributions (θ) that best explain the observed documents.

Mathematically, LDA can be described using the following notation:

- M: Number of documents

- N: Number of words in a document

- K: Number of topics

- α: Dirichlet before document-topic distribution, it affects the sparsity of topics within documents

- β: Dirichlet before topic-word distribution, it affects the sparsity of words within topics

- θ: Document-topic distributions (M × K matrix)

- φ: Topic-word distributions (K × V matrix, where V is the vocabulary size)

- z: Topic assignments for each word in each document (M × N matrix)

- w: Observed words in the documents (M × N matrix)

The joint probability of the topic assignments (z) and words (w) in the documents, given the topic-word distributions (φ) and document-topic distributions (θ), can be written as follows:

$$P(z, w | \theta, \varphi) = \prod_{i=1}^{M} \prod_{j=1}^{M} P\left(w_{ij} | \varphi, z_{ij}\right) P\left(z_{ij} | \theta_i\right)$$

The objective of LDA is to maximize the likelihood of the observed words given the Dirichlet priors α and β:

$$P(w | \alpha, \beta) = \iint P(w | \theta, \varphi) P(\theta | \alpha) P(\varphi | \beta) d\theta d\varphi$$

However, computing the likelihood directly is intractable due to the integration over the latent variables θ and φ. Therefore, LDA uses approximate inference algorithms, such as Gibbs sampling or variational inference, to estimate the posterior distributions $P(\theta \mid w, \alpha, \beta)$ and $P(\varphi \mid w, \alpha, \beta)$.

Once the posterior distributions have been estimated, we can obtain the document-topic distributions (θ) and topic-word distributions (φ), which can be used to analyze the discovered topics and their word distributions, as well as the topic proportions for each document.

Let's consider a simple example of topic modeling.

Suppose we have a collection of three documents:

- **Document 1**: "I love playing football with my friends."

- **Document 2**: "The football match was intense and exciting."

- **Document 3**: "My new laptop has an amazing battery life and performance."

We want to discover two topics (K = 2) in this document collection. Here are the steps that we need to perform:

1. **Preprocessing**: First, we need to preprocess the text data, which typically involves tokenization, stopword removal, and stemming/lemmatization (which was explained previously in this chapter). In this example, we will skip these steps for simplicity and assume our documents are already preprocessed.

2. **Initialization**: Choose the initial values for the Dirichlet priors, α and β. For example, we can set $\alpha = [1, 1]$ and $\beta = [0.1, 0.1, ..., 0.1]$ (assuming a V-dimensional vector with 0.1 for each word in the vocabulary).

3. **Random topic assignments**: Randomly assign a topic (1 or 2) to each word in each document.

4. **Iterative inference (for example, Gibbs sampling or variational inference)**: Iteratively update the topic assignments and the topic-word and document-topic distributions (φ and θ) until convergence or a fixed number of iterations. This process refines the assignments and distributions, ultimately revealing the underlying topic structure.

5. **Interpretation**: After the algorithm converges or reaches the maximum number of iterations, we can interpret the discovered topics by looking at the most probable words for each topic and the most probable topics for each document.

   For our example, LDA might discover the following topics:

   - **Topic 1**: {"football", "playing", "friends", "match", "intense", "exciting"}
   - **Topic 2**: {"laptop", "battery", "life", "performance"}

   With these topics, the document-topic distribution (θ) might look like this:

   - $\theta_1 = [0.9, 0.1]$ (Document 1 is 90% about Topic 1 and 10% about Topic 2)
   - $\theta_2 = [0.8, 0.2]$ (Document 2 is 80% about Topic 1 and 20% about Topic 2)
   - $\theta_3 = [0.1, 0.9]$ (Document 3 is 10% about Topic 1 and 90% about Topic 2)

In this example, topic 1 seems to be related to football and sports, while topic 2 seems to be related to technology and gadgets. The topic distributions for each document show that documents 1 and 2 are mostly about football, while document 3 is about technology.

Please note that this is a simplified example, and real-world data would require more sophisticated preprocessing and a larger number of iterations for convergence.

We are now ready to discuss the paradigm for putting together a complete project in a work or research setting.

Real-world ML system design for NLP text classification

This section is dedicated to the practical implementation of the various methods we discussed. It will revolve around Python code, which serves as a complete pipeline.

To provide a comprehensive learning experience, we will discuss the entire journey of a typical ML project. *Figure 5.1* depicts the different phases of the ML project:

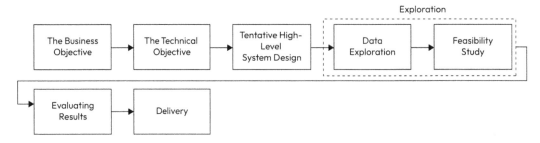

Figure 5.1 – The paradigm of a typical ML project

Let's break the problem down in a similar fashion to a typical project in the industry.

The business objective

An ML project, whether in a business or research setting, stems from an original objective, which is often qualitative rather than technical.

Here's an example:

1. "We need to know which of our patients is at a higher risk."
2. "We would like to maximize the engagement of our ad."
3. "We need the autonomous car to be alerted when a person is stepping in front of it."

Next comes the technical objective.

The technical objective

The original objective needs to be translated into a technical objective, like so:

1. "We will process every patient's medical record and build a risk estimator based on the history of realized risk."
2. "We will collect data about all the ads from the last year and will build a regressor to estimate the level of engagement based on the ad's features."

3. "We will collect a set of images taken by the car's front camera and present those to our online users who are visiting our site, telling them it's for security reasons and that they need to click on the parts that show a human to prove they are not robots. However, in practice, we'll collect their free labels for training, develop a computer vision classifier for humans, and won't give them any credit."

While the original business or research objective is somewhat of an open-ended question, the technical objective reflects an actionable plan. Note, however, that any given technical objective represents just one among several potential solutions aligned with the original business or research aim. It is the responsibility of the technical authority, such as the CTO, ML manager, or senior developer, to understand the original objective and translate it into a technical objective. Moreover, it may be that the technical objective would be refined or even replaced down the line. The next step after forming a technical objective is to form a plan for it.

Tentative high-level system design

To realize the technical objective, we need to derive a plan to decide which data would be used to feed into the ML system, and what the expected output of the ML system is. In the first steps of a project, there may be several candidate sources of potential data that are believed to be indicative of the desired output.

Following the set of three examples mentioned previously, here are some examples of data descriptions:

1. The input data would be columns A, B, and C of the `patient_records` SQL table and the risk would be assessed as $1/N$, where N is the number of days that passed from a given moment until the patient showed up in the emergency room.

2. The input data would be the geometric and color descriptions of the ads, and the level of engagement would be the number of clicks per day that the ad received.

3. The input data is the images of the car's front camera to be fed to a computer vision neural network classifier, and the output data would be whether the image captures a person or not.

Choosing a metric

When defining a potential solution approach, extra attention should be dedicated to identifying the best metric to focus on, also known as the objective function or error function. This is the metric by which the success of the solution will be evaluated. It is important to relate the metric to the original business or research objective.

As per the previous examples, we could have the following:

1. Minimize the 70th percentile confidence interval.

2. Minimize the mean absolute error.

3. Maximize precision while constraining on a fixed recall. This fixed recall will ideally be dictated by business leaders or the legal team, in the form of "the system must capture at least 99.9% of the cases where a person steps in front of a car."

Now that we have a tentative plan, we can explore the data and evaluate the feasibility of the design.

Exploration

Exploration is divided into two parts – exploring the data and exploring the feasibility of the design. Let's take a closer look.

Data exploration

Data is not always perfect for our objective. We discussed some of the data shortcomings in previous chapters. In particular, free text is often notorious for having many abnormal phenomena, such as encodings, special characters, typos, and so on. When exploring our data, we want to uncover all these phenomena and make sure that the data can be brought to a form that serves the objective.

Feasibility study

Here, we want to prospectively identify proxies for whether the planned design is expected to succeed. While with some problems there are known proxies for expected success, in most problems in the business and especially research setting, it takes much experience and ingenuity to suggest preliminary proxies for success.

An example of a very simple case is a simple regression problem with a single input variable and a single output variable. Let's say the independent variable is the number of active viewers that your streaming service currently has, and the dependent variable is the risk that the company's servers have for maxing out their capacity. The tentative design plan would be to build a regressor that estimates the risk at any given moment. A strong proxy for the feasibility of developing a successful regressor could be calculating the linear correlation between the historical data points. Calculating linear correlation based on sample data is easy and quick and if its result is close to 1 (or -1 in cases different than our business problem), then it means that a linear regressor is guaranteed to succeed, thus, making it a great proxy. However, note that if the linear correlation is close to 0, it doesn't necessarily mean that a regressor would fail, only that a linear regression would fail. In such a case, a different proxy should be deferred to.

In the *Reviewing our use case – ML system design for NLP classification in a Jupyter Notebook* section, we'll review our code solution. We'll also present a method to assess the feasibility of a text classifier. The method aims to mimic a relationship between the input text to the output class. But since we want to have that method suit a variable that is text and not numeric, we'll go back to the origin and calculate a measure for the statistical dependency between the input text and the output class. Statistical dependency is the most basic measure for a relationship between variables and thus doesn't require either of them to be numeric.

Assuming the **feasibility study** is successful, we can move on to implementing the ML solution.

Implementing an ML solution

This part is where the expertise of the ML developer comes into play. There are different steps for it and the developer chooses which ones are relevant based on the problem – whether it's data cleaning, text segmentation, feature design, model comparison, or metric choice.

We will elaborate on this as we review the specific use case we've solved.

Evaluating the results

We evaluate the solution given the metric that was chosen. This part requires some experience as ML developers tend to get better at this over time. The main pitfall in this task is the ability to set up an objective assessment of the result. That objective assessment is done by applying the finished model to data it had never "seen" before. But often folks who are only starting to apply ML find themselves improving their design after seeing what the results of that held-out set are. This leads to a feedback loop where the design is practically fitted to the no-longer-held-out set. While this may indeed improve the model and the design, it takes away from the ability to provide an objective forecast of how the model would perform when implemented in the real world. In the real world, it would see data that is truly held out and that it wasn't fitted to.

Done and delivered

Typically, when the design is done, the implementation is complete, and the results have been found satisfactory, the work is presented for business implementation, or in the research setting, for publication. In the business setting, implementation can take on different forms.

One of the simplest forms is where the output is used to provide business insights. Its purpose is to be presented. For instance, when looking to evaluate how much a marketing campaign was contributing to the growth in sales, the ML team may calculate an estimation for that measure of contribution and present it to leadership.

Another form of implementation is within a dashboard in real time. For instance, the model calculates the predicted risk of patients coming to the emergency room, and it does so on a daily cadence. The results are aggregated and a graph is presented on the hospital dashboard to show the expected number of people who would come to the emergency room for every day of the next 30 days.

A more advanced and common form is when the output of the data is directed so that it can be fed into downstream tasks. The model would then be implemented in production to become a microservice within a larger production pipeline. An example of that is when a classifier evaluates every post on your company's Facebook page. When it identifies offensive language, it outputs a detection that then passes down the pipeline to another system that removes that post and perhaps blocks that user.

Code design

The code's design should suit the purpose of the code once the work is complete. As per the different forms of implementation mentioned previously, some implementations dictate a specific code structure. For instance, when the completed code is handed off to production within a larger, already existing pipeline, it is the production engineer who would dictate the constraints to the ML team. These constraints may be around computation and timing resources, but they would also be around code design. Often, basic code files, such as .py files, are necessary.

As with cases where the code is used for presentations, such as in the example of presenting how contributive the marketing campaign was, Jupyter Notebooks may be the better choice.

Jupyter Notebooks can be very informative and instructional. For that reason, many ML developers start their projects with Jupyter Notebooks for the exploration phase.

Next, we will review our design in a Jupyter Notebook. This will allow us to encapsulate the entire process in a single coherent file that is meant to be presented to the reader.

Reviewing our use case – ML system design for NLP classification in a Jupyter Notebook

In this section, we will walk through a hands-on example. We will follow the steps we presented previously for articulating the problem, designing the solution, and evaluating the results. This section portrays the process that an ML developer goes through when working on a typical project in the industry. Refer to notebook: `Ch5_Text_Classification_Traditional_ML.ipynb`.

The business objective

In this scenario, we are working for a financial news agency. Our objective is to publish news about companies and products in real time.

The technical objective

The CTO derives several technical objectives from the business objective. One objective is for the ML team: given a stream of financial tweets in real time, detect those tweets that discuss information about companies or products.

The pipeline

Let's review the different parts of the pipeline, as shown in *Figure 5.2*:

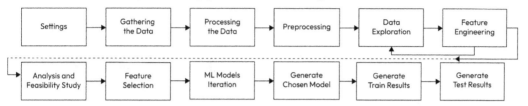

Figure 5.2 – The structure of a typical ML pipeline

> **Note**
>
> The phases of the pipeline in *Figure 5.2* are explored in the following subsections

Code settings

In this part of the code, we set the key parameters. We choose to have them as a part of the code as this is instructional code made for presentation. In cases where the code is expected to go to production, it may be better to host the parameters in a separate .yaml file. That would also suit heavy iterations during the development phase as it will allow you to iterate over different code parameters without having to change the code, which is often desirable.

As for the choice of these values, it should be stressed that some of these values should be optimized to suit the optimization of the solution. We have chosen fixed measures here to simplify the process. For instance, the number of features to be used for classification is a fixed quantity here, but it should also be optimized to fit the training set.

Gathering the data

This part loads the dataset. In our case, the loading function is simple. In other business cases, this part could be quite large as it may include a collection of SQL queries that are called. In such a case, it may be ideal to write a dedicated function in a separate .py file and source it via the imports section.

Processing the data

Here, we format the data in a way that suits our work. We also observe some of it for the first time. This allows us to get a feel of its nature and quality.

One key action we take here is to define the classes we care about.

Preprocessing

As we discussed in *Chapter 4*, preprocessing is a key part of the pipeline. For instance, we notice that many of the tweets have a URL, which we choose to remove.

Preliminary data exploration

At this point, we have observed the quality of the text and the distribution of the classes. This is where we explore any other characteristics of the data that may imply either its quality or its ability to indicate the desired class.

Feature engineering

Next, we start processing the text. We seek to represent the text of each observation as a set of numerical features. The main reason for this is that traditional ML models are designed to accept numbers as input, not text. For instance, a common linear regression or logistic regression model is applied to numbers, not words, categories, or image pixels. Thus, we need to suggest a numeric representation for the text. This design constraint is lifted when working with **language models** such as **BERT** and **GPT**. We will see this in the coming chapters.

We partition the text into N-grams, where *N* is a parameter of the code. *N* is fixed in this code but should be optimized to best fit the training set.

Once the text has been partitioned into N-grams, they are modeled as numeric values. When a binary (that is, **one-hot encoding**) method is chosen, the numerical feature that represents some N-gram gets a "1" when the observed text includes that N-gram, and "0" otherwise. See *Figure 5.3* for an example. If a BOW approach is chosen, then the value of the feature is the number of times the N-gram appears in the observed text. Another common feature engineering method that isn't implemented here is **TF-IDF**.

Here's what we get by using unigrams only:

Input sentence: "filing submitted."

N-gram	"report"	"filing"	"submitted"	"product"	"quarterly"	The rest of the unigrams
Feature value	0	1	1	0	0	(0's)

Figure 5.3 – Transforming an input text sentence into a numerical representation by partitioning to unigrams via one-hot encoding

The following figure shows what we get by using both unigrams and bigrams:

N-gram	"report"	"filing"	"filing submitted"	"report news"	"submitted"	The rest of the N-grams
Feature value	0	1	1	0	1	(0's)

Figure 5.4 – Transforming an input text sentence into a numerical representation
by partitioning to unigrams and bigrams via one-hot encoding

Note that at this point in the code, the dataset hasn't been partitioned into train and test sets, and the held-out set has not been excluded yet. This is because the binary and BOW feature engineering methods don't depend on data outside of the underlying observation. With TF-IDF, this is different. Every feature value is calculated using the entire dataset for the document frequency.

Exploring the new numerical features

Now that our text has been represented as a feature, we can explore it numerically. We can look at its frequencies and statistics and get a sense of how it's distributed.

Splitting into train/test sets

This is the part where we must pause and carve out a held-out set, also known as a test set, and sometimes as the validation set. Since these terms are used differently in different sources, it is important to explain that what we refer to as a test set is a held-out set. A held-out set is a data subset that we dedicate to evaluating our solution's performance. It is held out to simulate the results that we expect to get when the system is implemented in the real world and will encounter new data samples.

How do we know when to carve out the held-out set?

If we carve it out "too early," such as right after loading the data, then we are guaranteed to keep it held out, but we may miss discrepancies in the data as it won't take part in the preliminary exploration. If we carve it out "too late," our design decisions might become biased because of it. For example, if we choose one ML model over another based on results that include the would-be held-out set, then our design becomes tailored to that set, preventing us from offering an objective evaluation of the model.

Then, we need to carry out the test set right before the first action that will feed into design decisions. In the next section, we'll perform statistical analysis, which we can then feed into feature selection. Since that selection should be agnostic to the held-out set, we'll exclude that set from this part onwards.

Preliminary statistical analysis and feasibility study

This is the second part of the exploration phase we spoke about a few pages ago. The first part was data exploration, and we implemented that in the previous parts of the code. Now that we have the text represented as numerical features, we can perform the feasibility study.

We seek to measure the statistical dependence between the text inputs and the class values. Again, the motivation is to mimic the proxy that linear correlation provides with a regression problem.

We know that for two random variables, X and Y, if they are statistically independent, then we get the following:

$$P(X = x, Y = y) = P(X = x)P(Y = y), \text{ for every } x \text{ and } y$$

Alternatively, we get the following:

$$\frac{P(X = x, Y = y)}{P(X = x)P(Y = y)} = 1,$$

This happens for every x, y value that yields a non-zero probability.

Conversely, we could use Bayes's rules:

$$\frac{P(X = x \mid Y = y) \, P(Y = y)}{P(X = x)P(Y = y)} = 1$$

$$\frac{P(X = x \mid Y = y)}{P(X = x)} = 1.$$

Now, let's think about any two random variables that aren't necessarily statistically independent. We would like to evaluate whether there is a statistical relationship between the two.

Let one random variable be any of our numerical features, and the other random variable be the output class taking on values 0 or 1. Let's assume the feature engineering method is binary, so the feature also takes on values of 0 or 1.

Looking at the last equation, the expression on the left-hand side presents a very powerful measure of the ability of the relationship between X and Y:

$$\frac{P(feature = x \mid class = y)}{P(feature = x)}, x, y \text{ belong to } \left\{ 0,1 \right\}.$$

It is powerful because if the feature is completely nonindicative of the class value, then in statistical terms, we say the two are statistically independent, and thus this measure would be equal to 1.

Conversely, the bigger the difference between this measure and 1, the stronger the relationship is between this feature and this class. When performing a **feasibility study** of our design, we want to see that there are features in the data that have a statistical relationship with the output class.

For that reason, we calculate the value of this expression for every pair of every feature and every class.

We present the most indicative terms for class "0," which is the class of tweets that don't indicate a company or product information, and we also present the terms that are most indicative of class "1," meaning, when a tweet is discussing information about a company or a product.

This proves to us that there are indeed text terms that are indicative of the class value. This is a definite and clear success of the feasibility study. We are good to go and we are expecting productive outcomes when implementing a classification model.

As a side note, keep in mind that as with most evaluations, what we've just mentioned is just one sufficient condition for the potential of the text to predict the class. If it had failed, it would not necessarily indicate that there is no feasibility. Just like when the linear correlation between X and Y is near 0, this doesn't mean that X can't infer Y. It just means that X cannot infer Y via a linear model. The linearity is an assumption that's made to make things simple if it prevails.

In the method that we've suggested, we make two key assumptions. First, we assume a very particular manner for feature design, being a certain N for the N-gram partition, and a certain quantitative method for the value – binary. The second is that we perform the most simple evaluation of statistical dependency, a univariate statistical dependency. But it could be that only a higher order, such as univariate, would have statistical dependence on the outcome class.

With a **feasibility study** of text classification, it's ideal if the method is as simple as possible while covering as much of the "signal" it is hoping to uncover. The approach we designed in this example was derived after years of experience with different sets and various problem settings. We find that it hits the target very well.

Feature selection

With the **feasibility study**, we often kill two birds with one stone. As a **feasibility study** is successful, it not only helps us by confirming our plan, but it often hints toward the next steps that we should take. As we saw, some features are indicative of the class, and we learned which are the most significant. This allows us to reduce the feature space that the classification model will need to partition. We do that by keeping the most indicative features for each of the two classes. The number of features that we choose to keep would ideally be derived by computation constraints (for example, too many features would take too long to compute a model around), model capabilities (for example, too many features can't be handled well by the model due to co-linearity), and optimization of the train results. In our code, we fixed this number to make things quick and simple.

It should be stressed that in many ML models, feature selection is an inherited part of the model design. For instance, with the **least absolute shrinkage and selection operator** (**LASSO**), the hyperparameter scaler of the ℓ_1 norm component has an impact on which features get a zero coefficient, and thus get "thrown out." It is possible and sometimes recommended to skip this part of the feature selection process, leave all features in, and let the model perform feature selection. It is advised to do so when all the models that are being evaluated and compared possess that characteristic.

Remember that at this point, we are only observing the train set. Now that we have decided which features to keep, we need to apply that selection to the test set as well.

With that, our data has been prepared for ML modeling.

Iterating over ML models

To choose which model suits this problem best, we must train several models and see which one of them does best.

We should stress that we could do many things to try and identify the best model choice for a given problem. In our case, we only chose to evaluate a handful of models. Moreover, to make things simple and quick, we chose to not optimize the hyperparameters of each model in a comprehensive cross-validation approach. We simply fit each model to the training set with the default settings that its function comes with. Once we've identified the model we'd like to use, we optimize its hyperparameters for the train set via cross-validation.

By doing this, we identify the best model for the problem.

Generating the chosen model

Here, we optimize the hyperparameters of the chosen model and fit it to our train set.

Generating the train results – design choices

At this stage, we observe the results of the model for the first time. This result can be used to feed insight back into the design choice and the parameters chosen, such as the feature engineering method, the number of features left in the feature selection, and even the preprocessing scheme.

> **Important note**
> Note that when feeding back insights from the results of the train set to the design of the solution, you are risking overfitting the train set. You'll know whether you are by the gap between the results on the train set and the results on the test set.

While a gap is expected between these results in favor of the train results, a large gap should be treated as an alarm that the design isn't optimal. In such cases, the design should be redone with systematic code-based parameters to ensure fair choices are made. It is possible to even carve out another semi-held-out set from the train set, often referred to as the validation set.

Generating the test results – presenting performance

That's it!

Now that the design has been optimized and we are confident that it suits our objective, we can apply it to our held-out set and observe the test results. These results are our most objective forecast of how well the system would do in the real world.

As mentioned previously, we should avoid letting these results impact our design choices.

Summary

In this chapter, we embarked on a comprehensive exploration of text classification, an indispensable aspect of NLP and ML. We delved into various types of text classification tasks, each presenting unique challenges and opportunities. This foundational understanding sets the stage for effectively tackling a broad range of applications, from sentiment analysis to spam detection.

We walked through the role of N-grams in capturing local context and word sequences within text, thereby enhancing the feature set used for classification tasks. We also illuminated the power of the TF-IDF method, the role of Word2Vec in text classification, and popular architectures such as CBOW and skip-gram, giving you a deep understanding of their mechanics.

Then, we introduced topic modeling and examined how popular algorithms such as LDA can be applied to text classification.

Lastly, we introduced a professional paradigm for leading an NLP-ML project in a business or research setting. We discussed the objectives and the project design aspect, and then dove into the system design. We implemented a real-world example in code and experimented with this.

In essence, this chapter has aimed to equip you with a holistic understanding of text classification and topic modeling by touching on the key concepts, methodologies, and techniques in the field. The knowledge and skills imparted will enable you to effectively approach and solve real-world text classification problems.

In the next chapter, we will introduce advanced methods for text classification. We will review deep learning methods such as language models, discuss their theory and design, and present a hands-on system design in code.

6

Text Classification Reimagined: Delving Deep into Deep Learning Language Models

In this chapter, we delve into the realm of **deep learning** (**DL**) and its application in **natural language processing** (**NLP**), specifically focusing on the groundbreaking transformer-based models such as **Bidirectional Encoder Representations from Transformers** (**BERT**) and **generative pretrained transformer** (**GPT**). We begin by introducing the fundamentals of DL, elucidating its powerful capability to learn intricate patterns from large amounts of data, making it the cornerstone of state-of-the-art NLP systems.

Following this, we delve into transformers, a novel architecture that has revolutionized NLP by offering a more effective method of handling sequence data compared to traditional **recurrent neural networks** (**RNNs**) and **convolutional neural networks** (**CNNs**). We unpack the transformer's unique characteristics, including its attention mechanisms, which allow it to focus on different parts of the input sequence to better understand the context.

Then, we turn our attention to BERT and GPT, transformer-based language models that leverage these strengths to create highly nuanced language representations. We provide a detailed breakdown of the BERT architecture, discussing its innovative use of bidirectional training to generate contextually rich word embeddings. We will demystify the inner workings of BERT and explore its pretraining process, which leverages a large corpus of text to learn language semantics.

Finally, we discuss how BERT can be fine-tuned for specific tasks, such as text classification. We walk you through the steps, from data preprocessing and model configuration to training and evaluation, providing a hands-on understanding of how to leverage BERT's power for text classification.

This chapter provides a thorough exploration of DL in NLP, moving from foundational concepts to practical applications, equipping you with the knowledge to harness the capabilities of BERT and transformer models for your text classification tasks.

The following topics are covered in this chapter:

- Understanding deep learning basics
- The architecture of different neural networks
- Transformers
- Language models
- The challenges of training neural networks
- BERT
- GPT
- How to use language models for classification
- NLP-ML system design example

Technical requirements

To successfully navigate through this chapter, certain technical prerequisites are necessary, as follows:

- **Programming knowledge**: A strong understanding of Python is essential, as it's the primary language used for most DL and NLP libraries.

- **Machine learning fundamentals**: A good grasp of basic ML concepts such as training/testing data, overfitting, underfitting, accuracy, precision, recall, and F1 score will be valuable.

- **DL basics**: Familiarity with **DL** concepts and architectures, including neural networks, backpropagation, activation functions, and loss functions, will be essential. Knowledge of RNNs and CNNs would be advantageous but not strictly necessary as we will focus more on transformer architectures.

- **NLP basics**: Some understanding of basic NLP concepts such as tokenization, stemming, lemmatization, and word embeddings (such as **Word2Vec** or **GloVe**) would be beneficial.

- **Libraries and frameworks**: Experience with libraries such as **TensorFlow** and **PyTorch** for building and training neural models is crucial. Familiarity with NLP libraries such as **NLTK** or **SpaCy** can also be beneficial. For working with BERT specifically, knowledge of the `transformers` library from **Hugging Face** would be very helpful.

- **Hardware requirements**: DL models, especially transformer-based models such as BERT, are computationally intensive and typically require a modern **graphics processing unit** (**GPU**) to train in a reasonable amount of time. Access to a high-performance computer or cloud-based solutions with GPU capabilities is highly recommended.

- **Mathematics**: A good understanding of linear algebra, calculus, and probability is helpful for understanding the inner workings of these models, but most of the chapter can be understood without in-depth mathematical knowledge.

These prerequisites are intended to equip you with the necessary background to understand and implement the concepts discussed in the chapter. With these in place, you should be well-prepared to delve into the fascinating world of DL for text classification using **BERT**.

Understanding deep learning basics

In this part, we explain what neural network and deep neural networks are, what is the motivation for using them, and the different types (architectures) of deep learning models.

What is a neural network?

Neural networks are a subfield of **artificial intelligence** (**AI**) and ML that focuses on algorithms inspired by the structure and function of the brain. It is also known as "deep" learning because these neural networks often consist of many repetitive layers, creating a deep architecture.

These DL models are capable of "learning" from large volumes of complex, high-dimensional, and unstructured data. The term "learning" refers to the ability of the model to automatically learn and improve from experience without being explicitly programmed to do so for any one particular task of the tasks it learns.

DL can be supervised, semi-supervised, or unsupervised. It's used in numerous applications, including NLP, speech recognition, image recognition, and even playing games. The models can identify patterns and make data-driven predictions or decisions.

One of the critical advantages of DL is its ability to process and model data of various types, including text, images, sound, and more. This versatility has led to a vast range of applications, from self-driving cars to sophisticated web search algorithms and highly responsive speech recognition systems.

It's worth noting that DL, despite its high potential, also requires significant computational power and large amounts of high-quality data to train effectively, which can be a challenge.

In essence, DL is a powerful and transformative technology that is at the forefront of many of today's technological advancements.

The motivation for using neural networks

Neural networks are used for a variety of reasons in the field of ML and artificial intelligence. Here are some of the key motivations:

- **Nonlinearity**: Neural networks, with their intricate structure and use of activation functions, can capture nonlinear relationships in data. Many real-world phenomena are nonlinear in nature, and neural networks offer a way to model these complexities.

- **Universal approximation theorem**: This theorem states that a neural network with enough hidden units can approximate virtually any function with a high degree of accuracy. This makes them highly flexible and adaptable to a wide range of tasks.

- **Ability to handle high dimensional data**: Neural networks can handle data with a large number of features or dimensions effectively, which makes them useful for tasks such as image or speech recognition, where data is highly dimensional.

- **Pattern recognition and prediction**: Neural networks excel at identifying patterns and trends within large datasets, making them especially useful for prediction tasks, such as forecasting sales or predicting stock market trends.

- **Parallel processing**: Neural networks' architecture allows them to perform many operations simultaneously, making them highly efficient when implemented on modern hardware.

- **Learning from data**: Neural networks can improve their performance as they are exposed to more data. This ability to learn from data makes them highly effective for tasks where large amounts of data are available.

- **Robustness**: Neural networks can handle noise in the input data and are robust to small variations in the input.

Additionally, neural networks are extensively used in NLP tasks due to several reasons. Here are some of the primary motivations:

- **Handling sequential data**: Natural language is inherently sequential (words follow one another to make coherent sentences). RNNs and their advanced versions, such as **long short-term memory (LSTM)** and **gated recurrent units (GRUs)**, are types of neural networks that are capable of processing sequential data by maintaining a form of internal state or memory about the previous steps in the sequence.

- **Context understanding**: Neural networks, especially recurrent types, are capable of understanding the context in a sentence by taking into account the surrounding words or even previous sentences, which is crucial in NLP tasks.

- **Semantic hashing**: Neural networks, through the use of word embeddings (such as Word2Vec and GloVe), can encode words in a way that preserves their semantic meaning. Words with similar meanings are placed closer together in the vector space, which is highly valuable for many NLP tasks.

- **End-to-end learning**: Neural networks can learn directly from raw data. For example, in image classification, a neural network can learn features from the pixel level without needing any manual feature extraction steps. This is a significant advantage, as the feature extraction process can be time-consuming and require domain expertise.

  Similarly, neural networks can learn to perform NLP tasks from raw text data without the need for manual feature extraction. This is a big advantage in NLP, where creating hand-engineered features can be challenging and time-consuming.

- **Performance**: Neural networks, especially with the advent of transformer-based architectures such as BERT, GPT, and so on., have been shown to achieve state-of-the-art results in many NLP tasks, including but not limited to machine translation, text summarization, sentiment analysis, and question answering.

- **Handling large vocabularies**: Neural networks can effectively handle large vocabularies and continuous text streams, which is typical in many **NLP** problems.

- **Learning hierarchical features**: Deep neural networks can learn hierarchical representations. In the context of NLP, lower layers often learn to represent simple things such as n-grams, whereas higher layers can represent complex concepts such as sentiment.

Despite these advantages, it's worth noting that neural networks also have their challenges, including their "black box" nature, which makes their decision-making process difficult to interpret, and their need for large amounts of data and computational resources for training. However, the benefits they provide in terms of performance and their ability to learn from raw text data and model complex relationships make them a go-to choice for many NLP tasks.

The basic design of a neural network

A neural network consists of multiple layers of interconnected nodes, or "neurons," each of which performs a simple computation on the data it receives, passing its output to the neurons of the next layer. Each connection between neurons has an associated weight that is adjusted during the learning process.

The architecture of a basic neural network consists of three types of layers, as shown in *Figure 6.1*:

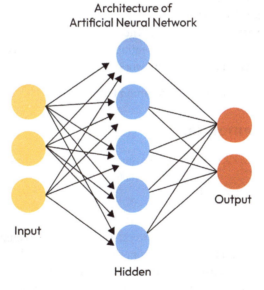

Figure 6.1 – Basic architecture of neural networks

In the following list, we explain each layer of the model in more detail:

- **Input layer**: This is where the network receives its input. If the network is designed to process an image with dimensions of 28x28 pixels, for instance, there would be 784 neurons in the input layer, each representing the value of one pixel.

- **Hidden layer(s)**: These are the layers between the input and output layers. Each neuron in a hidden layer takes the outputs of the neurons from the previous layer, multiplies each of these by the weight of the respective connection, and sums these values up. This sum is then passed through an "activation function" to introduce nonlinearity into the model, which helps the network learn complex patterns. There can be any number of hidden layers in a neural network, and a network with many hidden layers is often referred to as a "deep" neural network.

- **Output layer**: This is the final layer in the network. The neurons in this layer produce the final output of the network. For a classification problem, for instance, you might design the network to have one output neuron for each class in the problem, with each neuron outputting a value indicating the probability that the input belongs to its respective class.

The neurons in the network are interconnected. The weights of these connections, which are initially set to random values, represent what the network has learned once it has been trained on data.

During the training process, an algorithm such as backpropagation is used to adjust the weights of the connections in the network in response to the difference between the network's output and the desired output. This process is repeated many times, and the network gradually improves its performance on the training data.

To provide a simple visual idea, imagine three sets of circles (representing neurons) arranged in columns (representing layers). The first column is the input layer, the last column is the output layer and any columns in between are the hidden layers. Then, imagine lines connecting every circle in each column to every circle in the next column, representing the weighted connections between neurons. That's a basic visual representation of a neural network.

In the next part, we are going to describe the common terms related to neural networks.

Neural network common terms

In the following subsections, we'll look at some of the most commonly used terms in the context of neural networks.

Neuron (or node)

This is the basic unit of computation in a neural network; typically, a simple computation involves inputs, weights, a bias, and an activation function. A neuron, also known as a node or unit, is a fundamental element in a neural network. It receives input from some other nodes or from an external source if the neuron is in the input layer. The neuron then computes an output based on this input.

Each input has an associated weight (w), which is assigned based on its relative importance to other inputs. The neuron applies a weight to the inputs, sums them up, and then applies an activation function to the sum plus a bias value (b).

Here's a step-by-step breakdown:

1. **Weighted sum**: Each input (x) to the neuron is multiplied by a corresponding weight (w). These weighted inputs are then summed together with a bias term (b). The bias term allows for the activation function to be shifted to the left or the right, helping the neuron model a wider range of patterns. Mathematically, this step can be represented as follows:

$$z = w_1 x_1 + w_2 x_2 + \ldots + w_n x_n + b$$

2. **Activation function**: The result of the weighted sum is then passed through an activation function. The purpose of the activation function is to introduce nonlinearity into the output of a neuron. This nonlinearity allows the network to learn from errors and make adjustments, which is essential when it comes to performing complex tasks such as language translation or image recognition. Common choices for activation functions include the sigmoid function, hyperbolic **tangent (tanh)**, and **rectified linear unit (ReLU)**, among others.

The output of the neuron is the result of the activation function. It serves as the input to the neurons in the next layer of the network.

The weights and bias in the neuron are learnable parameters. In other words, their values are learned over time as the neural network is trained on data:

*   **Weights**: The strength or amplitude of the connection between two neurons. During the training phase, the neural network learns the correct weights that better map inputs to outputs. Weight is used in the neuron, as explained previously.

*   **Bias**: An additional parameter in the neuron that allows for the activation function to be shifted to the left or right, which can be critical for successful learning (also used in the neuron).

Activation function

The function (in each neuron) that determines the output a neuron should produce given its input is called an activation function. Common examples include sigmoid, ReLU and tanh.

Here are some of the most common types of activation functions:

*   **Sigmoid function**: This is where we're essentially classifying the input as either 0 or 1. The sigmoid function takes a real-valued input and squashes it to range between 0 and 1. It's often used in the output layer of a binary classification network:

$$f\left(x\right) = \frac{1}{(1 + exp(-x))}$$

However, it has two major drawbacks: **the vanishing gradients problem** (gradients are very small for large positive or negative inputs, which can slow down learning during backpropagation) and the **outputs are not zero-centered**.

- **Hyperbolic tanh function**: The tanh function also takes a real-valued input and squashes it to range between -1 and 1. Unlike the sigmoid function, its output is zero-centered because its range is symmetric around the origin:

$$f\left(x\right) = \frac{(exp(x) - exp(-x))}{(exp(x) + exp(-x))}$$

It also suffers from the vanishing gradients problem, as does the sigmoid function.

- **ReLU function**: The ReLU function has become very popular in recent years. It computes the function as follows:

$$f(x) = max(0, x)$$

In other words, the activation is simply the input if the input is positive; otherwise, it's zero.

It doesn't activate all the neurons at the same time, meaning that the neurons will only be deactivated if the output of the linear transformation is less than 0. This makes the network sparse and efficient. However, ReLU units can be fragile during training and can "die" (they stop learning completely) if a large gradient flows through them.

- **Leaky ReLU**: Leaky ReLU is a variant of ReLU that addresses the "dying ReLU" problem. Instead of defining the function as *0* for negative *x*, we define it as a small linear component of *x*:

$$f(x) = max(0.01x, x)$$

This allows the function to "leak" some information when the input is negative and helps to mitigate the dying ReLU problem.

- **Exponential linear unit (ELU)**: ELU is also a variant of ReLU that modifies the function to be a non-zero value for negative *x*, which can help the learning process:

$$f(x) = \begin{cases} x & if\ x > 0 \\ \alpha(e^x - 1) & otherwise \end{cases}$$

Here alpha (α) is a constant that defines function smoothness when inputs are negative. ELU tends to converge cost to zero faster and produce more accurate results. However, it can be slower to compute because of the use of the exponential operation.

- **Softmax function**: The softmax function is often used in the output layer of a classifier where we're trying to assign the input to one of several classes. It gives the probability that any given input belongs to each of the possible classes:

$$f(x_i) = \frac{e^{x_i}}{\sum_j e^{x_j}}$$

The denominator normalizes the probabilities, so they all sum up to 1 across all classes. The softmax function is also used in multinomial logistical regression.

Each of these activation functions has pros and cons, and the choice of activation function can depend on the specific application and context of the problem at hand.

Layer

A set of neurons that process signals at the same level of abstraction. The first layer is the input layer, the last layer is the output layer, and all layers in between are called hidden layers.

Epoch

In the context of training a neural network, an epoch is a term used to denote one complete pass through the entire training dataset. During an epoch, the neural network's weights are updated in an attempt to minimize the loss function.

The number of epochs hyperparameter sets how many times the deep learning algorithm processes the entire training dataset. Too many epochs can cause overfitting, where the model performs well on training data but poorly on new data. Conversely, training for too few epochs may mean the model is underfitting—it could improve with further training.

It's also important to note that the concept of an epoch is more relevant in the batch and mini-batch variants of gradient descent. In stochastic gradient descent, the model's weights are updated after seeing each individual example, so the concept of an epoch is less straightforward.

Batch size

The number of training instances used in one iteration. Batch size refers to the number of training examples used in one iteration.

When you start training a neural network, you have a couple of options for how you feed your data into the model:

- **Batch gradient descent**: Here, the entire training dataset is used to compute the gradient of the loss function for each iteration of the optimizer (as with gradient descent). In this case, the batch size is equal to the total number of examples in the training dataset.

- **Stochastic gradient descent (SGD)**: SGD uses a single example at each iteration of the optimizer. Therefore, the batch size for SGD is *1*.

- **Mini-batch gradient descent**: This is a compromise between batch gradient descent and SGD. In mini-batch gradient descent, the batch size is usually between 10 and 1,000 and is chosen depending on the computational resources you have.

The batch size can significantly impact the learning process. Larger batch sizes result in faster progress in training but don't always converge as fast. Smaller batch sizes update the model frequently but the progress in training is slower.

Moreover, smaller batch sizes have a regularizing effect and can help the model generalize better, leading to better performance on unseen data. However, using a batch size that is too small can lead to unstable training, less accurate estimates of the gradient, and, ultimately, a model with worse performance.

Choosing the right batch size is a matter of trial and error and depends on the specific problem and the computational resources at hand:

- **Iterations**: The number of batches of data the algorithm has seen (or the number of passes it has made on the dataset).

- **Learning rate**: A hyperparameter that controls the speed of convergence of the learning algorithm by adjusting the weight update rate based on the loss gradient.

- **Loss function (cost function)**: The loss function evaluates the neural network's performance on the dataset. Higher deviations between predictions and actual results result in a larger output from the loss function. The goal is to minimize this output, which will give the model more accurate predictions.

- **Backpropagation**: The primary algorithm for performing gradient descent on neural networks. It calculates the gradient of the loss function at the output layer and distributes it back through the layers of the network, updating the weights and biases in a way that minimizes the loss.

- **Overfitting**: A situation where a model learns the detail and noise in the training data to the extent that it performs poorly on new, unseen data.

- **Underfitting**: A situation where a model is too simple to learn the underlying structure of the data and, thus, performs poorly on both training and new data.

- **Regularization**: A technique used to prevent overfitting by adding a penalty term to the loss function, which, in turn, constrains the weights of the network.

- **Dropout**: A regularization technique where randomly selected neurons are ignored during training, which helps to prevent overfitting.

- **CNN**: A type of neural network well-suited to image processing and computer vision tasks.

- **RNN**: A type of neural network designed to recognize patterns in sequences of data, such as time series or text.

Let's move on to the architecture of different neural networks next.

The architecture of different neural networks

Neural networks come in various types, each with a specific architecture suited to a different kind of task. The following list contains general descriptions of some of the most common types:

- **Feedforward neural network (FNN)**: This is the most straightforward type of neural network. Information in this network moves in one direction only, from the input layer through any hidden layers to the output layer. There are no cycles or loops in the network; it's a straight, "feedforward" path.

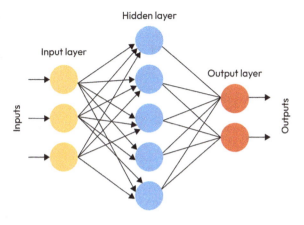

Figure 6.2 – Feedforward neural network

- **Multilayer perceptron (MLP)**: An MLP is a type of feedforward network that has at least one hidden layer in addition to its input and output layers. The layers are fully connected, meaning each neuron in a layer connects with every neuron in the next layer. MLPs can model complex patterns and are widely used for tasks such as image recognition, classification, speech recognition, and other types of machine learning tasks. The MLP is a feedforward network with layers of neurons arranged sequentially. Information flows from the input layer through hidden layers to the output layer in one direction:

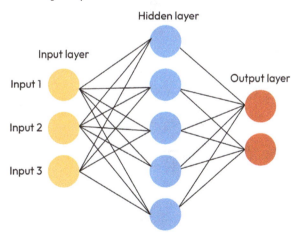

Figure 6.3 – Multilayer perceptron

- **CNN**: A CNN is particularly well-suited to tasks involving spatial data, such as images. Its architecture includes three main types of layers: convolutional layers, pooling layers, and fully connected layers. The convolutional layers apply a series of filters to the input, which allows the network to automatically and adaptively learn spatial hierarchies of features. Pooling layers decrease the spatial size of the representation, thereby reducing parameters and computation in the network to control overfitting and decrease the computation cost in the following layers. Fully connected layers get the output of the pooling layer and conduct high-level reasoning on the output.

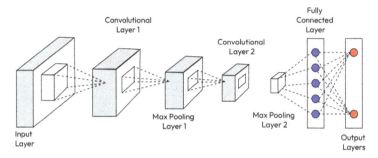

Figure 6.4 – Convolutional neural network

- **Recurrent neural network (RNN)**: Unlike feedforward networks, RNNs have connections that form directed cycles. This architecture allows them to use information from their previous outputs as inputs, making them ideal for tasks involving sequential data, such as time series prediction or NLP. A significant variation of RNNs is the LSTM network, which uses special units in addition to standard units. RNN units include a "memory cell" that can maintain information in memory for long periods of time, a feature that is particularly useful for tasks that require learning from long-distance dependencies in the data, such as handwriting or speech recognition.

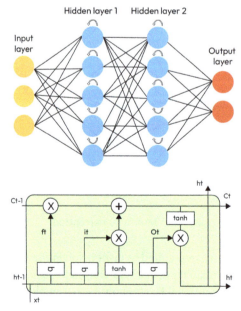

Figure 6.5 – Recurrent neural network

- **Autoencoder (AE)**: An AE is a type of neural network used to learn the efficient coding of input data. It has a symmetrical architecture and is designed to apply backpropagation, setting the target values to be equal to the inputs. Autoencoders are typically used for feature extraction, learning representations of data, and dimensionality reduction. They're also used in generative models, noise removal, and recommendation systems.

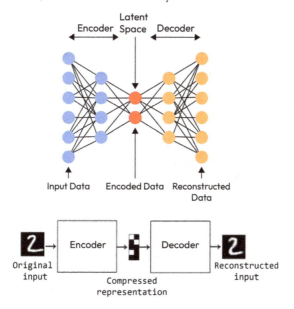

Figure 6.6 – Autoencoder architecture

- **Generative adversarial network (GAN)**: A GAN consists of two parts, a generator and a discriminator, which are both neural networks. The generator creates data instances that aim to come from the same distribution as the training dataset. The discriminator's goal is to distinguish between instances from the true distribution and instances from the generator. The generator and the discriminator are trained together, with the goal that the generator produces better instances as training progresses, whereas the discriminator becomes better at distinguishing true instances from generated ones.

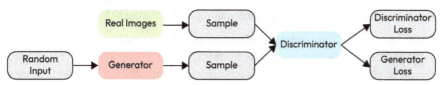

Figure 6.7 – Generative adversarial network in computer vision

These are just a few examples of neural network architectures, and many variations and combinations exist. The architecture you choose for a task will depend on the specific requirements and constraints of your task.

The challenges of training neural networks

Training neural networks is a complex task and comes with challenges during the training, such as local minima and vanishing/exploding gradients, as well as computational costs and interpretability. All challenges are explained in detail in the following points:

- **Local minima**: The objective of training a neural network is to find the set of weights that minimizes the loss function. This is a high-dimensional optimization problem, and there are many points (sets of weights) where the loss function has local minima. A suboptimal local minimum is a point where the loss is lower than for the nearby points but higher than the global minimum, which is the overall lowest possible loss. The training process can get stuck in such suboptimal local minima. It's important to remember that the local minima problem exists even in convex loss functions due to the discrete representation that is a part of digital computation.

- **Vanishing/exploding gradients**: This is a difficulty encountered, especially when training deep neural networks. The gradients of the loss function may become very small (vanish) or very large (explode) in deeper layers of the network during the backpropagation process. Vanishing gradients make it hard for the network to learn from the data because the weight updates become very small. Exploding gradients can cause the training process to fail because weight updates become too large, and the loss becomes undefined (e.g., NaN).

- **Overfitting**: One of the common problems in training machine learning models is when our model is too complex, and we train it too much. In this case, the model learns even the noises in the training data and works very well on training data but poorly on the unseen test data.

- **Underfitting**: Conversely, underfitting occurs when the model is too simple and can't capture the underlying structure of the data. Both overfitting and underfitting can be mitigated by using proper model complexity, regularization techniques, and a sufficient amount of training data.

- **Computational resources**: Training neural networks, particularly deep networks, requires significant computational resources (CPU/GPU power and memory). They also often require a large amount of training data to perform well, which can be a problem when such data are not available.

- **Lack of interpretability**: While not strictly a training issue, the lack of interpretability of neural networks is a significant problem. They are often referred to as "black boxes" because it is challenging to understand why they are making the predictions they do.

- **Difficulty in selecting appropriate architecture and hyperparameters**: There are many types of neural network architectures to choose from (such as CNN and RNN), and each has a set of hyperparameters that need to be tuned (such as learning rate, batch size, number of layers, and number of units per layer). Selecting the best architecture and tuning these hyperparameters for a given problem can be a challenging and time-consuming task.

- **Data preprocessing**: Neural networks often require the input data to be in a specific format. For instance, data might need to be normalized, categorical variables might need to be one-hot encoded, and missing values might need to be imputed. This preprocessing can be a complex and time-consuming step.

These challenges make training neural networks a non-trivial task, often requiring a combination of technical expertise, computational resources, and trial and error.

Language models

A language model is a statistical model in NLP that is designed to learn and understand the structure of human language. More specifically, it is a probabilistic model that is trained to estimate the likelihood of words when provided with a given word scenario. For instance, a language model could be trained to predict the next word in a sentence, given the previous words.

Language models are fundamental to many NLP tasks. They are used in machine translation, speech recognition, part-of-speech tagging, and named entity recognition, among other things. More recently, they have been used to create conversational AI models such as chatbots and personal assistants and to generate human-like text.

Traditional language models were often based on explicitly statistical methods, such as n-gram models, which consider only the previous n words when predicting the next word, or **hidden Markov models (HMMs)**.

More recently, neural networks have become popular for creating language models, leading to the rise of neural language models. These models use the power of neural networks to consider the context of each word when making predictions, resulting in higher accuracy and fluency. Examples of neural language models include RNNs, the transformer model, and various transformer-based architectures such as BERT and GPT.

Language models are essential for understanding, generating, and interpreting human language in a computational setting, and they play a vital role in many applications of NLP.

Here are several motivations for using language models:

- **Machine translation**: Language models are a crucial component in systems that translate text from one language to another. They can assess the fluency of translated sentences and help choose between multiple possible translations.

- **Speech recognition**: Language models are used in speech recognition systems to help distinguish between words and phrases that sound similar. By predicting what word is likely to come next in a sentence, they can improve the accuracy of transcription.

- **Information retrieval**: When you search for something on the internet, language models help to determine what documents are relevant to your query. They can understand the semantic similarity between your search terms and potential results.

- **Text generation**: Language models can generate human-like text, which is useful in various applications such as chatbots, writing assistants, and content creation tools. For example, a chatbot can use a language model to generate appropriate responses to user queries.

- **Sentiment analysis**: By understanding the structure of language, language models can help determine whether the sentiment of a piece of text is positive, negative, or neutral. This is useful in areas such as social media monitoring, product reviews, and customer feedback.

- **Grammar checking**: Language models can predict what word should come next in a sentence, which can help identify grammatical errors or awkward phrasing.

- **Named entity recognition**: Language models can help identify named entities in text, such as people, organizations, locations, and more. This can be useful for tasks such as information extraction and automated summarization.

- **Understanding context**: Language models, especially recent models based on **DL**, such as transformers, are excellent at understanding the context of words and sentences. This capability is vital for many **NLP** tasks, such as question answering, summarization, and dialogue systems.

All these motivations stem from a central theme: language models help machines understand and generate human language more effectively, which is crucial for many applications in today's data-driven world.

In the following section, we introduce the different types of learning and then explain how one can use self-supervised learning to train language models.

Semi-supervised learning

Semi-supervised learning is a type of ML approach that utilizes both labeled and unlabeled data for training. It is particularly useful when you have a small amount of labeled data and a large amount of unlabeled data. The strategy here is to use the labeled data to train an initial model and then use this model to predict labels for the unlabeled data. The model is then retrained using the newly labeled data, improving its accuracy in the process.

Unsupervised learning

Unsupervised learning, on the other hand, involves training models entirely on unlabeled data. The goal here is to find underlying patterns or structures in the data. Unsupervised learning includes techniques such as clustering (where the aim is to group similar instances together) and dimensionality reduction (where the aim is to simplify the data without losing too much information).

Using self-supervised learning to train language models

Self-supervised learning is a form of unsupervised learning where the data provides the supervision. In other words, the model learns to predict certain parts of the input data from other parts of the same input data. It does not require explicit labels provided by humans, hence the term "self-supervised."

In the context of language models, self-supervision is typically implemented by predicting parts of a sentence when given other parts. For example, given the sentence "The cat is on the __," the model would be trained to predict the missing word ("mat," in this case).

Let's look at a couple of popular self-supervised learning strategies for training language models next.

Masked language modeling (MLM)

This strategy, used in the training of BERT, randomly masks some percentage of the input tokens and tasks the model with predicting the masked words based on the context provided by the unmasked words. For instance, in the sentence "The cat is on the mat," we could mask "cat," and the model's job would be to predict this word. Please note that more than one word can also be masked.

Mathematically, the objective of an MLM is to maximize the following likelihood:

$$L = \sum_i \log\left(P\left(w_i \middle| w_{i-1}; \theta\right)\right)$$

where w_i is a masked word, w_{i-1} are the non-masked words, and θ represents the model parameters.

Autoregressive language modeling

In autoregressive language modeling, which is used in models such as GPT, the model predicts the next word in a sentence given all the preceding words. It's trained to maximize the likelihood of a word given its previous words in the sentence.

The objective of an autoregressive language model is to maximize

$$L = \sum_i \log\left(P\left(w_i \middle| w_1, \ldots, w_{i-1}; \theta\right)\right)$$

where w_i is the current word, $w_1, \ldots, w_{i-1}$ are the previous words, and θ represents the model parameters.

These strategies enable language models to obtain a rich understanding of language syntax and semantics directly from raw text without the need for explicit labels. The models can then be fine-tuned for various tasks such as text classification, sentiment analysis, and more, leveraging the language understanding gained from the self-supervised pretraining phase.

Transfer learning

Transfer learning is an ML technique where a pretrained model is reused as the starting point for a different but related problem. Compared to traditional ML approaches, where you start with initializing your model with random weights, transfer learning has the advantage of kick-starting the learning process from patterns that have been learned from a related task, which can both speed up the training process and improve the performance of the model, especially when you have limited labeled training data.

In transfer learning, a model is typically trained on a large-scale task, and then parts of the model are used as a starting point for another task. The large-scale task is often chosen to be broad enough that the learned representations are useful for many different tasks. This process works particularly well when the input data for both tasks are of the same type and the tasks are related.

There are several ways to apply transfer learning, and the best approach can depend on how much data you have for your task and how similar your task is to the original task the model was trained on.

Feature extraction

The pretrained model acts as a feature extractor. You remove the last layer or several layers of the model, leaving the rest of the network intact. Then, you pass your data through this truncated model and use the output as input to a new, smaller model that is trained for your specific task.

Fine-tuning

You use the pretrained model as a starting point and update all or some of the model's parameters for your new task. In other words, you continue the training where it left off, allowing the model to adjust from generic feature extraction to features more specific to your task. Often, a lower learning rate is used during fine-tuning to avoid overwriting the prelearned features entirely during training.

Transfer learning is a powerful technique that can be used to improve the performance of ML models. It is particularly useful for tasks where there are limited labeled data available. It is commonly used in DL applications. For instance, it's almost a standard in image classification problems where pretrained models on ImageNet, a large-scale annotated image dataset (ResNet, VGG, Inception, and so on), are used as the starting point. The features learned by these models are generic for image classification and can be fine-tuned on a specific image classification task with a smaller amount of data.

Here are some examples of how transfer learning can be used:

- A model trained to classify images of cats and dogs can be used to fine-tune a model to classify images of other animals, such as birds or fish

- A model trained to translate text from English to Spanish can be used to fine-tune a model to translate text from Spanish to French

- A model trained to predict the price of a house can be used to fine-tune a model to predict the price of a car

Similarly, in natural language processing, large pretrained models, such as BERT or GPT, are often used as the starting point for a wide range of tasks. These models are pretrained on a large corpus of text and learn a rich representation of language that can be fine-tuned for specific tasks such as text classification, sentiment analysis, question answering, and more.

Understanding transformers

Transformers are a type of neural network architecture that was introduced in a paper called *Attention is All You Need* by Ashish Vaswani, Noam Shazeer, Niki Parmar, Jakob Uszkoreit, Llion Jones, Aidan N. Gomez, Łukasz Kaiser, and Illia Polosukhin (*Advances in neural information processing systems 30* (2017), Harvard). They have been very influential in the field of NLP and have formed the basis for state-of-the-art models such as BERT and GPT.

The key innovation in transformers is the self-attention mechanism, which allows the model to weigh the relevance of each word in the input when producing an output, thereby considering the context of each word. This is unlike previous models such as RNNs or RNNs, which process the input sequentially and, therefore, have a harder time capturing the long-range dependencies between words.

Architecture of transformers

A transformer is composed of an encoder and a decoder, both of which are made up of several identical layers, as shown in *Figure 6.8*. Each layer in the encoder contains two sub-layers: a self-attention mechanism and a position-wise fully connected feedforward network. A residual connection is employed around each of the two sub-layers, followed by layer normalization:

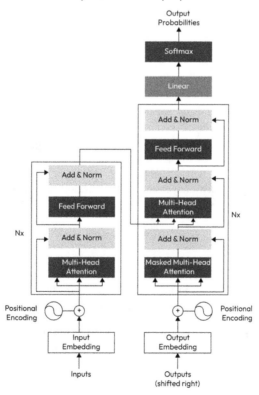

Figure 6.8 – Self-attention mechanism

Similarly, each layer in the decoder has three sub-layers. The first is a self-attention layer, the second is a cross-attention layer that attends to the output of the encoder stack, and the third is a position-wise fully connected feedforward network. Like the encoder, each of these sub-layers has a residual connection around it, followed by layer normalization. Please note that in the figure, just one head is being shown, and we can have multiple heads working in parallel (*N* heads).

Self-attention mechanism

The self-attention mechanism, or scaled dot-product attention, calculates the relevance of each word in the sequence to the current word being processed. The input to the self-attention layer is a sequence of word embeddings, each of which is split into a **query** (*Q*), a **key** (*K*), and a **value** (*V*) using separately learned linear transformations.

The attention score for each word is then calculated as follows:

$$Attention(Q, K, V) = softmax(QK^T / sqrt(d_k))V$$

Where d_k is the dimensionality of the queries and keys, which is used to scale the dot product to prevent it from growing too large. The softmax operation ensures that the attention scores are normalized and sum to 1. These scores represent the weight given to each word's value when producing the output for the current word.

The output of the self-attention layer is a new sequence of vectors, where the output for each word is a weighted sum of all the input values, with the weights determined by the attention scores.

Positional encoding

Since the self-attention mechanism does not take into account the position of the words in the sequence, the transformer adds a positional encoding to the input embeddings at the bottom of the encoder and decoder stacks. This encoding is a fixed function of the position and allows the model to learn to use the order of the words.

In the original transformer paper, positional encoding is a sinusoidal function of the position and the dimension, although learned positional encodings have also been used effectively.

Applications of transformers

Since their introduction, transformers have been used to achieve state-of-the-art results on a wide range of NLP tasks, including machine translation, text summarization, sentiment analysis, and more. They have also been adapted for other domains, such as computer vision and reinforcement learning.

The introduction of transformers has led to a shift in the NLP field towards pretraining large transformer models on a large corpus of text and then fine-tuning them on specific tasks, which is an effective form of transfer learning. This approach has been used in models such as BERT, GPT-2, GPT-3, and GPT-4.

Learning more about large language models

Large language models are a class of ML models that have been trained on a broad range of internet text.

The term "large" in "large language models" refers to the number of parameters that these models have. For example, GPT-3 has 175 billion parameters. These models are trained using self-supervised learning on a large corpus of text, which means they predict the next word in a sentence (such as GPT) or a word based on surrounding words (such as BERT, which is also trained to predict whether a pair of sentences is sequential). Because they are exposed to such a large amount of text, these models learn grammar, facts about the world, reasoning abilities, and also biases in the data they're trained on.

These models are transformer-based, meaning they leverage the transformer architecture, which uses self-attention mechanisms to weigh the importance of words in input data. This architecture allows these models to process long-range dependencies in text, making them very effective for a wide range of NLP tasks.

Large language models can be fine-tuned on specific tasks to achieve high performance. Fine-tuning involves additional training on a smaller, task-specific dataset and allows the model to adapt its general language understanding abilities to the specifics of the task. This approach has been used to achieve state-of-the-art results on many NLP benchmarks.

While large language models have demonstrated impressive abilities, they also raise important challenges. For example, because they're trained on internet text, they can reproduce and amplify biases present in the data. They can also generate outputs that are harmful or misleading. Additionally, due to their size, these models require significant computational resources to train and deploy, which raises issues around cost and environmental impact.

Despite these challenges, large language models represent a significant advance in the field of AI and are a powerful tool for a wide range of applications, including translation, summarization, content creation, question answering, and more.

The challenges of training language models

Training large language models is a complex and resource-intensive task that poses several challenges. Here are some of the key issues:

- **Computational resources**: The training of large language models requires substantial computational resources. These models have billions of parameters that need to be updated during training, which involves performing a large amount of computation over an extensive dataset. This computation is usually carried out on high-performance GPUs or **tensor processing units (TPUs)**, and the costs associated can be prohibitive.

- **Memory limitations**: As the size of the model increases, the amount of memory required to store the model parameters, intermediate activations, and gradients during training also increases. This can lead to memory issues on even the most advanced hardware. Techniques such as model parallelism, gradient checkpointing, and offloading can be used to mitigate these issues, but they add complexity to the training process.

- **Dataset size and quality**: Large language models are trained on extensive text corpora. Finding, cleaning, and structurally organizing such massive datasets can be challenging. Moreover, the quality of the dataset directly impacts the performance of the model. Since these models learn from the data they're trained on, biases or errors in the data can lead to a biased or error-prone model.

- **Overfitting**: While large models have a high capacity to learn complex patterns, they can also be overfitted to the training data, especially when the amount of available data is limited compared to the size of the model. Overfitting leads to poor generalization of unseen data. Regularization techniques, such as weight decay, dropout, and early stopping, can be used to combat overfitting.

- **Training stability**: As models get larger, stably training them becomes more difficult. The challenges include managing learning rates and batch sizes and dealing with issues such as vanishing or exploding gradients.

- **Evaluation and fine-tuning**: Evaluating the performance of these models can also be challenging due to their size. Moreover, fine-tuning these models on a specific task can be tricky, as it can lead to "catastrophic forgetting," where the model forgets the pretraining knowledge.

- **Ethical and safety concerns**: Large language models can generate content that is harmful or inappropriate. They can also propagate and amplify biases present in the training data. These issues necessitate the development of robust methods to control the behavior of the model, both during training and at runtime.

Despite these challenges, progress continues in the field of large language models. Researchers are developing new strategies to mitigate these issues and to train large models more effectively and responsibly.

Specific designs of language models

Here, we are going to explain two popular architectures of language models, BERT and GPT, in detail.

BERT

BERT, which we mentioned already and will now expand on, is a transformer-based ML technique for NLP tasks. It was developed by Google and introduced in a paper by Jacob Devlin, Ming-Wei Chang, Kenton Lee, and Kristina Toutanova titled *Bert: Pre-training of deep bidirectional transformers for language understanding*, arXiv preprint arXiv:1810.04805 (2018).

BERT is designed to pretrain deep bidirectional representations from the unlabeled text by joint conditioning on both left and right contexts in all layers. This is in contrast to previous methods, such as GPT and ELMo, which pretrain text representations from only the left context or from left and right contexts separately. This bi-directionality allows BERT to understand the context and the semantic meaning of a word more accurately.

BERT's design

BERT is based on the transformer model architecture, which is shown in *Figure 6.8*, originally introduced by Vaswani et al. in the paper *Attention is All You Need*. The model architecture consists of stacked self-attention and point-wise fully connected layers.

BERT comes in two sizes: **BERT Base** and **BERT Large**. BERT Base is composed of 12 transformer layers, each with 12 self-attention heads, and a total of 110 million parameters. BERT Large is much bigger and has 24 transformer layers, each with 16 self-attention heads, for a total of 340 million parameters.

BERT's training process involves two steps: **pretraining** and **fine-tuning**.

The very first step in training or using a language model is to create or load its dictionary. We usually use a tokenizer to achieve this goal.

Tokenizer

In order to use the language models efficiently, we need to use a tokenizer that converts the input text into a limited number of tokens. Subword tokenization algorithms, such as **byte pair encoding** (BPE), **unigram language model** (ULM), and **WordPiece**, split words into smaller subword units. This is useful for handling out-of-vocabulary words and allows the model to learn meaningful representations for subword parts that often carry semantic meaning.

The BERT tokenizer is a critical component of the BERT model, performing the initial preprocessing of text data necessary for input into the model. BERT uses WordPiece tokenization, a subword tokenization algorithm that breaks words into smaller parts, allowing BERT to handle out-of-vocabulary words, reduce the size of the vocabulary, and deal with the richness and diversity of languages.

Here's a detailed breakdown of how the BERT tokenizer works:

1. **Basic tokenization**: First, the BERT tokenizer performs basic tokenization, breaking text into individual words by splitting on whitespace and punctuation. This is similar to what you might find in other tokenization methods.

2. **WordPiece tokenization**: After basic tokenization, the BERT tokenizer applies WordPiece tokenization. This step breaks words into smaller subword units or "WordPieces." If a word isn't in the BERT vocabulary, the tokenizer will iteratively break the word down into smaller sub words until it finds a match in the vocabulary or until it has to resort to character-level representation.

   For example, the word "unhappiness" might be broken down into two WordPieces: "un" and "##happiness". The "##" symbol is used to denote sub-words that are part of a larger word and not a whole word on their own.

3. **Special tokens addition**: The **BERT** tokenizer then adds special tokens necessary for specific **BERT** functionalities. The [CLS] token is appended at the beginning of each sentence, serving as an aggregate representation for classification tasks. The [SEP] token is added at the end of each sentence to signify sentence boundaries. If two sentences are inputted (for tasks that require sentence pairs), they are separated by this [SEP] token.

4. **Token to ID conversion**: Finally, each token is mapped to an integer ID corresponding to its index in the **BERT** vocabulary. These IDs are what the **BERT** model actually uses as input.

So, in summary, the BERT tokenizer works by first tokenizing the text into words, then further breaking these words down into WordPieces (if necessary), adding special tokens, and finally converting these tokens into IDs. This process allows the model to understand and generate meaningful representations for a wide variety of words and sub-words, contributing to BERT's powerful performance on various NLP tasks.

Pretraining

During pretraining, **BERT** was trained on a large corpus of text (the entire English Wikipedia and BooksCorpus are used in the original paper). The model was trained to predict masked words in a sentence (masked language model) and to distinguish whether two sentences come in order in the text (next sentence prediction), as explained here:

*   **Masked language model**: In this task, 15% of the words in a sentence are replaced by a [MASK] token, and the model is trained to predict the original word from the context provided by the non-masked words.

*   **Next sentence prediction**: When the model is given a pair of two sentences, it is also trained to predict whether sentence *B* is the next sentence following sentence *A*.

Fine-tuning

After pretraining, BERT can be fine-tuned on a specific task with a significantly smaller amount of training data. Fine-tuning involves adding an additional output layer to BERT and training the entire model end-to-end on the specific task. This approach has been shown to achieve state-of-the-art results on a wide range of NLP tasks, including question answering, named entity recognition, sentiment analysis, and more.

BERT's design and its pretraining/fine-tuning approach revolutionized the field of NLP and have led to a shift toward training large models on a broad range of data and then fine-tuning them on specific tasks.

How to fine-tune BERT for text classification

As mentioned, BERT has been pretrained on a large corpus of text data, and the learned representations can be fine-tuned for specific tasks, including text classification. Here is a step-by-step process on how to fine-tune BERT for text classification:

1. **Preprocessing input data**: BERT requires a specific format for input data. The sentences need to be tokenized into sub-words using BERT's own tokenizer, and special tokens such as [CLS] (classification) and [SEP] (separation) need to be added. The [CLS] token is added at the beginning of each example and is used as the aggregate sequence representation for classification tasks. The [SEP] token is added at the end of each sentence to denote sentence boundaries. All sequences are then padded to a fixed length to form a uniform input.

2. **Loading the pretrained BERT model**: BERT has several pretrained models, and the right one should be chosen based on the task at hand. The models differ in terms of the size of the model and the language of the pretraining data. Once the pretrained BERT model is loaded, it can be used to create contextualized word embeddings for the input data.

3. **Adding a classification layer**: A classification layer, also known as the classification head, is added on top of the pretrained BERT model. This layer will be trained to make predictions for the text classification task. Usually, this layer is a fully connected neural network layer that takes the representation corresponding to the [CLS] token as input and outputs the probability distribution over the classes.

4. **Fine-tuning the model**: Fine-tuning involves training the model on the specific task (in this case, text classification) using the labeled data. This process can be done in multiple ways. The more common approach is to update the weights of the pretrained BERT model and the newly added classification layer to minimize a loss function, typically the cross-entropy loss for classification tasks. It is important to use a lower learning rate during fine-tuning, as larger rates can destabilize the prelearned weights. Additionally, the number of recommended epochs is two to four, so the model learns the task but does not overfit. The benefit of this approach is that the model weights will be adjusted to perform well on specific tasks. Alternatively, we can freeze BERT layers and just update the classifier layer weights.

5. **Evaluating the model**: Once the model has been fine-tuned, it can be evaluated on a validation set to assess its performance. This involves calculating metrics such as accuracy, precision, recall, and F1 score. During the training and evaluation task, similar to other ML and DL models, we can perform hyperparameter tuning.

6. **Applying the model**: The fine-tuned model can now be used to make predictions on new, unseen text data. As with the training data, this new data also need to be preprocessed into the format that BERT expects.

> **Important note**
>
> Note that working with **BERT** requires considerable computational resources, as the model has a large number of parameters. A GPU is typically recommended for fine-tuning and applying BERT models. There are some models that are lighter than BERT with slightly lower performance, such as DistilBERT, that we can use in the case of being constrained by the computation or memory resources. Additionally, BERT is able to process 512 tokens, which limits the length of our input text. If we want to process longer text, Longformer or BigBird are good choices. What we explained here works for similar language models such as RoBERTa, XLNet, and so on.

In summary, fine-tuning BERT for text classification involves preprocessing the input data, loading the pretrained BERT model, adding a classification layer, fine-tuning the model on the labeled data, and then evaluating and applying the model.

We will demonstrate the preceding paradigm of fine-tuning BERT and then apply it at the end of this chapter. You will have the opportunity to employ it firsthand and adjust it to your needs.

GPT-3

GPT-3, short for **generative pretrained transformer 3**, is an autoregressive language model developed by OpenAI that uses DL techniques to generate human-like text. It is the third version of the GPT series. The GPT versions that followed it, GPT-3.5 and GPT-4, will be covered in the next chapter, as we will expand on large language models.

Design and architecture of GPT-3

GPT-3 extends the transformer model architecture used by its predecessors. The architecture is based on a transformer model that uses layers of transformer blocks, where each block is composed of self-attention and feedforward neural network layers.

GPT-3 is massive compared to the previous versions. It consists of 175 billion ML parameters. These parameters are learned during the training phase, where the model learns to predict the next word in a sequence of words.

GPT-3's transformer model is designed to process sequences of data (in this case, sequences of words or tokens in text), making it well-suited for language tasks. It processes input data sequentially from left to right and generates predictions for the next item in the sequence. This is the difference between BERT and GPT, where, in BERT, words from both sides are used to predict masked words, but in GPT, just the previous words are used for prediction, which makes it a good choice for generative tasks.

Pretraining and fine-tuning

Similar to BERT and other transformer-based models, GPT-3 also involves a two-step process: **pretraining** and **fine-tuning**.

Pretraining

In this phase, GPT-3 is trained on a large corpus of text data. It learns to predict the next word in a sentence. However, unlike BERT, which uses a bidirectional context for prediction, GPT-3 only uses the left context (i.e., the previous words in the sentence).

Fine-tuning

After the pretraining phase, GPT-3 can be fine-tuned on a specific task using a smaller amount of task-specific training data. This could be any NLP task, such as text completion, translation, summarization, question answering, and so on.

Zero-shot, one-shot, and few-shot learning

One of the impressive features of GPT-3 is its capability to perform few-shot learning. When given a task and a few examples of that task, GPT-3 can often learn to perform the task accurately.

In the zero-shot setting, the model is given a task without any prior examples. In the one-shot setting, it's given one example, and in the few-shot setting, it's given a few examples to learn from.

Challenges of using GPT-3

Despite its impressive capabilities, GPT-3 also presents some challenges. Due to its large size, it requires substantial computational resources to train. It can sometimes generate incorrect or nonsensical responses, and it can reflect biases present in the training data. It also struggles with tasks that require a deep understanding of the world or common sense reasoning beyond what can be learned from text.

Reviewing our use case – ML/DL system design for NLP classification in a Jupyter Notebook

In this section, we are going to work on a real-world problem and see how we can use an NLP pipeline to solve it. The code for this part is shared as a Google Colab notebook at `Ch6_Text_Classification_DL.ipynb`.

The business objective

In this scenario, we are in the healthcare sector. Our objective is to develop a general medical knowledge engine that is very up to date with recent findings in the world of healthcare.

The technical objective

The CTO derives several technical objectives from the business objective. One objective is for the ML team: given the growing collection of conclusions that correspond to medical publications, identify the ones that represent advice. This will allow us to identify the medical advice that stems from the underlying research.

The pipeline

Let's review the parts of the pipeline, as depicted in *Figure 6.9*:

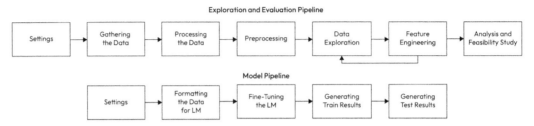

Figure 6.9 – The structure of a typical exploration and model pipeline

Notice how this design is different from the design we saw in *Figure 5.2*. There, the exploration and evaluation parts leverage the same feature engineering technique that is later used by the ML models. Here, with LMs, feature engineering is not a part of the preparation for the modeling. The pretrained model, and particularly the tokenizer, performs feature engineering, which yields very different and less interpretable features than the binary, BoW, or TF-IDF features.

> **Note**
> Code parts: From "Settings" through "Generating Results of the Traditional ML Models."

These parts are identical in their nature to the analog parts discussed in *Chapter 5*. The only differences relate to the differences in the data.

Deep learning

In this part of the code, we employ a deep learning language model.

When looking to apply transfer learning via LMs and fine-tuning them per our objective and data, there are several stacks to choose from. The ones that stand out the most are Google's TensorFlow, and Meta's PyTorch. A package called **Transformers** was built as a wrapper around these stacks to allow for a simpler implementation of the code. In this example, we leverage the simplicity and richness of transformers models.

It is worth highlighting the company that built and supports the Transformers package: Hugging Face. Hugging Face took it upon themselves to create an entire ecosystem around the collection and sharing of free, open source DL models, which includes the many components that accommodate for implementing these models. The most actionable tool is the Transformers package, which is a Python package dedicated to picking, importing, training, and employing a large and growing set of DL models.

The code we are reviewing here provides more than just an example of ML/DL system design in the real world; it also showcases Hugging Face's Transformers.

Formatting the data

Here, we set the data up in a format that suits the Transformers library. The column names must be very specific.

Evaluation metric

We decided which metric we wished to optimize and plugged it into the training process. For this problem of binary classification, we optimized for accuracy and evaluated our result in comparison to the dataset's baseline accuracy, also known as the prior.

Trainer object

This is the core object for training the LM in Transformers. It holds a set of predefined configurations. Some of the key training configurations are the following:

- The neural net's mathematical learning hyperparameters, such the following:

  - The learning rate

  - The gradient decent settings

- The number of training epochs

- The computation hardware usage

- Logging setting for capturing the progression of the objective metric throughout the training process

Fine-tuning the neural network parameters

The fundamental concept around fine-tuning LMs is transfer learning. Neural networks lend themselves so well to transfer learning because one can simply strip any number of layers from the end of the structure and replace them with untrained layers that would be trained based on the underlying problem. The rest of the layers that weren't removed and aren't trained continue to operate exactly in the same way they did when the LM was originally trained (when it was originally built). If we replace the last layer but leave the rest of the original layers, then we could view those layers as supervised feature engineering or, conversely, as an embedding mechanism. This trait reflects the concept of transfer learning. Ideally, the model is expected to lend itself well to our underlying problem so that we will choose to keep the vast majority of the original layers, and only a small minority would be replaced and trained. In this way, a large DL model that took many weeks to be pretrained can be transferred and adapted to a new problem in minutes.

In our code, we set the model up in a way that we dictate exactly which of its layers we are looking to fine-tune. It is a design choice for us for this to be based on performance and also computation resources. One choice is to fine-tune the last layer right before the final output, also known as the classification head. The alternative is to fine-tune all the layers. In our code, we explicitly call the model's configuration, which controls which layer is fine-tuned, so the code can be changed in any way that suits the design.

We configure the trainer to log the performance of the training in real time. It prints those logs out for us in a table so we can observe and monitor them. When the training is complete, we plot the progress of the training and the evaluation. This helps us see the relation between the evolution of the training results and the evaluation results. Since the evaluation set that the trainer uses can be viewed as a held-out set in the context of the trainer, this plot allows us to investigate underfitting and overfitting.

Generating the training results – used for design choices

We reviewed the results of the training set, along with the logs that the trainer printed out. We compared them to the baseline accuracy and observed an increase in accuracy. We learned about the quality of our design by iterating over several different design choices and comparing them. That process of iterating over many sets of design parameters would be automated into code to allow for a systematic evaluation of the optimal setting. We didn't do that in our notebook just to keep things simple in the example. Once we believed we had found the optimal setting, we could say that the process was finished.

Generating the testing results – used for presenting performance

As with the code in *Chapter 5*, here, too, we finished by reviewing the test results. It is worth noting the difference between the evaluation set and the test set. One could suggest that since the trainer doesn't use the evaluation set for training, it could be used as a held-out test set, thus saving the need to exclude so many observations from training and supplying the model with more labeled data. However, while the trainer didn't use the evaluation set, we did use it to make our design decisions. For instance, we observed the plot from the preceding section and judged which number of epochs is optimal to achieve optimal fitting. In *Chapter 5*, an evaluation set was used too, but we didn't need to explicitly define it; it was carried out as a part of the K-fold cross-validation mechanism.

Summary

In this enlightening chapter, we embarked on a comprehensive exploration of DL and its remarkable application to text classification tasks through language models. We began with an overview of DL, revealing its profound ability to learn complex patterns from vast amounts of data and its indisputable role in advancing state-of-the-art NLP systems.

We then delved into the transformative world of transformer models, which have revolutionized NLP by providing an effective alternative to traditional RNNs and CNNs for processing sequence data. By unpacking the attention mechanism—a key feature in transformers—we highlighted its capacity to focus on different parts of the input sequence, hence facilitating a better understanding of context.

Our journey continued with an in-depth exploration of the BERT model. We detailed its architecture, emphasizing its pioneering use of bidirectional training to generate contextually rich word embeddings, and we highlighted its pretraining process, which learns language semantics from a large text corpus.

However, our exploration did not end there; we also introduced GPT, another transformative model that leverages the power of transformers in a slightly different way—focusing on generating human-like text. By comparing BERT and GPT, we shed light on their distinct strengths and use cases.

The chapter culminated in a practical guide on how to design and implement a text classification model using these advanced models. We walked you through all the stages of this process, from data preprocessing and model configuration to training, evaluation, and finally, making predictions on unseen data.

In essence, this chapter provided a well-rounded understanding of DL in NLP, transitioning from fundamental principles to hands-on applications. With this knowledge, you are now equipped to leverage the capabilities of transformer models, BERT, and GPT for your text classification tasks. Whether you are looking to delve further into the world of NLP or apply these skills in a practical setting, this chapter has equipped you with a firm foundation on which to build.

In this chapter, we introduced you to large language models. In the next chapter, we dive deeper into these models to learn more about them.

7

Demystifying Large Language Models: Theory, Design, and Langchain Implementation

In this chapter, we delve deep into the intricate world of **large language models** (**LLMs**) and the underpinning mathematical concepts that fuel their performance. The advent of these models has revolutionized the field of **natural language processing** (**NLP**), offering unparalleled proficiency in understanding, generating, and interacting with human language.

LLMs are a subset of **artificial intelligence** (**AI**) models that can understand and generate human-like text. They achieve this by being trained on a diverse range of internet text, thus learning an extensive array of facts about the world. They also learn to predict what comes next in a piece of text, which enables them to generate creative, fluent, and contextually coherent sentences.

As we explore the operations of LLMs, we will introduce the key metric of **perplexity**, a measurement of uncertainty that is pivotal in determining the performance of these models. A lower perplexity indicates the confidence that a **language model** (**LM**) has in predicting the next word in a sequence, thus showcasing its proficiency.

This chapter draws on multiple insightful publications that delve into the mathematical insights of LLMs. Some of these include *A Neural Probabilistic Language Model*, *Attention is All You Need*, and *PaLM: Scaling Language Modeling with Pathways*. These sources will guide us in understanding the robust mechanisms that underpin LLMs and their exceptional capabilities.

We will also explore the emerging field of **reinforcement learning from human feedback** (**RLHF**) in the context of LMs. RLHF has proven to be a powerful tool in fine-tuning the performance of LLMs, thereby leading to more accurate and meaningful generated texts.

With a comprehensive understanding of the mathematical foundations of LLMs and a deep dive into RLHF, we will gain a robust knowledge of these advanced AI systems, paving the way for future innovations and advancements in the field.

Finally, we will discuss the detailed architecture and design of recent models, such as **Pathways Language Model (PaLM)**, **Large Language Model Meta AI (LLaMA)**, and GPT-4.

Now, let's look at the topics covered in this chapter:

- What are LLMs and how are they different from LMs?
- Motivations for developing and using LLMs
- Challenges in developing LLMs

Technical requirements

For this chapter, you are expected to possess a solid foundation in **machine learning (ML)** concepts, particularly in the areas of **Transformers** and **reinforcement learning**. An understanding of Transformer-based models, which underpin many of today's LLMs, is vital. This includes familiarity with concepts such as self-attention mechanisms, positional encoding, and the structure of encoder-decoder architectures.

Knowledge of reinforcement learning principles is also essential, as we will delve into the application of RLHF in the fine-tuning of LMs. Familiarity with concepts such as policy gradients, reward functions, and Q-learning will greatly enhance your comprehension of this content.

Lastly, coding proficiency, specifically in Python, is crucial. This is because many of the concepts will be demonstrated and explored through the lens of programming. Experience with PyTorch or TensorFlow, popular ML libraries, and Hugging Face's Transformers library, a key resource for working with transformer models, will also be beneficial.

However, don't be discouraged if you feel you're lacking in some areas. This chapter aims to walk you through the complexities of these subjects, bridging any knowledge gaps along the way. So, come prepared with a mindset for learning, and let's delve into the fascinating world of LLMs!

What are LLMs and how are they different from LMs?

An LM is a type of ML model that is trained to predict the next word (or character or subword, depending on the granularity of the model) in a sequence, given the words that came before it (or in some models, the surrounding words). It's a probabilistic model that is capable of generating text that follows a certain linguistic style or pattern.

Before the advent of Transformer-based models such as **generative pretrained Transformers (GPTs)** and **Bidirectional Encoder Representations from Transformers (BERT)**, there were several other types of LMs widely used in NLP tasks. The following subsections discuss a few of them.

n-gram models

These are some of the simplest LMs. An n-gram model uses the (n-1) previous words to predict the nth word in a sentence. For example, in a bigram (2-gram) model, we would use the previous word to predict the next word. These models are easy to implement and computationally efficient, but they typically don't perform as well as more complex models because they don't capture long-range dependencies between words. Their performance also degrades as n increases, as they suffer from data sparsity issues (not having enough data to accurately estimate the probabilities for all possible n-grams).

Hidden Markov models (HMMs)

These models consider the "hidden" states that generate the observed data. In the context of language modeling, each word would be an observed state, and the "hidden" state would be some kind of linguistic feature that's not directly observable (such as the part of speech of the word). However, like n-gram models, HMMs struggle to capture long-range dependencies between words.

Recurrent neural networks (RNNs)

These are a type of neural network where connections between nodes form a directed graph along a temporal sequence. This allows them to use their internal state (memory) to process sequences of inputs, making them ideal for language modeling. They can capture long-range dependencies between words, but they struggle with the so-called vanishing gradient problem, which makes it difficult to learn these dependencies in practice.

Long short-term memory (LSTM) networks

An LSTM network is a special kind of RNN that is designed to learn long-term dependencies. They do this by using a series of "gates" that control the flow of information in and out of the memory state of the network. LSTMs were a big step forward in the state of the art of language modeling.

Gated recurrent unit (GRU) networks

These are a variation of LSTMs that use a slightly different set of gates in their architecture. They're often simpler and faster to train than LSTMs, but whether they perform better or worse than LSTMs tends to depend on the specific task at hand.

Each of these models has its own strengths and weaknesses, and none of them are inherently better or worse than the others – it all depends on the specific task and dataset. However, Transformer-based models have generally outperformed all of these models in a wide range of tasks, leading to their current popularity in the field of NLP.

How LLMs stand out

LLMs, such as GPT-3 and GPT-4, are simply LMs that are trained on a very large amount of text and have a very large number of parameters. The larger the model (in terms of parameters and training data), the more capable it is of understanding and generating complex and varied texts. Here are some key ways in which LLMs differ from smaller LMs:

- **Data**: LLMs are trained on vast amounts of data. This allows them to learn from a wide range of linguistic patterns, styles, and topics.

- **Parameters**: LLMs have a huge number of parameters. Parameters in an ML model are the parts of the model that are learned from the training data. The more parameters a model has, the more complex patterns it can learn.

- **Performance**: Because they're trained on more data and have more parameters, LLMs generally perform better than smaller ones. They're capable of generating more coherent and diverse texts, and they're better at understanding context, making inferences, and even answering questions or generating texts on a wide range of topics.

- **Compute resources**: LLMs require a significant amount of computational resources to train, both in terms of processing power and memory. They also take longer to train.

- **Storage and inference time**: Large models also require more storage space, and it takes longer to generate predictions (although this inference time is still typically quite fast on modern hardware).

Thus, we can say that LLMs are essentially scaled-up versions of smaller LMs. They're trained on more data, have more parameters, and are generally capable of producing higher-quality results, but they also require more resources to train and use. Besides that, an important advantage of an LLM is that we can train them unsupervised on a large corpus of data and then fine-tune them with a limited amount of data for different tasks.

Motivations for developing and using LLMs

The motivation to develop and use LLMs arises from several factors related to the capabilities of these models, and the potential benefits they can bring in diverse applications. The following subsections detail a few of these key motivations.

Improved performance

LLMs, when trained with sufficient data, generally demonstrate better performance compared to smaller models. They are more capable of understanding context, identifying nuances, and generating coherent and contextually relevant responses. This performance gain applies to a wide range of tasks in NLP, including text classification, named entity recognition, sentiment analysis, machine translation, question answering, and text generation. As shown in *Table 7.1*, the performance of BERT – one of the first well-known LLMs – and GPT is compared to the previous models on the **General Language**

Understanding Evaluation (GLUE) benchmark. The GLUE benchmark is a collection of diverse **natural language understanding (NLU)** tasks designed to evaluate the performance of models across multiple linguistic challenges. The benchmark encompasses tasks such as sentiment analysis, question answering, and textual entailment, among others. It's a widely recognized standard in the field of NLU, providing a comprehensive suite for comparing and improving language understanding models. It can be seen that its performance is better in all tasks:

Model	Average (in all tasks)	Sentiment analysis	Grammatical	Similarity
BERT large	82.1	94.9	60.5	86.5
BERT base	79.6	93.5	52.1	85.8
OpenAI GPT	75.1	91.3	45.4	80.0
Pre-open AI **State of the Art (STOA)**	74.0	93.2	35.0	81.0
Bidirectional Long Short-Term memory (BiLSTM) + Embeddings from Language Model (ELMo) + Attention	71.0	90.4	36.0	73.3

Table 7.1 – Comparing different models' performance on GLUE (this comparison is based on 2018 when BERT and GPT were released)

Broad generalization

LLMs trained on diverse datasets can generalize better across different tasks, domains, or styles of language. They can effectively learn from the training data to identify and understand a wide range of linguistic patterns, styles, and topics. This broad generalization capability makes them versatile for various applications, from chatbots to content creation to information retrieval.

When an LM is bigger, it means it has more parameters. These parameters allow the model to capture and encode more complex relationships and nuances within the data. In other words, a bigger model can learn and retain more information from the training data. As such, it is better equipped to handle a wider array of tasks and contexts post-training. It is this increased complexity and capacity that makes bigger LMs more generalizable across different tasks. As we can see in *Figure 7.1*, the bigger LMs perform better in different tasks.

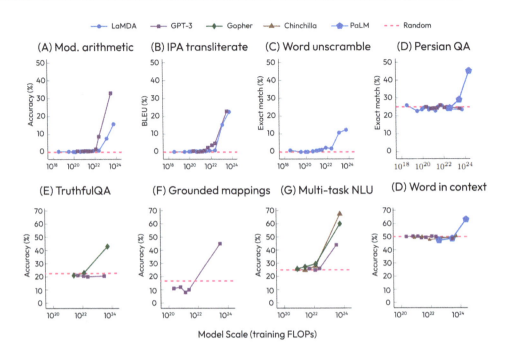

Figure 7.1 – LLMs performance based on their size and training

We can also see the progress in the development of the LLMs within the last three years in *Figure 7.2*.

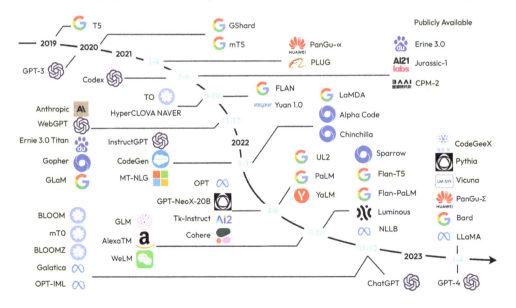

Figure 7.2 – The released LMs within 2019 to 2023 (the publicly available models are highlighted)

However, it's important to note that while larger models tend to be more generalizable, they also pose challenges such as increased computational requirements and the risk of overfitting. It is also essential to ensure that the training data is representative of the tasks and domains the model is expected to perform in, as models might carry over any biases present in the training data.

Few-shot learning

LLMs such as GPT-3, GPT-3.5, and GPT-4 have demonstrated impressive few-shot learning capabilities. Given a few examples (the "shots"), these models can generalize to complete similar tasks effectively. This makes adjusting and deploying these models in real-world applications more efficient. The prompts can be designed to include information for the model to refer to, such as example questions and their respective answers.

The model temporarily learns from given examples and refers to given information as an additional source. For example, when the LLM is used as a personal assistant or advisor, background information about the user can be appended to the prompt, allowing the model to "get to know you," as it uses your personal information prompts as a reference.

Understanding complex contexts

LLMs have the advantage of understanding complex contexts due to their extensive training on a wide range of data, including various topics, literary styles, and nuances as well as their deep architecture and large parameter space. This capacity allows them to comprehend and generate appropriate responses even in complex or nuanced situations.

For example, consider a scenario where a user asks the model to summarize a complicated scientific article. An LLM can understand the context and the technical language used in the article and generate a coherent and simplified summary.

Multilingual capabilities

LLMs can handle multiple languages effectively, making them suitable for global applications. Here are a few well-known multilingual LMs.

mBERT (multilingual BERT)

An extension of BERT, mBERT is pretrained on the top 104 languages with the largest Wikipedia using a masked LM objective.

Cross-lingual language model (XLM)

This is trained in 100 languages. It extends the BERT model to include several methods for cross-lingual model training.

XLM-RoBERTa

XLM-RoBERTa extends RoBERTa, which itself is an optimized version of BERT, and is trained on a much larger multilingual corpus covering more languages.

MarianMT

Part of Hugging Face's Transformers library, MarianMT is a state-of-the-art Transformer-based model optimized for translation tasks.

DistilBERT Multilingual

This is a smaller and faster version of mBERT, achieved through a distillation process.

T2T (T5) Multilingual

This is a variant of the **Text-to-Text Transfer Transformer** (**T5**) model, which is fine-tuned for translation tasks.

These models have achieved significant results in a variety of tasks, such as translation, named entity recognition, part-of-speech tagging, and sentiment analysis in multiple languages.

Human-like text generation

LLMs have shown a remarkable capability in generating human-like text. They can create contextually appropriate responses in conversations, write essays, and generate creative content such as poetry and stories. Models such as GPT-3, ChatGPT, and GPT-4 have shown good results in text generation tasks.

While the advantages are many, it's important to note that there are also challenges and potential risks associated with the use of LLMs. They require significant computational resources to train and deploy, and there are ongoing concerns related to their potential to generate harmful or biased content, their interpretability, and their environmental impact. Researchers are actively working on ways to mitigate these issues while leveraging the powerful capabilities of these models.

Due to these reasons, companies are trying to implement and train larger LMs (*Figure 7.3*):

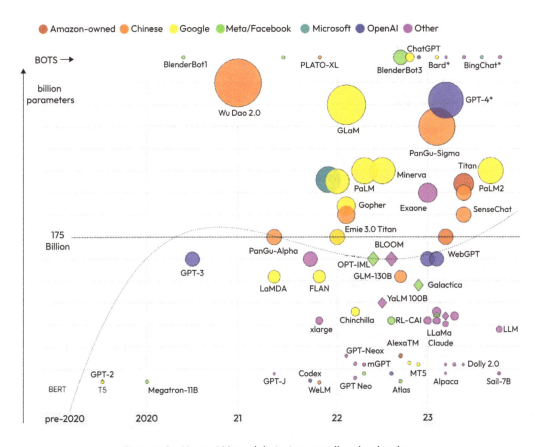

Figure 7.3 – Newer LMs and their size, as well as the developers

Challenges in developing LLMs

Developing LLMs poses a unique set of challenges, including but not limited to handling massive amounts of data, requiring vast computational resources, and the risk of introducing or perpetuating bias. The following subsections outline the detailed explanations of these challenges.

Amounts of data

LLMs require enormous amounts of data for training. As the model size grows, so does the need for diverse, high-quality training data. However, collecting and curating such large datasets is a challenging task. It can be time - consuming and expensive. There's also the risk of inadvertently including sensitive or inappropriate data in the training set. To have more of an idea, BERT has been trained using 3.3 billion words from Wikipedia and BookCorpus. GPT-2 has been trained on 40 GB of text data, and GPT-3 has been trained on 570 GB of text data. *Table 7.2* shows the number of parameters and size of training data of a few recent LMs.

Model	Parameters	Size of training data
GPT-3.5	175 B	300 billion tokens
GPT-3	175 B	300 billion tokens
PaLM	540 B	780 billion tokens
LLaMA	65 B	1.4 trillion tokens
Bloom	176 B	366 billion tokens

Table 7.2 – Number of parameters and training data of a few recent LMs

Computational resources

Training LLMs requires substantial computational resources. These models often have billions or even trillions of parameters and need to process vast amounts of data during training, which requires high-performance hardware (such as GPUs or TPUs) and a significant amount of time. This can be costly and could limit the accessibility of developing such models to only those who have these resources. For example, training GPT-3 took 1 million GPU hours, which cost around 4.6 million dollars (in 2020). *Table 7.3* shows the computational resources and training time of a few recent LMs.

Model	Hardware	Training time
PaLM	6144 TPU v4	-
LLaMA	2048 80G A100	21 days
Bloom	384 80G A100	105 days
GPT-3	1024x A100	34 days
GPT-4	25000 A100	90–100 days

Table 7.3 – The hardware and training time of a few recent LMs

Risk of bias

LLMs can learn and perpetuate biases present in their training data. This could be explicit bias, such as racial or gender bias in the way language is used, or more subtle forms of bias, such as the underrepresentation of certain topics or perspectives. This issue can be challenging to address because bias in language is a deeply rooted societal issue, and it's often not easy to even identify what might be considered bias in a given context.

Model robustness

It's challenging to ensure that LLMs will perform well in all possible scenarios, particularly on inputs that differ from their training data. This includes dealing with ambiguous queries, handling out-of-distribution data, and ensuring a level of consistency in the responses. Making sure that the model is not overtrained can help to have a more robust model, but much more is needed to have a robust model.

Interpretability and debugging

LLMs, like most **deep learning** (**DL**) models, are often described as "black boxes." It's not easy to understand why they're making a particular prediction or how they're arriving at a conclusion. This makes debugging challenging if the model starts to produce incorrect or inappropriate outputs. Improving interpretability is an active area of research. For example, some libraries attempt to elucidate the decision-making process of an LM by employing techniques such as feature importance analysis, which involves removing some words and analyzing the change in gradients.

One such method is the input perturbation technique. In this approach, a word (or words) from the input text is perturbed or removed, and the change in the model's output is analyzed. The rationale behind this is to understand the influence of a specific input word on the model's output prediction. If the removal of a certain word significantly changes the model's prediction, it can be inferred that the model deemed this word as important for its prediction.

Analyzing gradient changes is another popular method. By investigating how the gradient of the output with respect to the input changes when a certain word is removed, one can gain insight into how the model's decision-making process is influenced by that specific word.

These interpretation techniques provide a more transparent view into the complex decision-making process of LLMs, enabling researchers to better understand and improve their models. Libraries such as LIME and SHAP offer tools for model interpretation tasks, thus making the process more accessible to researchers.

Environmental impact

The high computational resources needed for training LLMs can have significant environmental implications. The energy required for training these models can contribute to carbon emissions, which is a concern from a sustainability perspective.

Besides that, there are concerns about privacy and security in LLMs. For example, it is recommended not to share models that are trained using patients' medical information, or not to feed sensitive information into publicly available LLMs such as ChatGPT, since it can return it to other users as the answer to their questions.

Different types of LLMs

LLMs are generally neural network architectures that are trained on a large corpus of text data. The term "large" refers to the size of these models in terms of the number of parameters and the scale of training data. Here are some examples of LLMs.

Transformer models

Transformer models have been at the forefront of the recent wave of LLMs. They are based on the "Transformer" architecture, which uses self-attention mechanisms to weigh the relevance of different words in the input when making predictions. Transformers are a type of neural network architecture introduced in the paper *Attention is All You Need* by Vaswani et al. One of their significant advantages, particularly for training LLMs, is their suitability for parallel computing.

In traditional RNN models, such as LSTM and GRU, the sequence of tokens (words, subwords, or characters in the text) must be processed sequentially. That's because each token's representation depends not only on the token itself but also on the previous tokens in the sequence. The inherent sequential nature of these models makes it difficult to parallelize their operations, which can limit the speed and efficiency of the training process.

Transformers, in contrast, eliminate the necessity for sequential processing by using a mechanism called self-attention (or scaled dot-product attention). In the self-attention process, each token's representation is computed as a weighted sum of all tokens in the sequence, with the weights determined by the attention mechanism. Importantly, these computations for each token are independent of the computations for other tokens, and thus they can be performed in parallel.

This parallelization capability brings several advantages for training LLMs as we will discuss next.

Speed

By parallelizing the computations, Transformers can process large amounts of data more quickly than RNNs. This speed can significantly reduce the training time of LLMs, which often need to process vast amounts of data.

Scalability

Transformers' parallelization makes it easier to scale up the model size and the amount of training data. This capability is crucial for developing LLMs, as these models often benefit from being trained on larger datasets and having a larger number of parameters.

Long-range dependencies

Transformers can better capture long-range dependencies between tokens because they consider all tokens in the sequence simultaneously, rather than processing them one at a time. This capability is valuable in many language tasks and can improve the performance of LLMs.

Each of these models has its own strengths and weaknesses, and the best choice of model can depend on the specific task, the amount and type of available training data, and the computational resources available.

Example designs of state-of-the-art LLMs

In this part, we are going to dig more into the design and architecture of some of the newest LLMs at the time of writing this book.

GPT-3.5 and ChatGPT

The core of ChatGPT is a Transformer, a type of model architecture that uses self-attention mechanisms to weigh the relevance of different words in the input when making predictions. It allows the model to consider the full context of the input when generating a response.

The GPT model

ChatGPT is based on the GPT version of the Transformer. The GPT models are trained to predict the next word in a sequence of words, given all the previous words. They process text from left to right (unidirectional context), which makes them well-suited for text generation tasks. For instance, GPT-3, one of the versions of GPT on which ChatGPT is based, contains 175 billion parameters.

Two-step training process

The training process for ChatGPT is done in two steps: pretraining and fine-tuning.

Pretraining

In this step, the model is trained on a large corpus of publicly available text from the internet. However, it's worth noting that it does not know specifics about which documents were in its training set or have access to any specific documents or sources.

Fine-tuning

After pretraining, the base model is further trained (fine-tuned) on custom datasets created by OpenAI, which include demonstrations of correct behavior as well as comparisons to rank different responses. Some prompts are from users of the Playground and ChatGPT apps, but they are anonymized and stripped of personally identifiable information.

RLHF

Part of the fine-tuning process involves RLHF, where human AI trainers provide feedback on model outputs for a range of example inputs, and this feedback is used to improve the model's responses. RLHF is a key component of the fine-tuning process used to train ChatGPT. It's a technique for refining the performance of the model by learning from feedback provided by human evaluators. Here, we first explain the general idea of RLHF, and in the next section, we explain it step by step.

The first step in RLHF is to collect human feedback. For ChatGPT, this often involves having human AI trainers participate in conversations where they play both sides (the user and the AI assistant). The trainers also have access to model-written suggestions to help them compose responses. This dialogue, in which AI trainers are essentially having a conversation with themselves, is added to the dataset for fine-tuning.

In addition to the dialogues, comparison data is created where multiple model responses are ranked by quality. This is done by taking a conversation turn, generating several different completions (responses), and having human evaluators rank them. The evaluators don't just rank the responses on factual correctness but also on how useful and safe they judged the response to be.

The model is then fine-tuned using **proximal policy optimization** (**PPO**), a reinforcement learning algorithm. PPO attempts to improve the model's responses based on human feedback, making small adjustments to the model's parameters to increase the likelihood of better-rated responses and decrease the likelihood of worse-rated responses.

RLHF is an iterative process. The procedure of collecting human feedback, creating comparison data, and fine-tuning the model using PPO is repeated multiple times to incrementally improve the model. Next, we will explain in more detail how PPO works.

PPO is a reinforcement learning algorithm used to optimize the π policy of an agent. The policy defines how the agent selects actions based on its current state. PPO aims to optimize this policy to maximize the expected cumulative rewards.

Before diving into PPO, it's important to define the reward model. In the context of reinforcement learning, the reward model is a R(s, a) function, which assigns a reward value to every state-action pair (s, a). The goal of the agent is to learn a policy π that maximizes the expected sum of these rewards.

Mathematically, the objective of reinforcement learning can be defined as follows:

$$J(\pi) = E_\pi\left(\sum_t R\left(s_t, a_t\right)\right)$$

In this formula, $E_{\pi[.]}$ is the expectation over trajectories (sequences of state-action pairs) generated by following policy π, s_t is the state at time t, a_t is the action taken at time t, and $R(s_t, a_t)$ is the reward received at time t.

PPO modifies this objective to encourage exploration of the policy space while preventing too drastic changes in the policy at each update. This is done by introducing a ratio, $r_{\_t(\theta)}$, which represents the ratio of the probabilities of the current policy π_θ to the old policy $\pi_{\theta old}$:

$$r_t\left(\theta\right) = \frac{\pi_\theta\left(a_t | s_t\right)}{\pi_{\theta\, old}\left(a_t | s_t\right)}$$

The objective of PPO is then defined as follows:

$$J_{PPO}(\pi) = E_{\pi\, old}\left(\min\left(r_t(\vartheta) A_t, clip\left(r_t(\vartheta), 1 - \epsilon, 1 + \epsilon\right) A_t\right)\right)$$

Here, A_t is the advantage function that measures how much better the taking action a_t is compared to the average action at state s_t, and $clip(r_t(\theta), 1 - \varepsilon, 1 + \varepsilon)$ is a clipped version of $r_t(\theta)$ that discourages too large policy updates.

The algorithm then optimizes this objective using stochastic gradient ascent, adjusting the policy parameters θ to increase $J_{PPO}(\pi)$.

In the context of ChatGPT and RLHF, the states correspond to the conversation histories, the actions correspond to the model-generated messages, and the rewards correspond to the human feedback on these messages. PPO is used to adjust the model parameters to improve the quality of the generated messages as judged by the human feedback.

The human rankings are used to create a reward model, which quantifies how good each response is. The reward model is a function that takes in a state and an action (in this case, a conversation context and a model-generated message), and outputs a scalar reward. During training, the model tries to maximize its expected cumulative reward.

The goal of RLHF is to align the model's behavior with human values and to improve its ability to generate useful and safe responses. By learning from human feedback, ChatGPT can adapt to a wider range of conversational contexts and provide more appropriate and helpful responses. It's worth noting that despite these efforts, the system might still make mistakes, and handling these errors and improving the RLHF process is an area of ongoing research.

Generating responses

When generating a response, ChatGPT takes as input a conversation history, which includes previous messages in the conversation along with the most recent user message and produces a model-generated message as output. The conversation history is tokenized and fed into the model, which generates a sequence of tokens in response, and these tokens are then detokenized to form the final output text.

System-level controls

OpenAI has also implemented some system-level controls to mitigate harmful or untruthful outputs from ChatGPT. This includes a Moderation API that warns or blocks certain types of unsafe content.

Step by step process of RLHF in ChatGPT

Since RLHF is an important part of ChatGPT and several other **State of the Art** (**SOTA**) models, understanding it better is useful to the you. In recent years, LMs have demonstrated remarkable abilities, creating varied and compelling text based on human-generated prompts. Nonetheless, it's challenging to precisely define what constitutes "good" text as it is inherently subjective and depends on the context. For instance, while crafting stories demands creativity, informative pieces require accuracy, and code snippets need to be executable.

Defining a loss function to encapsulate these attributes seems virtually impossible, hence most LMs are trained using a basic next-token prediction loss, such as cross-entropy. To overcome the limitations of the loss function, individuals have developed metrics that better align with human preferences, such as BLEU or **ROUGE**. The **BLEU** score, or Bilingual evaluation understudy, is a metric which is used to measure how well machine-translated text compares to a set of reference translations. Although these metrics are more effective at assessing performance, they are inherently limited as they merely compare the generated text to references using basic rules.

Wouldn't it be transformative if we could use human feedback on generated text as a performance measure, or even better, as a loss to optimize the model? This is the concept behind RLHF – leveraging reinforcement learning techniques to directly optimize an LM using human feedback. RLHF has begun to enable LMs to align a model trained on a general text corpus with intricate human values.

One of the recent successful applications of RLHF has been in the development of ChatGPT.

The concept of RLHF presents a formidable challenge due to its multifaceted model training process and various deployment phases. Here, we'll dissect the training procedure into its three essential components:

- Initial pretraining of an LM

- Data collection and reward model training

- Refining the LM using reinforcement learning

We'll begin by examining the pretraining phase for LMs.

LM pretraining

As a foundation, RLHF utilizes an LM that's already been pretrained using traditional pretraining objectives, which means that we create the tokenizer based on our training data, design model architecture, and then pretrain the model using the training data. For its initial well-received RLHF model, InstructGPT, OpenAI employed a smaller version of GPT-3. On the other hand, Anthropic used transformer models ranging from 10 million to 52 billion parameters trained for this task, and DeepMind utilized its 280 billion parameter model, Gopher.

This preliminary model may be further refined on extra text or particular conditions, although it's not always necessary. As an example, OpenAI chose to refine its model using human-generated text identified as "preferable." This dataset is used to further fine-tune the model using the RLHF model, distilling the original LM model based on contextual hints from humans.

Generally speaking, there's no definitive answer to the question of "which model" serves as the best launching point for RLHF. The array of options available for RLHF training has not been extensively explored.

Moving on, once an LM is in place, it's necessary to generate data to train a reward model. This step is crucial for integrating human preferences into the system.

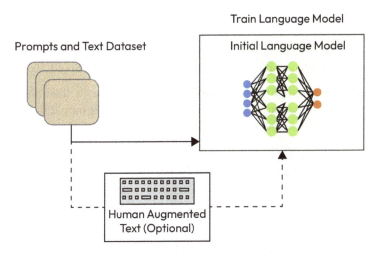

Figure 7.4 – Pretraining LM

Training the reward model

In the newly proposed method, RLHF is being used as the RM, which is known as a preference model as well. The main idea here is to get a text and return a scalar reward that reflects human preferences. This approach can be implemented in two ways. First, implement an end-to-end LLM, which gives us the preferred output. This process can be performed by fine-tuning a LLM or training a LLM from scratch. Second, have an extra component that ranks different outputs of the LLM and returns the best one.

The dataset used for training the RM is a set of prompt-generation pairs. Prompts are sampled from a predetermined dataset (Anthropic's data). These prompts undergo processing by the initial LM to generate fresh text.

Human annotators rank the text outputs generated by the LM. It might seem intuitive to have humans directly assign a scalar score to each text piece to generate a reward model, but it proves challenging in reality. Varied human values render these scores unstandardized and unreliable. Consequently, rankings are employed to compare multiple model outputs, thereby creating a substantially better regularized dataset.

There are several strategies for text ranking. One successful approach involves users comparing the text produced by two LMs given the same prompt. By evaluating model outputs in direct comparison, an **Elo rating system**, which we will soon describe, can generate a ranking of models and outputs relative to each other. These varying ranking methods are then normalized into a scalar reward signal for training. The Elo rating system, originally developed for chess, is also applicable to RLHF for LMs.

In the context of LMs, each model or variant (e.g., models at different stages of training) can be seen as a "player." Its Elo rating reflects how well it performs in terms of generating human-preferred outputs.

The fundamental mechanics of the Elo rating system remain the same. Here's how it can be adapted for RLHF in LMs:

- **Initialization**: All models start with the same Elo rating, often 1,000 or 1,500.

- **Comparison**: For a given prompt, two models (A and B) generate their outputs. A human evaluator then ranks these outputs. If the evaluator considers the output from model A to be better, model A "wins" the match, and model B "loses."

The Elo ratings are updated in this way after each evaluation. Over time, they provide an ongoing, dynamic ranking of the models based on human preferences. This is useful for tracking progress over the course of training and for comparing different models or model variants.

Successful RLHF systems have employed diverse-sized reward LMs relative to text generation. For example, OpenAI used a 175 B LM with a 6 B reward model, Anthropic utilized LM and reward models ranging from 10 B to 52 B, and DeepMind employed 70 B Chinchilla models for both the LM and reward model. This is because preference models must match the capacity needed to understand a text as a model would need to generate it. At this juncture in the RLHF process, we possess an initial LM capable of text generation and a preference model that assigns a score to any text based on human perception. We next apply reinforcement learning to optimize the original LM concerning the reward model.

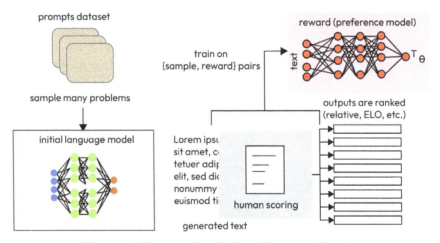

Figure 7.5 – The reward model for reinforcement learning

How to fine-tune the model using reinforcement learning

For a considerable period, the prospect of training an LM using reinforcement learning was considered unattainable due to both technical and algorithmic challenges. However, several organizations have achieved fine-tuning some or all parameters of a replica of the initial LM with a policy-gradient reinforcement learning algorithm – namely, PPO. Parameters of the LM are kept static because fine-tuning an entire model with 10 B or 100 B+ parameters is prohibitively expensive (for further details, refer to **Low-Rank Adaptation (LoRA)** for LMs or DeepMind's Sparrow LM). PPO, an established method for some time now, has abundant available guides explaining its functioning. This maturity made it an attractive choice for scaling up to the novel application of distributed training for RLHF. It appears that significant strides in RLHF have been made by determining how to update such a colossal model with a known algorithm (more on that later).

We can articulate this fine-tuning task as a reinforcement learning problem. Initially, the policy is an LM that accepts a prompt and produces a sequence of text (or merely probability distributions over text). The action space of this policy is all the tokens aligning with the LM's vocabulary (typically around 50 K tokens), and the observation space is the distribution of possible input token sequences, which is also notably large in light of reinforcement learning's prior uses (the dimension approximates the vocabulary size power ($^\wedge$) length of the input token sequence). The reward function melds the preference model with a constraint on policy shift.

The reward function is the juncture where the system integrates all the models discussed into a single RLHF process. Given a prompt, x, from the dataset, the text, y, is created by the current iteration of the fine-tuned policy. This text, coupled with the original prompt, is passed to the preference model, which returns a scalar measure of "preferability", r_θ.

Additionally, per-token probability distributions from the reinforcement learning policy are contrasted with those from the initial model to compute a penalty on their difference. In several papers from OpenAI, Anthropic, and DeepMind, this penalty has been constructed as a scaled version of the **Kullback–Leibler (KL)** divergence between these sequences of distributions over tokens, r_{KL}. The KL divergence term penalizes the reinforcement learning policy from veering significantly from the initial pretrained model with each training batch, ensuring the production of reasonably coherent text snippets.

Without this penalty, the optimization might start generating gibberish text that somehow deceives the reward model into granting a high reward. In practical terms, the KL divergence is approximated via sampling from both distributions. The final reward transmitted to the reinforcement learning update rule is as follows:

$$r = r_\theta - \lambda r_{KL}$$

Additional terms have been incorporated into the reward function by some RLHF systems. For instance, OpenAI's InstructGPT successfully tried the blending of additional pretraining gradients (from the human annotation set) into the update rule for PPO. It is anticipated that as RLHF continues to be studied, the formulation of this reward function will continue to evolve.

Finally, the update rule is the parameter update from PPO that optimizes the reward metrics in the current data batch (PPO is on-policy, meaning the parameters are only updated with the current batch of prompt-generation pairs). PPO is a trust region optimization algorithm that employs constraints on the gradient to ensure the update step does not destabilize the learning process. DeepMind utilized a similar reward setup for Gopher but employed a synchronous advantage actor.

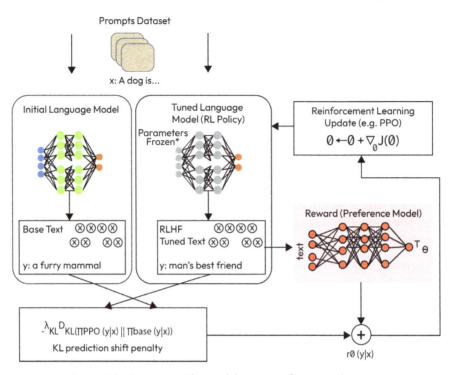

Figure 7.6 – Fine-tuning the model using reinforcement learning

The preceding diagram may suggest that both models produce different responses for the same prompt, but what actually occurs is that the reinforcement learning policy generates text, which is then supplied to the initial model to derive its relative probabilities for the KL penalty.

Optionally, RLHF can advance from this stage by cyclically updating both the reward model and the policy. As the reinforcement learning policy evolves, users can maintain the ranking of these outputs against the model's previous versions. However, most papers haven't yet addressed the implementation of this operation since the mode of deployment required to collect this type of data only works for dialogue agents who can access an active user base. Anthropic mentions this alternative as **iterated online RLHF** (as referred to in the original paper), where iterations of the policy are incorporated into the Elo ranking system across models. This brings about complex dynamics of the policy and reward model evolving, representing a complex and unresolved research question. In the next section, we will explain some well-known open-source tools for RLHF.

GPT-4

At the time of writing this book, we know very little about the GPT-4 model design. As OpenAI is slow to reveal, it is assumed that GPT-4 is not a single model but a combination of eight 220-billion-parameter models, an assumption that is confirmed by key figures in the AI community. This assumption suggests OpenAI used a "mixture of experts" strategy, an ML design tactic that dates even before

LLMs, to create the model. However, while we, the authors, support this assumption, it has not been officially confirmed by OpenAI.

Despite the speculation, GPT-4's impressive performance is undeniable, regardless of its internal structure. Its capabilities in writing and coding tasks are remarkable, and the specifics of whether it's one model or eight bundled together does not change its impact.

A common narrative suggests that OpenAI has managed expectations around GPT-4 deftly, focusing on its power and opting not to disclose specifications due to competitive pressures. The secrecy surrounding GPT-4 has led many to believe it to be a scientific marvel.

LLaMA

Meta has publicly launched LLaMA, a high-performing LLM aimed at aiding researchers in AI. This move allows individuals with limited access to extensive infrastructure to examine these models, thus broadening access in this rapidly evolving field.

LLaMA models are attractive because they require significantly less computational power and resources, allowing for the exploration of new approaches and use cases. Available in several sizes, these models are designed to be fine-tuned for various tasks and have been developed with responsible AI practices.

LLMs, despite their advancements, have limited research accessibility due to the resources required to train and run them. Smaller models, such as LLaMA, trained on more tokens, are simpler to retrain and adjust for specific use cases.

Similar to other models, LLaMA takes a sequence of words as input to predict the next word and generate text. Despite its capabilities, LLaMA shares the same challenges as other models regarding bias, toxic comments, and hallucinations. By sharing LLaMA's code, Meta enables researchers to test new ways of addressing these issues in LLMs.

Meta emphasizes the need for cooperation across the AI community to establish guidelines around responsible AI and LLMs. They anticipate that LLaMA will facilitate new learning and development in the field.

PaLM

PaLM is a 540-billion-parameter, densely-activated Transformer LM that was trained on 6,144 TPU v4 chips using Pathways, a new ML system, that enables highly efficient training across multiple TPU pods.

PaLM has been shown to achieve breakthrough performance on a variety of natural language tasks, including the following:

- Multi-step reasoning tasks
- The recently released **Beyond the Imitation Game Benchmark (BIG-bench)**

- Multilingual tasks

- Source code generation

The BIG-bench benchmark is worth expanding on as it serves as a recognized collection of benchmarks to measure against. The BIG-bench is an extensive assessment mechanism specifically designed for large-scale LMs. It is a broad-based, community-focused benchmark that presents a diversity of tasks to evaluate a model's performance in different disciplines and its competence in natural language comprehension, problem solving, and reasoning. With a total of 204 tasks from 450 contributors across 132 institutions, BIG-bench covers an eclectic mix of subjects including linguistics, childhood development, mathematics, common-sense reasoning, biology, physics, software development, and even social bias. It concentrates on challenges believed to be currently beyond the reach of existing LMs. The primary goal of BIG-bench extends beyond mere imitation or Turing test-style evaluations, aiming instead for a deeper, more nuanced appraisal of the abilities and constraints of these large models. This initiative is founded on the conviction that an open, collaborative approach to evaluation paves the way for a more comprehensive understanding of these LMs and their potential societal ramifications.

PaLM 540B excels beyond the fine-tuned state-of-the-art across various multi-step reasoning tasks and surpasses average human performance on the BIG-bench benchmark. Many BIG-bench tasks exhibit significant leaps in performance as PaLM scales to its largest size, demonstrating discontinuous improvements from the model scale. PaLM also has strong capabilities in multilingual tasks and source code generation. For example, PaLM can translate between 50 languages, and it can generate code in a variety of programming languages.

The authors of the PaLM paper also discuss the ethical considerations related to LLMs, and they discuss potential mitigation strategies. For example, they suggest that it is important to be aware of the potential for bias in LLMs and that it is important to develop techniques for detecting and mitigating bias.

PaLM architecture

PaLM employs the conventional Transformer model architecture in a decoder-exclusive setup, which allows each timestep to attend only to itself and preceding timesteps. Several modifications were applied to this setup, including the following:

- **SwiGLU activation**: Instead of standard ReLU, GeLU, or Swish activations, PaLM utilizes SwiGLU activations ($Swish(xW) \cdot xV$) for the **multilayer perceptron** (**MLP**) intermediate activations due to their superior performance in enhancing quality. This approach, however, requires three matrix multiplications in the MLP as opposed to the conventional two.

- **Parallel layers**: Rather than the typical "serialized" approach, PaLM uses a "parallel" formulation for each Transformer block.

  The standard structure is given by the following:

  $$y = x + MLP(LayerNorm(x + Attention(LayerNorm(x))))$$

The parallel structure is instead the following:

$$y = x + MLP(LayerNorm(x)) + Attention(LayerNorm(x))$$

This leads to roughly 15% quicker training speed at larger scales due to the fusion of MLP and attention input matrix multiplications.

- **Multi-query attention**: In the conventional Transformer formulation, k attention heads are employed. For each timestep, the input vector is linearly projected into query, key, and value tensors, which have a shape of $[k, h]$, where h denotes the size of the attention head. In the new approach, the projections for "key" and "value" are shared across all heads, meaning "key" and "value" are projected to $[1, h]$, while "query" maintains the shape $[k, h]$. The authors claimed that this approach doesn't notably affect model quality or training speed while it does result in significant cost reductions during autoregressive decoding. The reason for this lies in the inefficiency of standard multi-headed attention on accelerator hardware during autoregressive decoding, as the key/value tensors are not shared across examples and only one token is decoded at each moment.

- **Rotary Position Embedding (RoPE) embeddings**: RoPE embeddings, shown to perform better on longer sequence lengths, are preferred over absolute or relative position embeddings.

- **Shared input-output embeddings**: The input and output embedding matrices are shared, a practice that is common, though not universal, in previous work.

- **No biases**: The model abstains from using biases in any dense kernels or layer norms, which enhances training stability for larger models.

- **Vocabulary**: PaLM uses a 256k-token SentencePiece vocabulary designed for diverse languages in the training corpus, ensuring efficient training without excessive tokenization. This preserves all whitespaces and out-of-vocabulary Unicode characters while splitting numbers into individual digit tokens for clarity.

Overall, PaLM is a powerful LM that has the potential to be used for a wide variety of applications. It is still under development, but it has already demonstrated the ability to achieve breakthrough performance on a number of tasks.

Open-source tools for RLHF

OpenAI released the first open-source code to perform RLHF in 2019. They have implemented this approach to improve GPT-2 for different use cases such as summarization. Based on human feedback, the model is optimized to have outputs similar to humans, such as copying parts of the note. More information about this project can be found at the following link: `https://openai.com/research/fine-tuning-gpt-2`.

The code is also available at the following link: `https://github.com/openai/lm-human-preferences`.

Transformers Reinforcement Learning (TRL) is a tool crafted for fine-tuning pretrained LMs using PPO within the Hugging Face ecosystem. TRLX, an enhanced fork developed by CarperAI, is capable of handling larger models for both online and offline training. Currently, TRLX is equipped with a production-ready API supporting RLHF with PPO and **implicit language Q-learning (ILQL)** for deploying LLMs of up to 33 billion parameters. Future versions of TRLX aim to accommodate LMs of up to 200 billion parameters, making it ideal for ML engineers working at such scales.

- The code for TRL is available at the following link: `https://github.com/lvwerra/trl`

- The code for TRLX can be found at the following link: `https://github.com/CarperAI/trlx`.

Another good library is **Reinforcement Learning for Language Models (RL4LMs)**. The RL4LMs project addresses the challenge of training LLMs to align with human preference metrics. It recognizes that many NLP tasks can be seen as sequence learning problems, but their application is limited due to issues such as reinforcement learning training instability, high variance in automated NLP metrics, and reward hacking. The project offers solutions by doing the following:

- Giving guidelines on when to use reinforcement learning and suggesting suitable NLP tasks/metrics via a continually updated benchmark called GRUE

- Introducing a new reinforcement learning algorithm, **Natural Language Policy Optimization (NLPO)**, designed to handle large language action spaces and reward variance better

- Offering practical advice with high-quality implementations and hyperparameters of reinforcement learning, as well as other reinforcement learning algorithms, for training Transformers in the Hugging Face library

The code for this project can be found at the following link: `https://github.com/allenai/RL4LMs`.

Summary

In this chapter, we've delved into the dynamic and complex world of state-of-the-art LLMs. We've discussed their remarkable generalization capabilities, making them versatile tools for a wide range of tasks. We also highlighted the crucial aspect of understanding complex contexts, where these models excel by grasping the nuances of language and the intricacies of various subject matters.

Additionally, we explored the paradigm of RLHF and how it is being employed to enhance LMs. RLHF leverages scalar feedback to improve LMs by mimicking human judgments, thereby helping to mitigate some of the common pitfalls encountered in NLP tasks.

We discussed technical requirements for working with these models, emphasizing the need for foundational knowledge in areas such as Transformers, reinforcement learning, and coding skills.

This chapter also touched on some prominent LMs such as GPT-4 and LLaMA, discussing their architecture, methods, and performance. We highlighted the strategies some libraries employ to interpret LM predictions, such as the removal of certain words and analyzing gradient changes.

To sum up, this chapter offers a comprehensive overview of the current state of LLMs, exploring their capabilities, challenges, the methods used to refine them, and the evolving tools and measures for their evaluation and interpretation.

References

- *Hugging Face*: `huggingface.co`

- *Large language model*: `https://en.m.wikipedia.org/wiki/Large_language_model#`

- *Zhao, Wayne Xin, Kun Zhou, Junyi Li, Tianyi Tang, Xiaolei Wang, Yupeng Hou, Yingqian Min et al. "A survey of large language models."* arXiv preprint arXiv:2303.18223 (2023).

- *Introducing LLaMA: A foundational, 65-billion-parameter large language model*: `https://ai.facebook.com/blog/large-language-model-llama-meta-ai/`

- *Model Details*: `https://github.com/facebookresearch/llama/blob/main/MODEL_CARD.md`

- *Touvron, Hugo, Thibaut Lavril, Gautier Izacard, Xavier Martinet, Marie-Anne Lachaux, Timothée Lacroix, Baptiste Rozière et al. "Llama: Open and efficient foundation language models." arXiv* preprint arXiv:2302.13971 (2023).

- *Elo rating system*: `https://en.wikipedia.org/wiki/Elo_rating_system`

- *Chowdhery, Aakanksha, Sharan Narang, Jacob Devlin, Maarten Bosma, Gaurav Mishra, Adam Roberts, Paul Barham et al. "Palm: Scaling language modeling with pathways."* arXiv preprint arXiv:2204.02311 (2022).

- *BIG-bench*: `https://github.com/google/BIG-bench`

- *Srivastava, Aarohi, Abhinav Rastogi, Abhishek Rao, Abu Awal Md Shoeb, Abubakar Abid, Adam Fisch, Adam R. Brown et al. "Beyond the imitation game: Quantifying and extrapolating the capabilities of language models."* arXiv preprint arXiv:2206.04615 (2022).

Accessing the Power of Large Language Models: Advanced Setup and Integration with RAG

In this dynamic era of **Artificial Intelligence** (**AI**) and **Machine Learning** (**ML**), understanding the vast assortment of available resources and learning how to utilize them effectively is vital. **Large Language Models** (**LLMs**) such as GPT-4 have revolutionized the field of **Natural Language Processing** (**NLP**) by showcasing unprecedented performance in diverse tasks, from content generation to complex problem-solving. Their immense potential extends not only to understanding and generating human-like text but also to bridging the gap between machines and humans, in terms of communication and task automation. Embracing the practical applications of LLMs can empower businesses, researchers, and developers to create more intuitive, intelligent, and efficient systems that cater to a wide range of requirements. This chapter offers a guide to setting up access to LLMs, walking you through using them and building pipelines with them.

Our journey begins by delving into closed source models that utilize **Application Programming Interfaces** (**APIs**), taking OpenAI's API as a quintessential example. We will walk you through a practical scenario, illustrating how you can interact with this API using an API key within your Python code, demonstrating the potential applications of such models in real-world contexts.

As we advance, we will shift our focus to the realm of open source tools, giving you a rundown of widely employed open source models that can be manipulated via Python. We aim to provide a grasp of the power and versatility these models provide, emphasizing the community-driven benefits of open source development.

Subsequently, we will introduce you to retrieval-augmented generation and, specifically, LangChain, a robust tool specifically engineered for interaction with LLMs. LangChain is essential for the practical application of LLMs because it provides a unified and abstracted interface to them, as well as a suite of tools and modules that simplify the development and deployment of LLM-powered applications. We'll guide you through the foundational concept of LangChain, highlighting its distinctive methodology to circumvent the inherent challenges posed by LLMs.

The cornerstone of this methodology is the transformation of data into embeddings. We will shed light on the pivotal role that **Language Models** (**LMs**) and LLMs play in this transformation, demonstrating how they are engaged in creating these embeddings. Following this, we will discuss the process of establishing a local vector database, giving you a brief overview of vector databases and their crucial role in managing and retrieving these embeddings.

Then, we will address the configuration of an LLM for prompting, which could potentially be the same LLM used for the embedding process. We will take you through the stepwise setup procedure, detailing the advantages and potential applications of this strategy.

In the penultimate segment, we will touch upon the topic of deploying LLMs to the cloud. The scalability and cost-effectiveness of cloud services have led to an increased adoption of hosting AI models. We will provide an overview of the leading cloud service providers, including **Microsoft Azure**, **Amazon Web Services** (**AWS**), and **Google Cloud Platform** (**GCP**), giving you insights into their service offerings and how they can be harnessed for LLM deployment.

As we embark on this exploration of LLMs, it's crucial to acknowledge the continuously evolving data landscape that these models operate within. The dynamic nature of data – its growth in volume, diversity, and complexity – necessitates a forward-looking approach to how we develop, deploy, and maintain LLMs. In the subsequent chapters, particularly *Chapter 10*, we will delve deeper into the strategic implications of these evolving data landscapes, preparing you to navigate the challenges and opportunities they present. This foundational understanding will not only enhance your immediate work with LLMs but also ensure your projects remain resilient and relevant in the face of rapid technological and data-driven changes.

Let's go through the main topics covered in the chapter:

- Setting up an LLM application – API-based closed source models
- Prompt engineering and priming GPT
- Setting up an LLM application – local open source models
- Employing LLMs from Hugging Face via Python
- Exploring advanced system design – RAG and LangChain
- Reviewing a simple LangChain setup in a Jupyter notebook
- LLMs in the cloud

Technical requirements

For this chapter, the following will be necessary:

- **Programming knowledge**: Familiarity with Python programming is a must, since the open source models, OpenAI's API, and LangChain are all illustrated using Python code.

- **Access to OpenAI's API**: An API key from OpenAI will be required to explore closed source models. This can be obtained by creating an account with OpenAI and agreeing to their terms of service.

- **Open source models**: Access to the specific open source models mentioned in this chapter will be necessary. These can be accessed and downloaded from their respective repositories or via package managers such as `pip` or `conda`.

- **A local development environment**: A local development environment setup with Python installed is required. An **Integrated Development Environment** (**IDE**) such as PyCharm, Jupyter Notebook, or a simple text editor can be used. Note that we recommend a free Google Colab notebook, as it encapsulates all these requirements in a seamless web interface.

- **The ability to install libraries**: You must have permission to install the required Python libraries, such as NumPy, SciPy, TensorFlow, and PyTorch. Note that the code we provide includes the required installations, and you won't have to install them beforehand. We simply stress that you should have permission to do so, which we expect you would. Specifically, using a free Google Colab notebook would suffice.

- **Hardware requirements**: Depending on the complexity and size of the models you're working with, a computer with sufficient processing power (potentially including a good GPU for ML tasks) and ample memory will be required. This is only relevant when choosing to not use the free Google Colab.

Now that we've grasped the transformative potential of LLMs and the variety of tools available, let's delve deeper and explore how to effectively set up LLM applications using APIs.

Setting up an LLM application – API-based closed source models

When looking to employ models in general and LLMs in particular, there are various design choices and trade-offs. One key choice is whether to host a model locally in your local environment or to employ it remotely, accessing it via a communication channel. Local development environments would be wherever your code runs, whether that's your personal computer, your on-premises server, your cloud environment, and so on. The choice you make will impact many aspects, such as cost, information security, maintenance needs, network overload, and inference speed.

In this section, we will introduce a quick and simple approach to employing an LLM remotely via an API. This approach is quick and simple as it rids us of the need to allocate unusual computation resources to host the LLM locally. An LLM typically requires amounts of memory and computation resources that aren't common in personal environments.

Choosing a remote LLM provider

Before diving into implementation, we need to select a suitable LLM provider that aligns with our project requirements. OpenAI, for example, offers several versions of the GPT-3.5 and GPT-4 models with comprehensive API documentation.

OpenAI's remote GPT access in Python via an API

To gain access to OpenAI's LLM API, we need to create an account on their website. This process involves registration, account verification, and obtaining API credentials.

OpenAI's website provides guidance for these common actions, and you will be able to get set up quickly.

Once registered, we should familiarize ourselves with OpenAI's API documentation. This documentation will guide us through the various endpoints, methods, and parameters available to interact with the LLMs.

The first hands-on experience we will take on will be employing OpenAI's LLMs via Python. We have put together a notebook that presents the simple steps of employing OpenAI's GPT model via an API. Refer to the `Ch8_Setting_Up_Close_Source_and_Open_Source_LLMs.ipynb` notebook. This notebook, called *Setting Up Close Source and Open Source LLMs*, will be utilized in the current section about OpenAI's API, and also in the subsequent section about setting up local LLMs.

Let's walk through the code:

1. We start by installing the required Python libraries. In particular, to communicate with the LLM API, we need to install the necessary Python library:

   ```
   !pip install --upgrade openai
   ```

2. **Define OpenAI's API key**: Before making requests to the LLM API, we must embed our personal API key in the library's configuration. The API key is made available for you on OpenAI's website when you register. This can be done by either explicitly pasting the key's string to be hardcoded in our code or reading it from a file that holds that string. Note that the former is the simplest way to showcase the API, as it doesn't require an additional file to be set up, but it may not be the right choice when working in a shared development environment:

   ```
   openai.api_key = "<your key>"
   ```

3. **Settings – set the model's configurations**. Here, we set the various parameters that control the model's behavior.

As the foundation is set for connecting to LLMs through APIs, it's valuable to turn our attention to an equally important aspect – prompt engineering and priming, the art of effectively communicating with these models.

Prompt engineering and priming GPT

Let us pause and provide some context before returning to discuss the next part of the code.

Prompt engineering is a technique used in NLP to design effective prompts or instructions when interacting with LLMs. It involves carefully crafting the input given to a model to elicit the desired output. By providing specific cues, context, or constraints in the prompts, prompt engineering aims to guide the model's behavior and encourage the generation of more accurate, relevant, or targeted responses. The process often involves iterative refinement, experimentation, and understanding the model's strengths and limitations to optimize the prompt for improved performance in various tasks, such as question-answering summarization or conversation generation. Effective prompt engineering plays a vital role in harnessing the capabilities of LMs and shaping their output to meet specific user requirements.

Let's review one of the most impactful tools in prompt engineering, **priming**. Priming GPT via an API involves providing initial context to the model before generating a response. The priming step helps set the direction and style of the generated content. By giving the model relevant information or examples related to the desired output, we can guide its understanding and encourage more focused and coherent responses. Priming can be done by including specific instructions, context, or even partial sentences that align with the desired outcome. Effective priming enhances the model's ability to generate responses that better match the user's intent or specific requirements.

Priming is done by introducing GPT with several types of messages:

- The main message is the **system prompt**. This message instructs the model about the *role* it may play, the way it should answer the questions, the constraints it may have, and so on.

- The second type of message is a **user prompt**. A user prompt is sent to the model in the priming phase, and it represents an example user prompt, much like the prompt you may enter in ChatGPT's web interface. However, when priming, this message could be presented to the model as an example of how it should address such a prompt. The developer will introduce a user prompt of some sort and will then show the model how it is expected to answer that prompt.

For example, observe this priming code:

```
response = client.chat.completions.create(
    model="gpt-3.5-turbo",
    messages=[
            {"role": "system",
                "content": "You are a helpful assistant. You
provide short answers and you format them in Markdown syntax"},
            {"role": "user",
                "content": "How do I import the Python library
pandas?"},
            {"role": "assistant",
                "content": "This is how you would import
pandas: \n```\nimport pandas as pd\n```"},
```

```
                    {"role": "user",
                       "content": "How do I import the python library
     numpy?"}
              ])
     text = response.choices[0].message.content.strip()
     print(text)
     )
```

This is the output:

```
To import numpy, you can use the following syntax:
```python
import numpy as np
```
```

You can see that we prime the model to provide concise answers in a Markdown format. The example that is used to teach the model is in the form of a question and an answer. The question is via a user prompt, and the way we tell the model what the potential answer is is provided via an assistant prompt. We then provide the model with another user prompt; this one is the actual prompt we'd like the model to address for us, and as shown in the output, it gets it right.

By looking at OpenAI's documentation about prompt engineering, you'll find that there are additional types of prompts to prime the GPT models with.

Going back to our notebook and code, in this section, we leverage *GPT-3.5 Turbo*. We prime it in the simplest manner, only giving it a system prompt to provide directions in order to showcase how additional functionality could stem from the system prompt. We tell the model to finish a response by alerting us about typos in the prompt and correcting them.

We then provide our desired prompt in the user prompt section, and we insert a few typos into it. Run that code and give it a shot.

Experimenting with OpenAI's GPT model

At this stage, we send our prompts to the model.

The following simple example code is run once in the *Setting Up Close Source and Open Source LLMs* notebook. You can wrap it in a function and call it repeatedly in your own code.

Some aspects worth noticing are as follows:

- **Parsing and processing the returned output from the model**: We structure the output response in a coherent manner for the user to read:

```
print(f"Prompt: {user_prompt_oai}\n\n{openai_model}'s Response:
\n{response_oai}")
```

- **Error handling**: We designed the code to allow for several failed attempts before accepting a failure to use the API:

```
except Exception as output:
    attempts += 1
    if attempts >= max_attempts:
        [...]
```

- **Rate limits and cost mitigation**: We don't implement such restrictions here, but it would be ideal to have both of these in an experimental setting and perhaps in production.

The result of the preceding code is demonstrated as follows:

```
Prompt: If neuroscience could extract the last thoughts a person
had before they dyed, how would the world be different?
gpt-3.5-turbo's Response:
If neuroscience could extract the last thoughts a person had
before they died, it would have profound implications for
various aspects of society.
This ability could potentially revolutionize fields such as
psychology, criminology, and end-of-life care.
Understanding a person's final thoughts could provide valuable
insights into their state of mind, emotional well-being, and
potentially help unravel mysteries surrounding their death.
It could also offer comfort to loved ones by providing a glimpse
into the innermost thoughts of the deceased.
However, such technology would raise significant ethical
concerns regarding privacy, consent, and the potential misuse of
this information.
Overall, the world would be both fascinated and apprehensive
about the implications of this groundbreaking capability.
Typos in the prompt:
1. "dyed" should be "died"
2. "diferent" should be "different"
Corrections:
If neuroscience could extract the last thoughts a person had
before they died, how would the world be different?
```

The model provided us with a legitimate, concise response. It then notified us about the typos, which are perfectly in line with the system prompt we provided it with.

That was an example showcasing the employment of a remote, off-premises, closed source LLM. While leveraging the power of paid APIs such as OpenAI offers convenience and cutting-edge performance, there's also immense potential in tapping into free open source LLMs. Let's explore these cost-effective alternatives next.

Setting up an LLM application – local open source models

Now, we shall touch on the complementary approach to a closed source implementation, that is, an open source, local implementation.

We will see how you can achieve a similar functional outcome to the one we reviewed in the previous section, without having to register for an account, pay, or share prompts that contain possibly sensitive information with a third-party vendor, such as OpenAI.

About the different aspects that distinguish between open source and closed source

When selecting between open source LLMs, such as LLaMA and GPT-J, and closed source, API-based models such as OpenAI's GPT, several critical factors must be considered.

Firstly, cost is a major factor. Open source LLMs often have no licensing fees, but they require significant computational resources for training and inference, which can be expensive. Closed source models, while potentially carrying a subscription or pay-per-use fee, eliminate the need for substantial hardware investments.

Processing speed and maintenance are closely linked to computational resources. Open source LLMs, if deployed on powerful enough systems, can offer high processing speeds but require ongoing maintenance and updates by the implementing team. In contrast, closed source models managed by the provider ensure continual maintenance and model updates, often with better efficiency and reduced downtime, but processing speed can be dependent on the provider's infrastructure and network latency.

Regarding model updates, open source models offer more control but require a proactive approach to incorporate the latest research and improvements. Closed source models, however, are regularly updated by the provider, ensuring access to the latest advancements without additional effort from the user.

Security and privacy are paramount in both scenarios. Open source models can be more secure, as they can be run on private servers, ensuring data privacy. However, they demand robust in-house security protocols. Closed source models, managed by external providers, often come with built-in security measures but pose potential privacy risks, due to data handling by third parties.

Overall, the choice between open source and closed source LLMs hinges on the trade-off between cost, control, and convenience, with each option presenting its own set of advantages and challenges.

With that in mind, let's revisit Hugging Face, the company that put together the largest and most approachable hub for free LMs. In the following example, we will leverage Hugging Face's easy and free library: transformers.

Hugging Face's hub of models

When looking to choose an LLM for our task, we recommend referring to Hugging Face's Models online page. They offer an enormous amount of Python-based, open source LLMs. Every model has a page dedicated to it, where you can find information about it, including the syntax needed to employ that model via Python code in your personal environment.

It should be noted that in order to implement a model locally, you must have an internet connection from the machine that runs the Python code. However, as this requirement may become a bottleneck in some cases – for instance, when the development environment is restricted by a company's intranet or has limited internet access due to firewall restrictions – there are alternative approaches. Our recommended approach is to clone the model repository from Hugging Face's domain. That is a less trivial and less-used approach. Hugging Face provides the necessary cloning commands on each model's web page.

Choosing a model

When looking to choose a model, there may be several factors that come into play. Depending on your intentions, you may care about configuration speed, processing speed, storage space, computation resources, legal usage restrictions, and so on. Another factor worth noting is the popularity of a model. It attests to how frequently that model is chosen by other developers in the community. For instance, if you look for LMs that are labeled for zero-shot classification, you will find a very large collection of available models. But, if you then narrow the search some more so to only be left with models that were trained on data from news articles, you would be left with a much smaller set of available models. In which case, you may want to refer to the popularity of each model and start your exploration with the model that was used the most.

Other factors that may interest you could be publications about the model, the model's developers, the company or university that released the model, the dataset that the model was trained on, the architecture the model was designed by, the evaluation metrics, and other potential factors that may be available on each model's web page on Hugging Face's website.

Employing LLMs from Hugging Face via Python

Now, we will review a code notebook that exemplifies implementing an open source LLM locally using Hugging Face's free resources. We will continue with the same notebook from the previous section, *Setting Up Close Source and Open Source LLMs*:

1. **Install the required Python libraries**: To freely work with Hugging Face's open source models and other various resources, we need to install the necessary Python library.

   Via `pip` on the Terminal, we will run the following:

   ```
   pip install -upgrade transformers
   ```

   Alternatively, if running directly from a Jupyter notebook, add ! to the beginning of the command.

2.   **Experiment with Microsoft's DialoGPT-medium**: This LLM is dedicated to conversational applications. It was generated by Microsoft and achieved high scores when compared to other LLMs on common benchmarks. For that reason, it is also quite popular on Hugging Face's platform, in the sense that it is downloaded frequently by ML developers.

3.   In the **Settings** code section in the notebook, we will define the parameters for this code and import the model and its tokenizer:

```
hf_model = "microsoft/DialoGPT-medium"
max_length = 1000
tokenizer = AutoTokenizer.from_pretrained(hf_model)
model = AutoModelForCausalLM.from_pretrained(hf_model)
```

Note that this code requires access to the internet. Even though the model is deployed locally, an internet connection is required to import it. Again, if you wish, you can clone the model's repo from Hugging Face and then no longer be required to have access to the internet.

4.   **Define the prompt**: As can be seen in the following code block, we picked a straightforward prompt here, much like a user prompt for the GPT-3.5-Turbo model.

5.   **Experiment with the model**: Here, we have the syntax that suits this code. If you want to create a rolling conversation with this model, you wrap this code in a function and iterate over it, collecting prompts from the user in real time.

6.   **The result**: The resulting prompt is, If dinosaurs were alive today, would they possess a threat to people?:

```
microsoft/DialoGPT-medium's Response:
I think they would be more afraid of the humans
```

This section established the tremendous value proposition that LLMs can bring. We now have the necessary background to learn and explore a new frontier in efficient LLM application development – constructing pipelines using tools such as LangChain. Let's dive into this advanced approach.

Exploring advanced system design – RAG and LangChain

Retrieval-Augmented Generation (**RAG**) is a development framework designed for seamless interaction with LLMs. LLMs, by virtue of their generalist nature, are capable of performing a vast array of tasks competently. However, their generality often precludes them from delivering detailed, nuanced responses to queries that necessitate specialized knowledge or in-depth expertise in a domain. For instance, if you aspire to use an LLM to address queries concerning a specific discipline, such as law or medicine, it might satisfactorily answer general queries but fail to respond accurately to those needing detailed insights or up-to-date knowledge.

RAG designs offer a comprehensive solution to the limitations typically encountered in LLM processing. In a RAG framework, the text corpus undergoes initial preprocessing, where it's segmented into summaries or distinct chunks and then embedded within a vector space. When a query is made, the model identifies the most relevant segments of this data and utilizes them to form a response. This process involves a combination of offline data preprocessing, online information retrieval, and the application of the LLM for response generation. It's a versatile approach that can be adapted to a variety of tasks, including code generation and semantic search. RAG models function as an abstraction layer that orchestrates these processes. The efficacy of this method is continually increasing, with its applications expanding as LLMs evolve and require more contextually rich data during prompt processing. In *Chapter 10*, we will present a deeper discussion of RAG models and their role in the future of LLM solutions.

Now that we've introduced the premise and capabilities of RAG models, let's focus on one particular example, called LangChain. We will review the nuts and bolts of its design principles and how it interfaces with data sources.

LangChain's design concepts

In this section, we will dissect the core methodologies and architectural decisions that make LangChain stand out. This will give us insights into its structural framework, the efficiency of data handling, and its innovative approach to integrating LLMs with various data sources.

Data sources

One of the most significant virtues of LangChain is the ability to connect an arbitrary LLM to a defined data source. By arbitrary, we mean that it could be any *off-the-shelf* LLM that was designed and trained with no specific regard to the data we are looking to connect it to. Employing LangChain allows us to customize it to our domain. The data source is to be used for reference when structuring the answer to the user prompt. That data may be proprietary data owned by a company or local personal information on your personal machine.

However, when it comes to leveraging a given database, LangChain does more than point the LLM to the data; it employs a particular processing scheme and makes it quick and efficient. It creates a vector database.

Given raw text data, be it free text in a `.txt` file, formatted files, or other various data structures of text, a vector database is created by chunking the text into appropriate lengths and creating numerical text embeddings, using a designated model. Note that if the designated embedding model is chosen to be an LLM, it doesn't have to be the same LLM that is used for prompting. For instance, the embedding model could be picked to be a free, sub-optimal, open source LLM, and the prompting model could be a paid LLM with optimal performance. Those embeddings are then stored in a vector database. You can clearly see that this approach is extremely storage-efficient, as we transform text, and perhaps encoded text, into a finite set of numerical values, which by its nature is dense.

When a user enters a prompt, a search mechanism identifies the relevant data chunks in the embedded data source. The prompt gets embedded with the same designated embedding model. Then, the search mechanism applies a similarity metric, such as cosine similarity, for example, and finds the most similar text chunks in the defined data source. Then, the original text of these chunks is retrieved. The original prompt is then sent again, this time to the prompting LLM. The difference is that, this time, the prompt consists of more than just the original user's prompt; it also consists of the retrieved text as a reference. This enables the LLM to get a question and a rich text supplement for reference. The LLM then can refer to the added information as a reference.

If it weren't for this design, when the user wanted to find an answer to their question, they would need to read through the vast material and find the relevant section. For instance, the material may be a company's entire product methodology, consisting of many PDF documents. This process leverages an automated smart search mechanism that narrows the relevant material down to an amount of text that can fit into a prompt. Then, the LLM frames the answer to the question and presents it to the user immediately. If you wish, the pipeline can be designed to quote the original text that it used to frame the answer, thus allowing for transparency and verification.

This paradigm is portrayed in *Figure 8.1*:

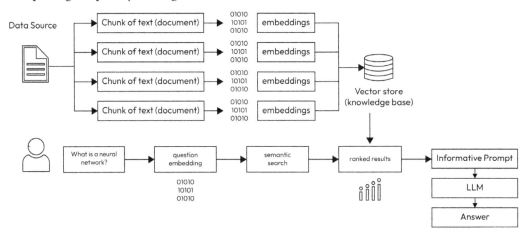

Figure 8.1 – The paradigm of a typical LangChain pipeline

In order to explain the prompt engineering behind the LangChain pipeline, let's review a financial information use case. Your data source is a cohort of **Securities & Exchange Commission (SEC)** filings of public companies from the US. You are looking to identify companies that gave dividends to their stock holders, and in what year.

Your prompt would be as follows:

```
Which filings mention that the company gave dividends in the year
2023?
```

The pipeline then embeds this question and looks for text chunks with similar context (e.g., that discuss paid dividends). It identifies many such chunks, such as the following:

```
"Dividend Policy. Dividends are paid at the discretion of the Board of
Directors. In fiscal 2023, we paid aggregate quarterly cash dividends
of $8.79 per share […]"
```

The LangChain pipeline then forms a new prompt that includes the text of the identified chunks. In this example, we assume the prompted LLM is OpenAI's GPT. LangChain embeds the information in the system prompt sent to OpenAI's GPT model:

```
"prompts": [
     "System: Use the following pieces of context to answer the user's
question. \nIf you don't know the answer, just say that you don't
know, don't try to make up an answer.\n----------------\n Dividend
Policy. Dividends are paid at the […]"
    ]
```

As we can see, the system prompt is used to instruct the model how to act and then to provide the context.

Now that we have an understanding of the foundational approach and benefits of LangChain, let's go deeper into its intricate design concepts, starting with how it bridges LLMs to diverse data sources efficiently.

Data that is not pre-embedded

While the preceding description is of data that is preprocessed to take the form of a vector database, another approach is to set up access to external data sources that are not yet processed into an embedding form. For instance, you may wish to leverage a SQL database to supplement other data sources. This approach is referred to as **multiple retrieval sources**.

We've now explored the ways LangChain efficiently interfaces with various data sources; now, it is essential to grasp the core structural elements that enable its functionalities – chains and agents.

Chains

The atomic building blocks within LangChain are called components. Typical components could be a prompt template, access to various data sources, and access to LLMs. When combining various components to form a system, we form a chain. A chain can represent a complete LLM-driven application.

We will now present the concept of agents and walk through a code example that showcases how chains and agents come together, creating a capability that would have been quite complex not too long ago.

Agents

The next layer of complexity over chains is agents. Agents leverage chains by employing them and complementing them with additional calculations and decisions. While a chain may yield a response to a simple request prompt, an agent would process the response and act upon it with further downstream processing based on a prescribed logic.

You can view agents as a reasoning mechanism that employs what we call a tool. Tools complement LLMs by connecting them with other data or functions.

Given the typical LLM shortcomings that prevent LLMs from being perfect multitaskers, agents employ tools in a prescribed and monitored manner, allowing them to retrieve necessary information, leverage it as context, and execute actions using designated existing solutions. Agents then observe the results and employ the prescribed logic for further downstream processes.

As an example, assume we want to calculate the salary trajectory for an average entry-level programmer in our area. This task is comprised of three key sub-tasks – finding out what that average starting salary is, identifying the factors for salary growth (e.g., a change in the cost of living, or a typical merit increase), and then projecting onward. An ideal LLM would be able to do the entire process by itself, not requiring anything more than a coherent prompt. However, given the typical shortcomings, such as hallucinations and limited training data, current LLMs would not be able to perform this entire process to a level where it could be productionized within a commercial product. A best practice is to break it down and monitor the thought process via agents.

In its most simple design, this would require the following:

1. Defining an agent that can access the internet and that can calculate future values of time series, given growth factors

2. Providing the agent with a comprehensive prompt

3. The agent breaks the prompt down into the different sub-tasks:

    I.   Fetching the average salary from the internet

    II. Fetching the growth factors

    III. Employing the calculation tool by applying the growth factors to the starting salary and creating a future time series for salary values

To exemplify the agentic approach, let's review a simple task that involves fetching a particular detail from the web, and using it to perform a calculation.

1. First, install these packages:

```
!pip install openai
!pip install wikipedia
!pip install langchain
!pip install langchain-openai
```

2. Then, run the following code:

```
from langchain.agents import load_tools, initialize_agent
from langchain_openai import OpenAI
import os
os.environ["OPENAI_API_KEY"] = "<your API key>"
llm = OpenAI(model_name='gpt-3.5-turbo-instruct')
tools = load_tools(["wikipedia", "llm-math"], llm=llm)
agent = initialize_agent(tools, llm=llm, agent="zero-shot-react-
description", verbose=True)
agent.run("Figure out how many pages are there in the book
Animal Farm. Then calculate how many minutes would it take me to
read it if it takes me two minutes to read one page.")
```

The output is then shown as follows:

```
> Finished chain.
'It would take me approximately 224 minutes or 3 hours and 44
minutes to read Animal Farm.'
```

Note that we didn't apply any method to fix the LLM to reproduce this exact response. Running this code again will yield a slightly different answer.

In the next chapter, we will dive deeper into several examples with code. In particular, we will program a multi-agent framework, where a team of agents is working on a joint project.

Long-term memory and referring to prior conversations

Another very important concept is long-term memory. We discussed how LangChain complements an LLM's knowledge by appending additional data sources, some of which may be proprietary, making it highly customized for a particular use case. However, it still lacks a very important function, the ability to refer to prior conversations and learn from them. For instance, you can design an assistant for a project manager. As the user interacts with it, they would ideally update each day about the progress of the work, the interactions, the challenges, and so on. It would be best if the assistant could digest all that newly accumulated knowledge and sustain it. That would allow for a scenario such as this:

*   **User**: "Where do we stand with regard to Jim's team's task?"

*   **Assistant**: "According to the original roadmap, Jim's team is to address the client's feedback to the design of the prototype. Based on the update from last week, the client provided only partial feedback, which you felt would not yet be sufficient for Jim's team to start work."

We will touch more on the concept of memory in the next chapter.

Ensuring continuous relevance through incremental updates and automated monitoring

To maintain the accuracy and relevance of LLM outputs in dynamic information environments, it's imperative to implement strategies for the ongoing update and maintenance of vector databases. As the corpus of knowledge continues to expand and evolve, so too must the embeddings that serve as the foundation for LLM responses. Incorporating techniques for incremental updates allows these databases to refresh their embeddings as new information becomes available, ensuring that the LLMs can provide the most accurate and up-to-date responses.

Incremental updates involve periodically re-embedding existing data sources with the latest information. This process can be automated to scan for updates in the data source, re-embed the new or updated content, and then integrate these refreshed embeddings into the existing vector database, without the need for a complete overhaul. By doing so, we ensure that the database reflects the most current knowledge available, enhancing the LLM's ability to deliver relevant and nuanced responses.

Automated monitoring plays a pivotal role in this ecosystem by continually assessing the quality and relevance of the LLM's outputs. This involves setting up systems that track the performance of the LLM, identifying areas where responses may be falling short due to outdated information or missing contexts. When such gaps are identified, the monitoring system can trigger an incremental update process, ensuring that the database remains a robust and accurate reflection of the current knowledge landscape.

By embracing these strategies, we ensure that LangChain and similar RAG frameworks can sustain their effectiveness over time. This approach not only enhances the relevance of LLM applications but also ensures that they can adapt to the rapidly evolving landscape of information, maintaining their position at the forefront of NLP technology.

We can now get hands-on with LangChain.

Reviewing a simple LangChain setup in a Jupyter notebook

We are now ready to set up a complete pipeline that can later be lent to various NLP applications.

Refer to the `Ch8_Setting_Up_LangChain_Configurations_and_Pipeline.ipynb` notebook. This notebook implements the LangChain framework. We will walk through it step by step, explaining the different building blocks. We chose a simple use case here, as the main point of this code is to show how to set up a LangChain pipeline.

In this scenario, we are in the healthcare sector. We have many care givers; each has many patients they may see. The physician in chief made a request on behalf of all the physicians in the hospital to be able to use a smart search across their notes. They heard about the new emerging capabilities with LLMs, and they would like to have a tool where they can search within the medical reports they wrote.

For instance, one physician said the following:

"I often come across research that may be relevant to a patient I saw months ago, but I don't recall who that was. I would like to have a tool where I can ask, 'Who was that patient that complained about ear pain and had a family history of migraines?', and it would find me that patient."

Thus, the business objective here is as follows:

"The CTO tasked us with putting together a quick prototype in the form of a Jupyter notebook. We will collect several clinical reports from the hospital's database, and we will use LangChain to search through them in the manner that the physician in the example described."

Let's jump right in by designing the solution in Python.

Setting up a LangChain pipeline with Python

Diving into the practicalities of LangChain, this section will guide you step by step in setting up a LangChain pipeline using Python, from installing the necessary libraries to executing sophisticated similarity searches.

Installing the required Python libraries

As always, we have a list of libraries that we will need to install. Since we are writing the code in a Jupyter notebook, we can install them from within the code:

1. **Load the text files with mock physician notes**: Here, we put together some mock physician notes. We load them and process them per the LangChain paradigm. We stress that these aren't real medical notes and that the people described there don't exist.

2. **Process the data so that it can be prepared for embedding**: Here, we split the text per the requirements of the embedding model. As we mentioned in previous chapters, LMs, such as those used for embedding, have a finite window of input text that they can process in a single batch. That size is hardcoded in their design architecture and is fixed for each particular model.

3. **Create the embeddings that would be stored in the vector database**: The vector database is one of the key pillars of the LangChain paradigm. Here, we take the text and create an embedding for each item. Those embeddings are then stored in a dedicated vector database. The LangChain library allows you to work with several different vector databases. While we chose one particular database, you can refer to the **Vector Store** page to read more about the different choices.

4. **Create the vector database**: Here, we create the vector database. This process may be slightly different for each database choice. However, the creators of these databases make sure to take away all of the hard work and leave you with a simple turnkey function that creates the database for you, given the appropriate embeddings in vector form. We leverage Meta's **Facebook AI Similarity Search** (**FAISS**) database, as it is simple, quick to deploy, and free.

5. **Perform a similarity search based on our in-house documents**: This is the key part of the pipeline. We introduce several questions and use LangChain's similarity search to identify the physician notes that would best answer our question.

As we can see, the similarity search function is able to do a good job with most of the questions. It embeds the question and looks for reports whose embeddings are similar.

However, a similarity search could only go so far when it comes to answering the question correctly. It is easy to think of a question that discusses a matter that is very similar to one of the notes, yet a minor difference confuses the similarity search mechanism. For instance, the similarity search process actually makes a mistake in question two, mistaking different months and, thus, providing a wrong answer.

In order to overcome this matter, we would want to do more than just a similarity search. We would want an LLM to review the results of the similarity search and apply its judgment. We will see how that's done in the next chapter.

With our foundation set for LangChain's practical applications in Python, let's now move on to understanding how the cloud plays a pivotal role, especially when harnessing the true potential of LLMs in contemporary computational paradigms.

LLMs in the cloud

In this era of big data and computation, cloud platforms have emerged as vital tools for managing large-scale computations, providing infrastructure, storage, and services that can be rapidly provisioned and released with minimal management effort.

This section will focus on computation environments in the cloud. These have become the dominant choice for many leading companies and institutions. As an organization, having a computation environment in the cloud versus on-premises makes a major difference. It impacts the ability to share resources and manage allocations, maintenance, and cost. There are many trade-offs for employing cloud services instead of owning physical machines. You can learn about them by searching online or even asking a chat LLM about them.

One significant difference with cloud computing is the ecosystem that the providers have built around it. When you pick a cloud provider as your computation hub, you tap into a whole suite of additional products and services, opening up a new world of capabilities that would not be as accessible to you otherwise.

In this section, we will focus on the LLM aspect of those services.

The three primary cloud platforms are AWS, Microsoft Azure, and GCP. These platforms offer a myriad of services, catering to the varying needs of businesses and developers. When it comes to NLP and LLMs, each platform provides dedicated resources and services to facilitate experimentation, deployment, and production.

Let's explore each of these platforms to see how they cater to our specific needs.

AWS

AWS remains a dominant force in the cloud computing landscape, providing a comprehensive and evolving suite of services that cater to the needs of ML and AI development. AWS is renowned for its robust infrastructure, extensive service offerings, and deep integration with ML tools and frameworks, making it a preferred platform for developers and data scientists looking to innovate with LLMs.

Experimenting with LLMs on AWS

AWS provides a rich ecosystem of tools and services designed to facilitate the development and experimentation with LLMs, ensuring that researchers and developers have access to the most advanced ML capabilities:

- **Amazon SageMaker**: The cornerstone of ML on AWS, SageMaker is a fully managed service that streamlines the entire ML workflow. It offers Jupyter notebook instances for experimentation, broad framework support, including TensorFlow and PyTorch, and a range of tools for model building, training, and debugging. SageMaker's capabilities have been continually enhanced to support the complexities of training and fine-tuning LLMs, providing scalable compute options and optimized ML environments.

- **AWS Deep Learning Containers and Deep Learning AMIs**: For those looking to customize their ML environments, AWS offers Deep Learning Containers and **Amazon Machine Images** (**AMIs**) pre-installed with popular ML frameworks. These resources simplify the setup process for LLM experiments, allowing developers to focus on innovation rather than infrastructure configuration.

- **Pre-trained models and SageMaker JumpStart**: AWS has expanded its library of pre-trained models accessible through SageMaker JumpStart, facilitating quick experimentation with LLMs for a variety of NLP tasks. JumpStart also offers solution templates and executable example notebooks, making it easier for developers to start and scale their ML projects.

Deploying and productionizing LLMs on AWS

AWS provides a suite of services designed to efficiently deploy and manage LLMs at scale, ensuring that models are easily accessible and performant under varying loads:

- **SageMaker endpoints**: To deploy LLMs, SageMaker endpoints offer fully managed hosting services with auto-scaling capabilities. This service allows developers to deploy trained models into production quickly, with the infrastructure automatically adjusting to the demands of the application.

- **Elastic Inference and Amazon EC2 Inf1 instances**: To optimize inference costs, AWS offers Elastic Inference, which adds GPU-powered inference acceleration to SageMaker instances. For even greater performance and cost efficiency, Amazon EC2 Inf1 instances, powered by AWS Inferentia chips, provide high-throughput and low-latency inference for DL models.

- **AWS Lambda and Amazon Bedrock**: For serverless deployment, AWS Lambda supports running inference without provisioning or managing servers, ideal for applications with variable demand. Amazon Bedrock, represents a significant leap forward, offering serverless access to foundational models through APIs, model customization, and seamless integration within an organizational network, ensuring data privacy and security.

Let's move on to the next topic, Microsoft Aure.

Microsoft Azure

Microsoft Azure stands at the forefront of cloud computing services, offering a robust platform for the development, deployment, and management of ML and LLMs. Leveraging its strategic partnership with OpenAI, Azure provides exclusive cloud access to GPT models, positioning itself as a critical resource for developers and data scientists aiming to harness the power of advanced NLP technologies. Recent enhancements have expanded Azure's capabilities, making it an even more attractive choice for those looking to push the boundaries of AI and ML applications.

Experimenting with LLMs on Azure

Azure has significantly enriched its offerings to support research and experimentation with LLMs, providing a variety of tools and platforms that cater to the diverse needs of the AI development community:

- **Azure OpenAI Service**: This directly integrates OpenAI's cutting-edge models, including the latest GPT versions, DALL·E, and Codex, into the Azure ecosystem. This service enables developers to easily incorporate sophisticated AI functionalities into their applications, with the added benefits of Azure's scalability and management tools.

- **Azure Machine Learning (Azure ML)**: This offers an advanced environment for the custom training and fine-tuning of LLMs on specific datasets, allowing for enhanced model performance on niche tasks. Azure ML Studio's pre-built and customizable Jupyter notebook templates support a wide range of programming languages and frameworks, facilitating a seamless experimentation process.

- **Azure Cognitive Services**: This provides access to a suite of pre-built AI services, including text analytics, speech services, and decision-making capabilities powered by LLMs. These services enable developers to add complex AI functions to applications quickly, without deep ML expertise.

Deploying and productionizing LLMs on Azure

Azure's infrastructure and services offer comprehensive solutions for the deployment and productionization of LLM applications, ensuring scalability, performance, and security:

- **Deployment options**: Azure supports various deployment scenarios through **Azure Container Instances (ACI)** for lightweight deployment needs and **Azure Kubernetes Service (AKS)** for larger, more complex applications requiring high scalability. These services allow for the efficient scaling of LLM applications to meet user demand.

- **Model management**: Through Azure ML, developers can manage the life cycle of their models, including version control, auditing, and governance. This ensures that deployed models are not only performant but also comply with industry standards and regulatory requirements.

- **Security and compliance**: Azure emphasizes security and compliance across all its services, providing features such as data encryption, access control, and comprehensive compliance certifications. This commitment ensures that applications built and deployed on Azure meet the highest standards for data protection and privacy.

GCP

GCP continues to be a powerhouse in cloud computing, providing an extensive suite of services that cater to the evolving needs of AI and ML development. Known for its cutting-edge innovations in AI and ML, GCP offers a rich ecosystem of tools and services that facilitate the development, deployment, and scaling of LLMs, making it an ideal platform for developers and researchers aiming to leverage the latest in AI technology.

Experimenting with LLMs on GCP

GCP has further enhanced its capabilities for experimenting with and developing LLMs, offering a comprehensive set of tools that support the entire ML workflow, from data ingestion and model training to hyperparameter tuning and evaluation:

- **Vertex AI**: At the heart of GCP's ML offerings, Vertex AI provides an integrated suite of tools and services that streamline the ML workflow. It offers advanced features for training and fine-tuning LLMs, including AutoML capabilities for automating the selection of optimal model architectures and hyperparameters. Vertex AI's integration with GCP's robust data and analytics services makes it easier to manage large datasets that are essential for training LLMs.

- **An IDE**: The built-in notebooks service within Vertex AI offers a fully managed JupyterLab environment, enabling developers to write, run, and debug ML code seamlessly. This environment is optimized for ML development, supporting popular frameworks such as TensorFlow and PyTorch, which are crucial for building and experimenting with LLMs.

- **AI and ML libraries**: GCP continues to expand its library of pre-trained models and ML APIs, including those specifically designed for NLP and understanding. These tools allow developers to integrate advanced NLP capabilities into their applications rapidly.

Deploying and productionizing LLMs on GCP

GCP provides robust and scalable solutions for deploying and productionizing LLMs, ensuring that applications built on its platform can meet the demands of real-world usage:

- **Vertex AI prediction**: Once an LLM is trained, Vertex AI's prediction service allows for the easy deployment of models as fully managed, auto-scaling endpoints. This service simplifies the process of making your LLMs accessible to applications, with the infrastructure automatically adjusting to the workload demands.

- **Google Kubernetes Engine (GKE)**: For more complex deployment scenarios requiring high availability and scalability, GKE offers a managed environment to deploy containerized LLM applications. GKE's global infrastructure ensures that your models are highly available and can scale to meet the needs of enterprise-level applications.

Concluding cloud services

The landscape of cloud computing continues to evolve rapidly, with AWS, Azure, and GCP each offering unique advantages for the development and deployment of LLMs. AWS stands out for its broad infrastructure and deep integration with ML tools, making it ideal for a wide range of ML and AI projects. Azure, with its exclusive access to OpenAI's models and deep integration within the Microsoft ecosystem, offers unparalleled opportunities for enterprises looking to leverage the cutting edge of AI technology. GCP, recognized for its innovation in AI and ML, provides tools and services that mirror Google's internal AI advancements, appealing to those seeking the latest in AI research and development. As the capabilities of these platforms continue to expand, the choice between them will increasingly depend on specific project needs, organizational alignment, and strategic partnerships, underscoring the importance of a thoughtful evaluation based on the current and future landscape of cloud-based AI and ML.

Summary

As the world of NLP and LLMs continues to grow rapidly, so do the various practices of system design. In this chapter, we reviewed the design process of LLM applications and pipelines. We discussed the components of these approaches, touching on both API-based closed source and local open source solutions. We then gave you hands-on experience with code.

We later delved deeper into the system design process and introduced LangChain. We reviewed what LangChain comprises and experimented with an example pipeline in code.

To complement the system design process, we surveyed leading cloud services that allow you to experiment, develop, and deploy LLM-based solutions.

In the next chapter, we'll focus on particular practical use cases, accompanied with code.

9

Exploring the Frontiers: Advanced Applications and Innovations Driven by LLMs

In the rapidly evolving landscape of **natural language processing (NLP)**, **large language models (LLMs)** have marked a revolutionary step forward, reshaping how we interact with information, automate processes, and derive insights from vast data pools. This chapter represents the culmination of our journey through the emergence and development of NLP methods. It is here that the theoretical foundations laid in previous chapters converge with practical, cutting-edge applications, illuminating the remarkable capabilities of LLMs when harnessed with the right tools and techniques.

We delve into the most recent and thrilling advancements in LLM applications, presented through detailed Python code examples designed for hands-on learning. This approach not only illustrates the power of LLMs but also equips you with the skills to implement these technologies in real-world scenarios. The subjects covered in this chapter are meticulously selected to showcase a spectrum of advanced functionalities and applications.

The importance of this chapter cannot be overstated. It not only reflects the state of the art in NLP but also serves as a bridge to the future, where the integration of these technologies into everyday solutions becomes seamless. By the end of this chapter, you will have a comprehensive understanding of how to apply the latest LLM techniques and innovations, empowering you to push the boundaries of what's possible in NLP and beyond. Join us on this exciting journey to unlock the full potential of LLMs.

Let's go through the main headings covered in the chapter:

- Enhancing LLM performance with RAG and LangChain – a dive into advanced functionalities
- Advanced methods with chains
- Retrieving information from various web sources automatically

- Prompt compression and API cost reduction
- Multiple agents – forming a team of LLMs who collaborate

Technical requirements

For this chapter, the following will be necessary:

- **Programming knowledge**: Familiarity with Python programming is a must since the open source models, OpenAI's API, and LangChain are all illustrated using Python code.

- **Access to OpenAI's API**: An API key from OpenAI will be required to explore closed source models. This can be obtained by creating an account with OpenAI and agreeing to their terms of service.

- **Open source models**: Access to the specific open source models mentioned in this chapter will be necessary. These can be accessed and downloaded from their respective repositories or via package managers such as pip or conda.

- **Local development environment**: A local development environment setup with Python installed is required. An **integrated development environment** (**IDE**) such as **PyCharm**, **Jupyter Notebook**, or a simple text editor can be used. Note that we recommend a free **Google Colab** notebook, as it encapsulates all these requirements in a seamless web interface.

- **Ability to install libraries**: You must have permission for the installation of the required Python libraries such as **NumPy**, **SciPy**, **TensorFlow**, and **PyTorch**. Note that the code we provide includes the required installations so you won't have to install them ahead of time. We simply stress that you should have permission to do so, which we expect you would. Specifically, using a free Google Colab notebook would suffice.

- **Hardware requirements**: Depending on the complexity and size of the models you're working with, a computer with sufficient processing power (potentially including a good GPU for ML tasks) and ample memory will be required. This is only relevant when choosing to not use the free Google Colab.

Now that we've set up LLM applications using APIs and locally, we can finally deploy the advanced applications of LLMs that let us leverage their immense power.

Enhancing LLM performance with RAG and LangChain – a dive into advanced functionalities

The **retrieval-augmented generation** (**RAG**) framework has become instrumental in tailoring **large language models** (**LLMs**) for specific domains or tasks, bridging the gap between the simplicity of prompt engineering and the complexity of model fine-tuning.

Prompt engineering stands as the initial, most accessible technique for customizing LLMs. It leverages the model's capacity to interpret and respond to queries based on the input prompt. For example, to inquire if Nvidia surpassed earnings expectations in its latest announcement, directly providing the earnings call content within the prompt can compensate for the LLM's lack of immediate, up-to-date context. This approach, while straightforward, hinges on the model's ability to digest and analyze the provided information within a single or a series of carefully crafted prompts.

When the scope of inquiry exceeds what prompt engineering can accommodate—such as analyzing a decade's worth of tech sector earnings calls—RAG becomes indispensable. Prior to RAG's adoption, the alternative was fine-tuning, a resource-intensive process requiring significant adjustments to the LLM's architecture to incorporate extensive datasets. RAG simplifies this by preprocessing and storing large amounts of data in a vector database. It intelligently isolates and retrieves the data segments pertinent to the query, effectively condensing the vast information into a manageable, prompt-size context for the LLM. This innovation drastically reduces the time, resources, and expertise needed for such extensive data familiarization tasks.

In *Chapter 8*, we introduced the general concept of RAGs and, in particular, LangChain, a RAG framework distinguished by its advanced capabilities.

We will now discuss the additional unique features LangChain offers for enhancing LLM applications, providing you with practical insights into its implementation and utility in complex NLP tasks.

LangChain pipeline with Python – enhancing performance with LLMs

In this section, we will pick up where we left off with our last example from *Chapter 8*. In this scenario, we are in the healthcare sector, and in our hospital, our care providers are expressing a need to be able to quickly surface patients' records based on rough descriptions of the patient or their condition. For example, "Who was that patient I saw last year who was pregnant with triplets?" "Did I ever have a patient with a history of cancer from both of their parents and they were interested in a clinical trial?" and so on.

> **Important note**
> We stress that these aren't real medical notes and that the people described in the notes aren't real.

In our example in *Chapter 8*, we kept the pipeline at minimum complexity by simply leveraging the vector databases of embeddings of clinical notes, and then we applied similarity search to look for notes based on simple requests. We noticed how one of the questions, the second question, received a wrong answer with the similarity search algorithm.

We will now enhance that pipeline. We will not settle for the results of the similarity search and surface those to the physicians; we will take those results that were deemed to be similar in content to the request, and we will employ an LLM to go through these results, vet them, and tell us which ones are indeed relevant to the physician.

Paid LLMs versus free

We'll use this pipeline to exemplify the utility of either type of LLM, paid or free. We give you the choice, via the `paid_vs_free` variable, to either use OpenAI's paid GPT model or a free LLM. Using OpenAI's paid model would leverage their API and would require an API key. However, the free LLM is imported to the local environment where the Python code is run, thus making it available to anyone who has an internet connection and sufficient computational resources.

Let's start getting hands-on and experimenting with the code.

Applying advanced LangChain configurations and pipelines

Refer to the following notebook: `Ch9_Advanced_LangChain_Configurations_and_Pipeline.ipynb`.

Note that the first part of the notebook is identical to the notebook from *Chapter 8*, so we will skip the description of that part.

Installing the required Python libraries

Here, we need to expand the set of installed libraries and install `openai` and `gpt4all`. Moreover, in order to utilize `gpt4all`, we will need to download a `.bin` file from the web.

These two steps are easy to perform via the notebook.

Setting up an LLM – choose between a paid LLM (OpenAI's GPT) and a free LLM (from Hugging Face)

As explained above, we let you choose whether you want to run this example via a paid API by OpenAI or a free LLM.

Remember, since OpenAI's service includes hosting the LLM and processing the prompts, it requires minimal resources and time and a basic internet connection. It also involves sending our prompts to OpenAI's API service. Prompts typically include information that, in real-world settings, may be proprietary. Thus, an executive decision needs to be made regarding the security of the data. Similar considerations were central, in the last decade, to the transition of companies' computation from on-premises to the cloud.

In contrast to that requirement, with a free LLM, you would host it locally, you would avoid exporting any information outside of your computation environment, but you would take on the processing.

Another aspect to consider is the terms of use of each LLM, as each may have different license terms. While an LLM may allow you to experiment with it for free, it may present constrictions on whether you may use it in a commercial product.

In the context of constraints around runtime and computational resources, choosing the paid LLM for this example will yield quicker responses.

In order to accommodate your wish to experiment with a free LLM, and since we aspire to let you run the code quickly and for free on Google Colab, we must restrict our choice of LLMs to those that can be run on the limited RAM that Google lets us have with a free account. In order to do that, we chose an LLM with reduced precision, also known as a quantized LLM.

Based on your choice between an API-based LLM and a free local LLM, the LLM will be assigned to the `llm` variable.

Creating a QA chain

Here, we set up a RAG framework. It is designed to accept various text documents and set them up for retrieval.

Search based on the same requirements when using the LLM as the "brain" instead of embedding similarity

We will now run the exact same requests as we did in the example in *Chapter 8*. Those will be performed across the same notes, and the same vector DB that holds the same embedding. None of that has been changed or enhanced. The difference is that we will have the LLM oversee the processing of the answers.

In *Chapter 8*, we saw that question number two received a wrong answer. The question was, "Are there any pregnant patients who are due to deliver in September?"

The answer we saw in *Chapter 8* was about a patient who is due to give birth in August. The mistake was due to the deficiency of the similarity algorithm. Indeed, that patient's notes had content similar to that of the question, but the fine detail of giving birth in a different month should have been the factor that made those note irrelevant.

Here, in our current pipeline, where OpenAI's LLM is applied, it gets it right, telling us that there are no patients who are due to deliver in September.

Note that when opting for the free LLM, it gets it wrong. This exemplifies the sub-optimal aspects of that model, as it is quantized in an effort to save on RAM requirements.

To conclude this example, we have put together an in-house search mechanism that lets the user, in our example, a physician, search through their patients' notes to find patients based on some criteria. A unique aspect of this system design is the ability to let the LLM retrieve the relevant answer from an external data source and not be limited to the data it was trained on. This paradigm is the basis of RAG.

In the next section, we will showcase more uses for LLMs.

Advanced methods with chains

In this section, we will continue our exploration of ways one can utilize LLM pipelines. We will focus on chains.

Refer to the following notebook: `Ch9_Advanced_Methods_with_Chains.ipynb`. This notebook presents an evolution of a chain pipeline, as every iteration exemplifies another feature that LangChain allows us to employ.

For the sake of using minimal computational resources, memory, and time, we use OpenAI's API. You can choose to use a free LLM instead and may do so in a similar way to how we set up the notebook from the previous example in this chapter.

The notebook starts with the basic configurations, as always, so we can skip to reviewing the notebook's content.

Asking the LLM a general knowledge question

In this example, we want to use the LLM to tell us an answer to a simple question that would require common knowledge that a trained LLM is expected to have:

```
"Who are the members of Metallica. List them as comma separated."
```

We then define a simple chain called `LLMChain`, and we feed it with the LLM variable and the prompt.

The LLM, indeed, knows the answer from its knowledge base and returns:

```
'James Hetfield, Lars Ulrich, Kirk Hammett, Robert Trujillo'
```

Requesting output structure – making the LLM provide output in a particular data format

This time, we would like the output to be in a particular syntax, potentially allowing us to use it in a computational manner for downstream tasks:

```
"List the first 10 elements from the periodical table as comma
separated list."
```

Now, we add a feature for achieving the syntax. We define the `output_parser` variable, and we use a different function for generating the output, `predict_and_parse()`.

The output is the following:

```
['Hydrogen',
 'Helium',
 'Lithium',
```

```
'Beryllium',
'Boron',
'Carbon',
'Nitrogen',
'Oxygen',
'Fluorine',
'Neon']
```

Evolving to a fluent conversation – inserting an element of memory to have previous interactions as reference and context for follow-up prompts

This feature brings a new level of value to the chain. Until this point, the prompts didn't have any context. The LLM processed each prompt independently. For instance, if you wanted to ask a follow-up question, you couldn't. The pipeline didn't have your prior prompts and the responses to them as reference.

In order to go from asking disjointed questions to having an ongoing, rolling conversation-like experience, LangChain offers ConversationChain(). Within this function, we have a memory parameter that maps the prior interactions with the chain to the current prompt. Therefore, the prompt template is where that memory "lives."

Instead of prompting with a basic template, such as

```
"List all the holidays you know as comma separated list."
```

the template now accommodates the memory feature:

```
"Current conversation:
{history}
Your task:
{input}}"
```

Here, you can think of this string as being formatted similarly to a Python f "..." string, where history and input are string variables. The ConversationChain() function processes this prompt template and inserts these two variables to complete the prompt string. The input variable is produced by the function itself as we activate the memory mechanism, and the input variable is then supplied by us as we run the following:

```
conversation.predict_and_parse(input="Write the first 10 holidays you
know, as a comma separated list.")
```

Where the output is the following:

```
['Christmas',
'Thanksgiving',
```

```
"New Year's Day",
'Halloween',
'Easter',
'Independence Day',
"Valentine's Day",
"St. Patrick's Day",
'Labor Day',
'Memorial Day']
```

Now, let's make a follow-up request that would only be understood in the context of the previous request and output:

```
conversation.predict_and_parse(input=" Observe the list of holidays
you printed and remove all the non-religious holidays from the list.")
```

Indeed, we get the appropriate output:

```
['Christmas',
'Thanksgiving',
"New Year's Day",
'Easter',
"Valentine's Day",
"St. Patrick's Day,"]
```

To complete this example, let's assume the intention we had was to quickly generate a table of some holidays that includes their names and descriptions:

```
"For each of these, tell about the holiday in 2 sentences.
Form the output in a json format table.
The table's name is "holidays" and the fields are "name" and
"description".
For each row, the "name" is the holiday's name, and the "description"
is the description you generated.
The syntax of the output should be a json format, without newline
characters."
```

Now, we get a formatted string from the chain:

```
{
  "holidays": [
    {
      "name": "Christmas",
      "description": "Christmas is a religious holiday that celebrates
the birth of Jesus Christ and is widely observed as a secular cultural
and commercial phenomenon."
    },
    {
```

```
    "name": "Thanksgiving",
    "description": "Thanksgiving is a national holiday in the United
States, celebrated on the fourth Thursday of November, and originated
as a harvest festival."
    },
    {
    "name": "Easter",
    "description": "Easter is […]
```

We can then use pandas to convert this string to a table:

```
dict = json.loads(output)
pd.json_normalize(dict[ "holidays"])
```

After pandas processes `dict` to be a DataFrame, we can observe it in *Table 9.1*:

	Name	Description
0	Christmas	Christmas is a Christian holiday that celebrates the birth of Jesus Christ. It is observed on December 25 each year.
1	Thanksgiving	Thanksgiving is a holiday in which people gather together to express gratitude for the blessings in their lives. It is celebrated on the fourth Thursday in November in the United States.
2	New Year's Day	New Year's Day marks the beginning of the Gregorian calendar year. It is celebrated on January 1 with various traditions and festivities.
3	Easter	Easter is a Christian holiday that commemorates the resurrection of Jesus Christ from the dead. It is observed on the first Sunday following the first full moon after the vernal equinox.
4	Valentine's Day	Valentine's Day is a day to celebrate love and affection. It is traditionally associated with romantic love, but it is also a time to express appreciation for friends and family.
5	St. Patrick's Day	St. Patrick's Day is a cultural and religious holiday that honors the patron saint of Ireland, St. Patrick. It is celebrated on March 17 with parades, wearing green, and other festive activities.

Table 9.1 – pandas transformed the table from dict to a DataFrame, thus suiting down-stream processing

This concludes the various chain features that this notebook presents. Notice how we leveraged the features that both chains bring us and that LLMs bring us. For instance, while the memory and parsing features are completely handled on the chain's side, the ability to present a response in a particular format, such as a JSON format, is solely accredited to the LLM.

In our next example, we will continue to present novel utilities with LLMs and LangChain.

Retrieving information from various web sources automatically

In this example, we will review how simple it is to leverage LLMs to access the web and extract information. We may wish to research a particular topic, and so we would like to consolidate all the information from a few web pages, several YouTube videos that present that topic, and so on. Such an endeavor can take a while, as the content may be massive. For instance, several YouTube videos can sometimes take hours to review. Often, one doesn't know how useful the video is until one has watched a significant portion of it.

Another use case is when looking to track various trends in real time. This may include tracking news sources, YouTube videos, and so on. Here, speed is crucial. Unlike the previous example where speed was important to save us personal time, here, speed is necessary for getting our algorithm to be relevant for identifying real-time emerging trends.

In this section, we put together a very simple and limited example.

Retrieving content from a YouTube video and summarizing it

Refer to the following notebook: Ch9_Retrieve_Content_from_a_YouTube_Video_and_Summarize.ipynb. We will build our application on a library called EmbedChain (https://github.com/embedchain/embedchain). EmbedChain leverages a RAG framework and enhances it by allowing the vector database to include information from various web sources.

In our example, we will choose a particular YouTube video (*Robert Waldinger: What makes a good life? Lessons from the longest study on happiness | TED*: https://www.youtube.com/watch?v=8KkKuTCFvzI&ab_channel=TED). We would like the content of that video to be processed into the RAG framework. Then, we will prompt an LLM with questions and tasks related to the content of that video, thus allowing us to extract everything we care to learn about the video without having to watch it.

It should be stressed that a key feature that this method relies on is that YouTube accompanies many of its verbal videos with a written transcript. This makes the importing of the video's text context seamless. If, however, one wishes to apply this method to a video that isn't accompanied by a transcript, this is not a problem. One would need to pick a speech-to-text model, many of which are free and of very high quality. The audio of the video would be processed, a transcript would be extracted, and you may then import it into the RAG process.

Installs, imports, and settings

As with previous notebooks, here too, we install the necessary packages, import all the relevant packages, and set our OpenAI API key.

We then do the following:

1.   Make our choice of model.

2.   Choose an embedding model that will serve the RAG's vector database feature.

3.   Choose a prompting LLM. Notice how you can set up further parameters that control the model's output, such as the maximal number of returned tokens or the temperature.

4.   Pick the YouTube video to which you would like to apply this code and set a string variable using the video's URL.

Setting up the retrieval mechanism

We need to set EmbedChain's RAG process. We specify that we are passing a path to a YouTube video, and we provide the video's URL.

We can then print out the text that was fetched and verify that it is, indeed, aligned with the video we are looking to analyze.

Reviewing, summarizing, and translating

We will now observe the value that this code yields.

We ask the LLM to review the content, to put together a summary, and to present that summary in English, Russian, and German:

```
Please review the entire content, summarize it to the length of 4
sentence, then translate it to Russian and to German.
Make sure the summary is consistent with the content.
Put the string '\n----\n' between the English part of the answer and
the Russian part.
Put the string '\n****\n' between the Russian part of the answer and
the German part.
```

The returned output is spot on, as it completely captures the essence of the TED talk. We edit it to remove the delimiter strings and get:

```
The content emphasizes the importance of good
relationships in keeping us happy and healthy
throughout our lives. It discusses how social
connections, quality of close relationships, and
avoiding conflict play crucial roles in our well-
being. The study follows the lives of 724 men over
75 years, highlighting the significance of
relationships over wealth and fame in leading a
fulfilling life.
Russian:
```

```
Содержание подчеркивает
Важность [...]
German:
Der
Inhalt betont die Bedeutung  [...]
```

Now, to make the content simple for, say, a German speaker, we ask the LLM to form the German summary into several bullet points that best describe the content of the video.

It does this well, and the outputs are as follows:

```
- Betonung der Bedeutung guter Beziehungen für Glück und Gesundheit
- Diskussion über soziale Verbindungen, Qualität enger Beziehungen und
Konfliktvermeidung
- Verfolgung des Lebens von 724 Männern über 75 Jahre in der Studie
- Hervorhebung der Bedeutung von Beziehungen im Vergleich zu Reichtum
und Ruhm
- Fokus auf Beziehungen als Schlüssel zu einem erfüllten Leben
```

While this code is meant to serve as a basic proof of concept, one can see how simple it would be to add more data sources, automate it to run constantly, and act based on the findings. While a readable summary is helpful, one could change the code to act based on the identified content and execute downstream applications.

Now that we have observed several capabilities that LLMs can perform, we can take a step back and refine the way we utilize those LLMs. In our next section, we will exemplify how one may reduce LLM processing, thus saving API costs, or, when employing a local LLM, reducing inference computation.

Prompt compression and API cost reduction

This part is dedicated to a recent development in resource optimization for when employing API-based LLMs, such as OpenAI's services. When considering the many trade-offs between employing a remote LLM as a service and hosting an LLM locally, one key metric is cost. In particular, based on the application and usage, the API costs can accumulate to a significant amount. API costs are mainly driven by the number of tokens that are being sent to and from the LLM service.

In order to illustrate the significance of this payment model on a business plan, consider business units for which the product or service relies on API calls to OpenAI's GPT, where OpenAI serves as a third-party vendor. As a particular example, imagine a social network that lets its users have LLM assistance to comment on posts. In that use case, a user is interested in commenting on a post, and instead of having to write a complete comment, a feature lets the user describe their feelings about the post in three–five words, and a backend process augments a full comment.

In this particular example, the engine collects the user's three–five words, and it also collects the content of the post that the comment is meant for, meaning it will also collect all other relevant information that the social network's experts would think is relevant for augmenting a comment. For instance, the user's profile description, their past few comments, and so on.

This would mean that every time a user wishes to have a comment augmented, a detailed prompt is sent from the social network's servers to the third party's LLM via theAPI.

Now, this type of process can accumulate high costs.

In this section, we will analyze an approach to reducing this cost by reducing the number of tokens sent to the LLM through the API. The basic assumption is that one can always reduce the number of words sent to the LLM and, thus, reduce cost, but the reduction in performance could be significant. Our motivation is to reduce that amount while maintaining high-quality performance. We then asked if only the "right" words could be sent, ignoring other "non-material" words. This notion reminds us of the concept of file compression, where a smart and tailored algorithm is employed to reduce the size a file takes while maintaining its purpose and value.

Prompt compression

Here, we introduce **LLMLingua**, a development by Microsoft that is meant to address prompts that are "sparse" in information by compressing them.

LLMLingua utilizes a compact, well-trained language model, such as LLaMA-7B, to identify and remove non-essential tokens within prompts. This approach enables efficient inference with LLMs, achieving up to 20x compression with minimal performance loss (`https://github.com/microsoft/LLMLingua`).

In their papers (`https://arxiv.org/abs/2310.05736` and `https://arxiv.org/abs/2310.06839`), the authors explain the algorithm and the advantages it proposes. It is interesting to note that besides the reduction in cost, the compression also aims to focus the remaining content, which is shown by the authors to lead to an improvement in performance by the LLM, as it avoids a sparse and noisy prompt.

Let's experiment with prompt compression in a real-world example and evaluate its impact and various trade-offs.

Experimenting with prompt compression and evaluating trade-offs

For the sake of this experiment, we'll illustrate a real-world example.

In our current use case, we are developing a feature that sits on top of a database of academic publications. The feature allows the user to pick a specific publication and ask questions about it. A backend engine evaluates the question, reviews the publication, and derives an answer.

To narrow down the scope of the feature for the sake of putting together a series of experiments, the publications are from the particular category of AI publications, and the question that the user asks is the following:

```
"Does this publication involve Reinforcement Learning?"
```

This question requires a deep and insightful review of each publication, as there are cases where a publication discusses a novel algorithm where the term reinforcement learning isn't explicitly mentioned at any point in the publication, yet the feature is expected to infer from the description of the algorithm whether it indeed leverages the concepts of reinforcement learning and flag it as such.

Refer to the following notebook: `Ch9_RAGLlamaIndex_Prompt_Compression.ipynb`.

In this code, we run a set of experiments, each per the above feature description. Each experiment is in the form of a full, end-to-end RAG task. While we employed LangChain in the previous RAG examples, here, we introduce LlamaIndex. LlamaIndex is an open source Python library that employs a RAG framework (`https://docs.llamaindex.ai/en/stable/index.html`). LlamaIndex is similar to LangChain in that way.

The LLMLingua code stack that the folks at Microsoft put together is integrated with LlamaIndex.

Let's review the code in detail.

Code settings

Similar to the previous notebooks, here too, we set the initial settings with the following:

1. In this code section, we start by defining some key variables.

2. We set the number of experiments that we want to run. We want to make sure we choose a number that is large enough so as to get a good statistical representation of the impact that the compression has.

3. We set the top-k, which is the number of chunks to be retrieved by the RAG framework for prompt context.

4. We predefined the target number of the token we would like the compression to reduce.

5. Finally, as in the previous code, we set our OpenAI API key.

We take this opportunity to stress that some of the parameters in this evaluation were fixed for the sake of limiting its complexity and keeping it appropriate for educational purposes. When conducting such an evaluation in business or academic settings, there should be either qualitative or quantitative reasoning for the value chosen. Qualitative may be of the form "We shell fix the desired reduction to 999 tokens due to budget constraints," whereas quantitative may seek to not fix it but rather optimize it as a part of the other trade-offs. In our case, we fixed this particular parameter to a value that was found to allow for an impressive compression rate while maintaining a decent agreement rate between the two evaluated approaches. Another example was the number of experiments we chose, which was a trade-off between runtime, GPU memory allocation, and statistical power.

Gathering the data

We need to gather the dataset of the publications, and we also filter it so as to be left with only the limited cohort of publications that are in the AI category.

LLM configurations

Here, we set the ground for the two LLMs we will be employing.

The compression method, LLMLingua, employs Llama2 as the compressing LLM. It will obtain the context retrieved by the LlamaIndex RAG pipeline, the user's question, and it will compress and reduce the size of the context content.

OpenAI's GPT is to be used as the downstream LLM for prompting, meaning it will obtain the question about reinforcement learning and the additional relevant context and return an answer.

Additionally, here, we define the user's question. Note that we added instructions for OpenAI's GPT on how to present the answer.

The experiments

This is the core of the notebook. A `for` loop iterates over the various experiments. In each iteration, two scenarios are evaluate:

1. **First scenario**: an ordinary RAG task is deployed where the context is retrieved without being compressed. The prompt is comprised of the retrieved context and the user's question, and the answer that the LLM returns is recorded along with the number of sent tokens and the processing time.

2. **Second scenario**: LLMLingua is employed. The retrieved context is compressed. The compressed context is sent to the LLM along with the user's question. Again, the returned answer is recorded along with the number of sent tokens and the processing time.

When this code cell is completed, we have a dictionary, `record`, that holds the relevant values for each iteration that will be used to aggregate and derive conclusions.

Analyzing the impact of context compression – a reduction in classification performance versus an increase in resource efficiency

Here, we sum up the values of the experiments and deduce what impact the prompt compression has on the performance of the LLM, the processing time, and the cost of the API:

- We found that the reduction in the context length had yielded an agreement rate of 92%.
- We found that the process of compression had extended the processing time by 11 times.
- We found that the reduction in the context length saved 92% of the total cost of sent tokens!

Note that cost reduction is negatively dependent on the agreement rate, as we expect an increase in cost savings to reduce the agreement rate.

This reduction is significant and, in some cases, may tilt the scale from a loss-making service to a profitable service.

Here are some notes to keep in mind regarding the meaning of a disagreement and additional trade-offs. Regarding the drop in agreement rate between the two approaches, while an agreement between the two approaches insinuates that they are both correct, a disagreement could go either way. It could be that in the second scenario, the compression distorted the context and, thus, made the model unable to properly classify it. However, the opposite may be true, as the compression may have reduced the irrelevant content and made the LLM focus on the relevant aspects of the content, thus making the scenario with the compressed context yield a correct answer.

Regarding additional trade-offs, the above metrics of LLM performance, processing time, and API cost don't reveal additional considerations such as the computational resources that the compression requires. The local compressing LLM, in our case, Llama2, requires local hosting and local GPUs. These are non-trivial resources that don't exist on an ordinary laptop. Remember the original approach, i.e., the first scenario, does not require those. An ordinary RAG approach can perform embeddings using either a smaller LM, such as one that is BERT-based, or even an API-based embedding. The prompted LLM, under our original assumption, is chosen to be remote and API-based, thus enabling the deployment environment to have minimal computation resources, like a common laptop would provide.

This evaluation proves that the LLMLingua prompt compression method is very impactful and useful as a means of cost reduction.

In the next and last code demonstration of this chapter, we will continue to observe the results of this experience, and we will do so by forming a team of experts, each played by an LLM, so as to enhance the process of deriving a conclusion to the analysis.

Multiple agents – forming a team of LLMs that collaborate

This section deals with one of the most exciting recent methods in the world of LLMs, employing multiple LLMs simultaneously. In the context of this section, we seek to define multiple agents, each backed by an LLM and given a different designated role to play. Instead of the user working directly with the LLM, as we see in ChatGPT, here, the user sets up multiple LLMs and sets their role by defining a different system prompt for each of them.

Potential advantages of multiple LLM agents working simultaneously

Much like with people working together, here too, we see the advantages of employing several LLMs simultaneously.

Some advantages are the following:

- **Enhancing validation and reducing hallucinations**: It has been shown that when providing feedback to an LLM and asking it to reason or to check its response, the reliability of its response improves. When designating roles for the various LLM agents on a team, the system prompt of at least one of them may include the requirement to criticize and validate the answers.

- **Allowing the person to be involved as much or as little as they want in the process**: When designating the various roles, the user may insert themselves into the team, such that when it is the user's turn to participate in the conversation, the rest of the agents wait while the user enters their input. However, if desired, the user may remove themselves altogether and just let the LLMs work automatically.

  In the following examples, we will see examples of the latter.

- **Allowing different LLM models to be best utilized**: Today, we have several leading LLMs available. Some are free and hosted locally, and some are API-based. They are different in their size and capabilities, and some of them are stronger in particular tasks than others. When forming a team of agents where each agent is assigned a different role, a different LLM may be set that best suits that role. For instance, in the context of a coding project, where one of the agents is a programmer of a particular coding language, the user may choose to set the LLM for that agent to be an LLM that is superior for code generation in that particular coding language.

- **Optimizing resources – employing several smaller LLMs**: Imagine a project that involves technical functions and also domain expertise. For example, building a user platform in the medical space. You would want there to be a frontend engineer, a backend engineer, a designer, and a medical expert, all governed by the project manager and the product manager. If you were to develop this platform using the multiple-agents framework, you would define the agents, assign the various roles to them, and pick an LLM to drive them. If you were to use the same LLM for all of the agents, say, OpenAI's most recent GPT, then that model would have to be very generic, thus requiring it to be very large and perhaps very expensive and maybe even slow. However, if you had access to individual LLMs, each pre-trained to only fulfill a limited function, for instance, one LLM dedicated to the medical service domain and a different LLM dedicated to backend development in Python, then you would assign each of those particular LLMs to their corresponding agents.

  That may present a major reduction in model size, as the combined architecture of several specialized LLMs may be smaller in size than the architecture of one generic LLM when assuming equal performance between the two scenarios.

- **Optimizing resources – optimal designation of a single LLM**: A unique and particular case of employing multiple LLMs is that in which we are seeking to optimize the LLM being chosen per the current task. This case is different than all the above, as it does not refer to a case where several LLMs are working simultaneously. In this case, a routing algorithm chooses one LLM based on a current state of constraints and variables. These may include the following:

  - The current load on each of the different parts of the computation system

  - The cost constraints, which may vary over time

  - The source of the prompt, as different clients/regions may have different priorities

  - The purpose of the prompt, as different use cases may be prioritized by the business

  - The prompt's requirements, as a code-generating task, may be obtaining excellent responses with a small and efficient code-generating LLM, whereas a request to review a legal document and to suggest precedents may call for a completely different model

AutoGen

The particular framework we employ in this section is called AutoGen, and it is made available by Microsoft (GitHub repo: `https://github.com/microsoft/autogen/tree/main`).

Figure 9.1 conveys the AutoGen framework. The following was obtained from the statement made in the GitHub repo:

AutoGen is a framework that enables the development of LLM applications using multiple agents that can converse with each other to solve tasks. AutoGen agents are customizable, conversable, and seamlessly allow human participation. They can operate in various modes that employ combinations of LLMs, human inputs, and tools.

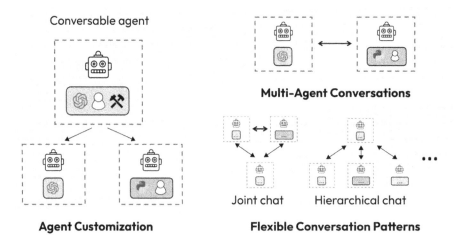

Figure 9.1 – AutoGen functionality

On the left of *Figure 9.1*, we observe the designation of roles and capabilities to individual agents; on the right, we observe a few of the conversation structures that are available.

AutoGen's key capabilities as presented in the code repo:

- AutoGen enables building next-gen LLM applications based on multi-agent conversations with minimal effort. It simplifies the orchestration, automation, and optimization of a complex LLM workflow. It maximizes the performance of LLM models and overcomes their weaknesses.

- It supports diverse conversation patterns for complex workflows. With customizable and conversable agents, developers can use AutoGen to build a wide range of conversation patterns concerning conversation autonomy, the number of agents, and agent conversation topology.

- It provides a collection of working systems with different complexities. These systems span a wide range of applications from various domains and complexities. This demonstrates how AutoGen can easily support diverse conversation patterns.

- AutoGen provides enhanced LLM inference. It offers utilities such as API unification and caching, and advanced usage patterns such as error handling, multi-config inference, context programming, and so on.

AutoGen is powered by collaborative research studies from Microsoft, Penn State University, and the University of Washington.

Next, we can dive into a practical example in the code.

Completing a complex analysis – visualizing the results and forming a conclusion

Here, we will show how a team of multiple agents, each with a different designated role, could serve as a professional team. The use case we chose is a continuation of the previous code we ran. In the last code, we performed a complex evaluation of employing prompt compression, and when that code finished, we had two resulting items: the `dict` that holds the numeric measurements of the experiments, called `record,` and the verbal statements about the resulting agreement rate, the reduction in tokens and cost, and the change in processing time.

With that previous notebook, we intentionally stopped short. We didn't visualize the reduction in tokens and cost, and we didn't form an opinion as to whether we would advocate for employing the prompt reductions. However, in business or academic settings, one would be required to offer both. When you present your findings to stakeholders, decision-makers, or the research community, you are expected, when feasible, to visualize the statistical significance of the experiments. As a subject expert in NLP and ML, you are also expected to provide your recommendation on whether to adopt the experimented method or not.

We will take the results from that evaluation, and we will task a team of agents to do the work for us!

Refer to the following notebook: `Ch9_Completing_a_Complex_Analysis_with_a_Team_of_LLM_Agents.ipynb`. The notebook starts with the common aspects of installs, imports, and settings. You will notice that AutoGen has a particular format of settings in the form of a dictionary. They provide the details, as you can see in our notebook.

Now, we move on to the interesting parts!

Creating a visualization of the significance of the experiments

The `record.pickle file` is of a `dict` variable. It is the collection of numerical results from the previous evaluation notebook. Our wish is to visualize the distributions of the token counts for each of the experiments. There are token counts for original prompts and token counts for compressed prompts. There are also the ratios between the two for each experiment.

In this section, we'll form a team to put code together that would visualize the distributions of each of the three.

Defining the task to be fulfilled by the team

First, we define the task to be fulfilled by the team. We tell the team where the file is saved and the context and the nature of the values in the `dict`, thus giving the team the understanding they need to ideate a solution to the task. Then, we describe the task of creating a plot and visualizing the distributions. All those details are in the one string that describes the task. Note that in an Agile Scrum work setting, this task string is similar to the purpose of the story.

Now that we have formed a comprehensive description, it should be clear what is expected. For instance, we ask for the figures and axes to be labeled, but we don't explicitly state what labels are expected. The agents will understand on their own, just as we would have understood this on our own, as the labels are inferred from the task and the data field names.

Defining the agents and assigning the team members roles

For this task, we would need three team members: a programmer to write the code, a QA engineer to run the code and provide feedback, and a team lead to verify when the task is complete.

For each of the roles, we articulate a system prompt. This system prompt, as we learned in *Chapter 8*, has a significant impact on the LLM's function. Notice that we also provide the QA engineer and the team lead with the ability to run code on their own. In this way, they will be able to verify the programmer's code and provide objective feedback. If we told the same agent to write the code and to confirm that it is correct, we might find that, in practice, it would generate a first draft, wouldn't bother to run and verify it, and it would conclude that task without having verified it.

Defining a group conversation

Here, we define the conversation to be a multi-agent conversation; this is one of the features of AutoGen. This is slightly different from the case where you define a series of conversations where each conversation involves just two agents. The group conversation involves more agents.

When defining a group conversation, we also define a manager for the conversation.

Deploying the team

The team lead tasks the manager with the task we defined. The manager then delegates the work to the programmer and the QA engineer.

Here are the highlights of that automated conversation as it appears on the screen:

```
lead (to manager_0):
Refer to the Python dict that is in this [...]
programmer (to manager_0):
```python
import pandas as pd
import matplotlib.pyplot as plt
# Load the record dict from URL
import requests
import pickle
[...]
qa_engineer (to manager_0):
exitcode: 0 (execution succeeded)
Code output:
Figure(640x480)
programmer (to manager_0):
TERMINATE
```

As can be seen, the conversation had four interactions, each between two agents. Each interaction starts by telling the user which agent is talking to which other agent; these parts are in bold letters in the preceding printout.

In the second interaction, the programmer provided a complete Python script. We pasted only the first four commands to keep it short, but you can observe the full script in the notebook. The QA engineer ran the script and reported that it ran well. If it hadn't run well, it would have returned an exitcode: 1 and would have provided the programmer with the error specification for the programmer to fix the code; the conversation would have continued until a solution was found, or, if not, the team would report failure and conclude the conversation.

This task provided us with the code to create the visual we wanted. Note that we didn't ask the agents to run the code and provide us with the visual; we asked for the code itself. One could, if desired,
```

configure the LLMs to run the code and provide us with the resulting image. See AutoGen's repo for the various examples and capabilities.

In the next code cell, we pasted the code that the team created. The code runs well and visualizes the three distributions exactly as we asked the team (see *Figure 9.2*):

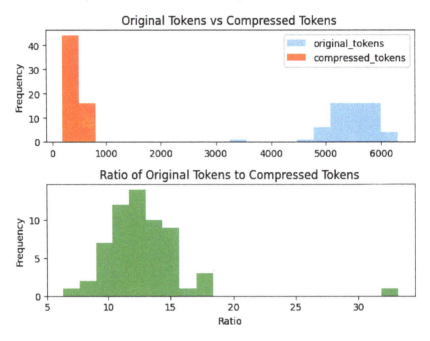

Figure 9.2 – Visualizing the value that prompt compression provides

The top visualization displays the distributions of the token count for the original prompts (blue/light shade) and the compressed prompts (orange/dark shade), and the bottom part of the figure shows the distribution of the ratio between each pair of prompts. *Figure 9.2* shows just how effective the reduction rate is, as this ratio translates to a reduction in API cost.

This concludes the visualization of the significance of the experiments.

Human intervention in the team's tasks

Note that all three agents are driven by LLMs, thus making this entire task automatically performed without human intervention. One could change the lead's configuration to represent a human user, meaning you. If you did that, then you would be able to intervene and demand certain verifications from the QA engineer or certain additional features in the code from the programmer.

This could be particularly useful if you wanted to run the code yourself in your environment instead of letting the QA engineer agent run it in its own environment. Your environments are different. One advantage of doing this is when the code is required to load a data file that you have locally. If you told the agent to write code that loads this file, then when the QA engineer agent ran it, it would tell you the code failed since that data file doesn't exist in its environment. In this case, you may elect to be the one who iterates with the programmer and the one who runs the code during the iterations and provides feedback.

Another case where you would want to be the one running the code and providing feedback is when the QA engineer encounters an error or a bug in the programmer's code, but the two agents aren't able to figure out the solution. In that case, you would want to intervene and provide your insight. For instance, in a case where a for loop iterates over a dict's keys instead of its values, you may intervene and enter *The code runs but the for loop is iterating on the dict's keys. It should iterate over its values for the key 'key1*.

We can now move on to the second part of concluding the evaluation.

Reviewing the results of the experiments and forming an educated conclusion

As with every complex evaluation where we perform experiments to target the impact of a particular feature, we would now like to derive a qualitative summary of the results and suggest a conclusion for our audience, whether it is the decision-makers in the company or the research community in academia.

What is unique about this part is that the act of deriving a conclusion has never been left to any mathematical or algorithmic model to derive. As we humans govern the various evaluations, and although we may seek to automate as much as possible to feed into the final conclusion, we are the entity that forms the final impression and conclusion.

Here, we attempt to automate that final part. We will assign a team of expert agents to provide an educated summary of the results that the evaluation notebook printed out. We'll then push the team to provide us with a recommendation as to whether we should implement the new feature of prompt compression or not. We provide the team with the actual results of the evaluation notebook, but in order to examine its reliability, we then task it again, this time providing it with mocked results that are much poorer, hoping that the team will apply judgment and provide a different recommendation. All of this is done without any human intervention.

As we did before, we start by defining the task for our team to fulfill.

Defining the task to be fulfilled by the team

Our aim is to provide the team with the printout of the evaluation notebook from the previous section. That printout describes, in words, the change in agreement rate, the impact on the number of prompt tokens, and the processing runtime, all due to employing the LLMLingua prompt compression method.

We then copy that from the previous notebook and paste it as a text string.

Note that we have also created another text string of results (which are mocked results that are much worse than the true results), but we see that the agreement rate is very low, and the reduction in token count due to compression is much less significant.

As we did in the visualization case, we then create the instructions for the team; we paste the results into the task description for the team to refer to when deriving its conclusion. We have two task descriptions, as we will have two separate runs, one with the true results and one with the mocked bad results.

We will now allocate the roles.

Defining the agents and assigning team members roles

For this task, we would need three team members: a principal engineer who is an experienced technical person, a technical writer who writes the conclusion as per the principal engineer's feedback, and a team lead to verify when the task is complete, which was defined in the previous task.

Defining a group conversation

Here, we define the group conversation, just like we did in the visualization part. This time, we have a new group conversation manager, as the group consists of different agents.

Deploying the team

The team lead tasks the manager with the task we defined. The manager then delegates the work to the writer and the principal engineer.

Here are the highlights of that automated conversation as it appears on the screen:

```
lead (to manager_1):
Refer to the results printed below.
These are the results that stem from [...]
writer (to manager_1):
The experiments on prompt compression using LLMLingua have produced
the following results:
- Classification Performance:
  - Agreement rate of [...]
principal_engineer (to manager_1):
[...]
```

The agents have a few iterations between them and come to an agreement regarding the summary and the conclusion.

They provide a summary of the numeric results and seal it with the following recommendation:

```
It is imperative to carefully consider the trade-offs presented by
prompt compression, as while it may lead to resource savings, there
might be implications on processing efficiency. The decision to adopt
prompt compression should be made with a thorough understanding of
these trade-offs.
```

The team agrees on a cautious approach to presenting the various trade-offs and avoids making a decision in spite of being tasked to do so.

One would wonder, could a definite decision to adopt or not to adopt the method be made here?

Evaluation of the team's judgment

Now, we will ask the team to perform the same action, this time providing it with the mocked results that make the compression method seem much less effective and with a great reduction in agreement with the classification of the noncompressed method.

The team has a conversation, and the final agreement summary is sealed with the following statement:

```
Overall, the results indicate that while prompt compression may lead
to cost savings and resource reduction, it comes at the expense of
decreased classification performance and significantly increased
processing times.
**Recommendation:** Prompt compression using LLMLinguam is **not
recommended** as it can negatively impact classification performance
and significantly increase processing times, outweighing the potential
cost savings.
```

Here, the team found it much easier to draw a definite conclusion. It did so without any human intervention and solely based on the numerical results it was given.

Concluding thoughts on the multiple-agent team

This emerging method of simultaneously employing several LLMs is gaining interest and traction in the world of AI. In the code experiments that we present in this section, it was proven without a doubt that AutoGen's group conversation can provide tangible and actionable value in the professional setting. Although setting these code experiments required a series of trials and errors for properly setting the agent roles and properly describing the tasks, it suggests that this framework is moving in a direction where less human intervention is required. What seems to remain a monumental component is the human oversight, feedback, and evaluation of the resulting relics of those agent teams' *work*. We would like to stress to the reader that of the various application and innovations that we share in this book, we have marked the multiple-agent framework as the one that is most likely to grow and to also become the most popular. This is based on the overwhelming expectations that industries have from AI to automate and demonstrate human-like expertise, while innovations such as Autogen, and later Autodev, both by Microsoft, are exemplifying growing feasibility and competency.

Summary

Throughout this pivotal chapter, we have embarked on an in-depth exploration of the most recent and groundbreaking applications of LLMs, presented through comprehensive Python code examples. We began by unlocking advanced functionalities by using the RAG framework and LangChain, enhancing LLM performance for domain-specific tasks. The journey continued with advanced methods in chains for sophisticated formatting and processing, followed by the automation of information retrieval from diverse web sources. We also tackled the optimization of prompt engineering through prompt compression techniques, significantly reducing API costs. Finally, we ventured into the collaborative potential of LLMs by forming a team of models that work in concert to solve complex problems.

By mastering these topics, you have now acquired a robust set of skills, enabling you to harness the power of LLMs for a variety of applications. These newfound abilities not only prepare you to tackle current challenges in NLP but also equip you with the insights to innovate and push the boundaries of what's possible in the field. The practical knowledge gained from this chapter will empower you to apply advanced LLM techniques to real-world issues, opening up new opportunities for efficiency, creativity, and problem-solving.

As we turn the page, the next chapter will take us into the realm of emerging trends in AI and LLM technology. We will delve into the latest algorithmic developments, assess their impact on various business sectors, and consider the future landscape of AI. This forthcoming discussion promises to provide you with a comprehensive understanding of where the field is headed and how you can stay at the forefront of technological innovation.

10

Riding the Wave: Analyzing Past, Present, and Future Trends Shaped by LLMs and AI

Natural language processing (**NLP**) and **large language models** (**LLMs**) stand at the intersection of linguistics and artificial intelligence, serving as milestones in our understanding of human-computer interactions. Their story begins with basic rule-based systems, which, while innovative for their time, often stumbled due to the complex nuances and immensity of human language. The limitations of these systems highlighted the need for a shift, paving the way for the **machine learning** (**ML**) era, where data and pattern recognition prescribe the design and the models.

In this chapter, we will review key trends that have been emerging in NLP and LLMs, some of which are broad enough to capture the direction of AI as a whole. We will discuss those trends from a qualitative perspective as we aim to highlight their purpose, value, and impact. In the next sections, we'll share our thoughts on what the future might look like. We hope to spark your curiosity and inspire you to explore these emerging paths with us.

Let's go through the main topics covered in the chapter:

- Key technical trends around LLMs and AI
- Computation power – the engine behind LLMs
- Large datasets and their indelible mark on NLP and LLMs
- Evolution of large language models – purpose, value, and impact
- Cultural trends in NLP and LLMs
- NLP and LLMs in the business world
- Behavioral trends induced by AI and LLMs – the social aspect

Let's dive into the many trends we are seeing, starting with the technical ones.

Key technical trends around LLMs and AI

In this section, we cover what we identify as key trends in the field of NLP and LLMs.

We will start with the technical trends, and later, we will touch on the softer cultural trends.

Computation power – the engine behind LLMs

As technology has advanced, especially in computing, many areas in tech have thrived, particularly NLP and LLMs. It's not just about faster calculations and bigger parameter space; it's about new possibilities and reshaping our digital world. In this section, we'll explore how this growth in computing has been foundational for NLP and LLMs today, focusing on their purpose, worth, and influence.

Purpose – paving the way for progress

In the initial days of AI and ML, the models were rudimentary—not due to a lack of imagination or intent, but because of restrictive computational boundaries. Tasks that we now consider basic, such as simple pattern recognitions, were significant undertakings, as they demanded great algorithmic sophistication to allow for low complexity. In computer science classes, we were taught that an algorithm with complexity beyond linear has poor sustainability and impractical scalability.

As computational power grew, so did the ambition of researchers. No longer were they confined to toy problems or theoretical settings. The computational evolution meant they could now design and test models of considerable complexity and depth, which we now view as a prerequisite for advanced NLP and LLMs.

The emergence of parallel processing and the development of **graphics processing units** (**GPUs**) marked a fundamental shift. Due to being designed to handle multiple operations simultaneously, it was as if these innovations were tailor-made for the demands of NLP, allowing for the training of extensive computation tasks such as neural networks and facilitating real-time processing.

Value – amplifying potential and efficiency

Computation power didn't just improve what was possible; it transformed what was practical. Training large models became economically feasible, ensuring that research institutions and companies could experiment, iterate, and refine their models without prohibitive costs.

The digital age has introduced an overflow of data. Efficiently processing, parsing, and gleaning insights from this ocean of information became viable primarily due to exponential growth in computation power. This has been instrumental in LLMs' ability to self-train on extensive datasets, extracting nuanced linguistic patterns and treating them as signals for downstream tasks such as prediction and assistance.

Today's users are becoming accustomed to a growing processing speed and they demand instant interaction. Whether it's a digital assistant offering suggestions or an AI-driven customer service platform, real-time responses are a standard. Enhanced computational capacities have ensured that complex NLP tasks, which would have taken minutes, if not hours, in the past, are now completed within seconds on end devices.

Impact – reshaping digital interactions and insights

The improvements in computational power have seen AI-driven interfaces become the norm. From chatbots on websites to voice-activated home assistants, NLP and LLMs, supercharged by advanced processing capabilities, have become a part of daily life.

The domains of art, literature, and entertainment have seen AI's ingress, with tools such as AI-driven content creators and music generators becoming possible due to the close relationship between NLP/LLMs and computational strength.

With the computational means to process diverse linguistic data, NLP models now offer multilingual support, breaking down language barriers and fostering global digital inclusivity. During 2023, we witnessed a major milestone when Meta released SeamlessM4T, a multi-lingual LLM that is a single model that performs speech-to-text, speech-to-speech, text-to-speech, and text-to-text translations for up to 100 languages; you can read more about this here: `https://about.fb.com/news/2023/08/seamlessm4t-ai-translation-model/#:~:text=SeamlessM4T%20is%20the%20first%20all,languages%20depending%20on%20the%20task`.

To conclude, this story of computational power and its relationship with NLP and LLMs is one of mutual growth and evolution. It's a tale that underscores the bond between hardware advancements and software innovations. As we look onward, with quantum computing and neuromorphic chips suggesting the next frontier of computational leaps, one can only imagine the further revolutions in store for NLP and LLMs. The purpose, value, and impact of computational progress that we are witnessing are a testament to its role as the cornerstone of the AI-driven linguistic revolution.

Now, let's see where things are headed.

The future of computational power in NLP

We identify several advancements that will take place and push computation power that will be leveraged by AI and, in particular, NLP.

Exponential increase in speed

Moore's law has traditionally held that the number of transistors on a microchip doubles approximately every two years. Although there's speculation about its sustainability in the traditional sense, it provides a useful guide for estimating the growth in computational capability. Advancements in chip architecture, such as 3D stacking and innovative transistor designs, might help sustain or even accelerate this growth.

The need for real-time NLP applications, from translation services to voice assistants, will continue to drive demand for faster computational speeds. We are witnessing a new trend of AI-dedicated hardware. Google released the Tensor Processing Unit in 2015 (`https://spectrum.ieee.org/google-details-tensor-chip-powers`), and since then, we have seen several more such dedicated pieces of hardware by either big players, such as Meta and Nvidia, or by small emerging startups.

Economies of scale and cost-efficiency

As AI and NLP become more abundant, there's a significant incentive for tech giants and startups alike to invest in more efficient, scalable, and cost-effective computational infrastructure.

The transition to cloud computing has already made vast computational resources accessible to even small startups. This trend is likely to continue, with costs per computation expected to decrease, making NLP applications more accessible and affordable.

Quantum computing – the next frontier

Quantum computing represents a paradigm shift in the way we understand and harness computational power. Quantum bits, or qubits, can represent both 0s and 1s simultaneously through the phenomenon of superposition, potentially offering exponential speedups for specific problems.

Although quantum computing is in its growing stages, its potential implications for NLP are profound. Training complex models, which currently takes days or weeks, could be reduced to hours or even minutes.

Google has established itself as a significant spearheader in the world of quantum computing (The following quote is taken from here: `https://quantumai.google/learn/map`):

Beginning with around 100 physical qubits, we can study different approaches to building logical qubits. A logical qubit allows us to store quantum data, without errors, long enough that we can use them for complex calculations. After that, we'll reach quantum computing's transistor moment: the moment that we demonstrate that the technology is ready to be scaled and commercialized.

Google drafted a roadmap of milestones that laid out the future forecasts of key achievements. See *Figure 10.1*. It should be noted that Google has been adhering to it, which, for such an ambitious research field, is astonishing:

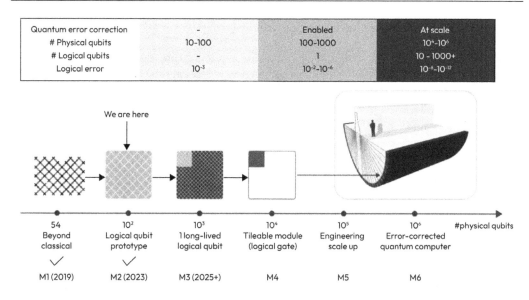

Quantum error correction	-		Enabled		At scale	
# Physical qubits	10-100		100-1000		10^4-10^6	
# Logical qubits	-		1		10 - 1000+	
Logical error	10^{-3}		10^{-2}-10^{-6}		10^{-6}-10^{-12}	

54	10^2	10^3	10^4	10^5	10^6	#physical qubits
Beyond classical	Logical qubit prototype	1 long-lived logical qubit	Tileable module (logical gate)	Engineering scale up	Error-corrected quantum computer	
✓	✓					
M1 (2019)	M2 (2023)	M3 (2025+)	M4	M5	M6	

Figure 10.1 – Key milestones for building an error-corrected quantum computer

Cryptography, a key component in secure data transmission that is essential for cloud-based NLP services, will also undergo massive changes, given quantum computing's potential to break several existing encryption methods. Thus, the rise of quantum-safe cryptographic methods will be vital.

Energy efficiency and sustainability

As the demand for computational power grows, so does the energy consumption of data centers. There will be a dual drive towards more energy-efficient computation and sustainable energy sources for powering these computational efforts.

In the context of NLP, this might mean more efficient model architectures that require less energy to train and run, alongside hardware innovations that maximize operations per watt.

Specialized hardware for NLP

We've already seen the rise of specialized **tensor processing units** (**TPUs**) for DL. Going forward, there might be hardware specifically optimized for NLP tasks, ensuring faster and more efficient language model operations.

Neuromorphic computing, which attempts to mimic the human brain's architecture, may offer unique advantages for tasks such as NLP, which require a blend of logic and intuition. Davies et al. review some of the key opportunities in their publication "*Advancing Neuromorphic Computing With Loihi: A Survey of Results and Outlook.*"

Democratization of high-end computation

With advancements in edge computing and the abundance of powerful processors in everyday devices, high-end NLP tasks might not always require a connection to a centralized data center. Potentially, advanced NLP capabilities could become standard in smartphones, smart home devices, and even smartwatches. You will have an LLM available on your personal device, running locally and responding immediately in the same way as your calculator.

Cloud computing – the catalyst for NLP and LLMs evolution

Cloud platforms offer unprecedented flexibility in terms of computational resources, making it easier to train larger and more sophisticated NLP models.

Platforms such as AWS's SageMaker, Microsoft's Azure Machine Learning Studio, and Google's Vertex AI have fostered a spirit of collaboration, giving researchers and developers tools to share models, datasets, and tools seamlessly.

The combination of local, edge, and cloud computation ensures that NLP tasks are handled efficiently, balancing both latency and computational power.

Cloud platforms are evolving to make high-end computational power more accessible, with pricing models that reflect actual usage and offer temporary high-powered computational access at reduced costs.

To conclude our view on the future of computational power, as it relates to NLP, it is clearly on an upward trajectory. While challenges remain, especially in the realms of energy consumption and the potential roadblocks in traditional chip scaling, innovations such as quantum computing promise to open doors to capabilities that will definitely get their own share of dedicated books.

The future of computation power, which is the engine that NLP runs on, is looking bright, so let's discuss another instrumental component: data.

Large datasets and their indelible mark on NLP and LLMs

The era of big data and the subsequent rise of NLP and LLMs are deeply linked. The transformation of NLP and LLMs into today's powerful developments cannot be discussed without mentioning the vast datasets that became available. Let's explore this relationship.

Purpose – training, benchmarking, and domain expertise

At its core, the emergence of large datasets has provided the raw material required to train increasingly sophisticated models. Typically, the larger the dataset, the more comprehensive and diverse the information the model can learn from.

Large datasets not only serve as training grounds but also provide benchmarks for evaluating model performance. This has led to standardized measures, giving researchers clear targets and allowing for apples-to-apples comparisons between models. There is a collection of benchmarks that are common and can be used for evaluating LLMs. One famous and very comprehensive benchmark was created by Google, the Beyond the Imitation Game benchmark (BIG-bench). It is a benchmark designed to evaluate responses from LLMs and infer their future capabilities. It encapsulates over 200 tasks, such as reading comprehension, summarization, logical reasoning, and even social reasoning.

Large datasets covering specific domains, such as healthcare or legal texts, pave the way for specialized models that can understand and operate within niche areas with high precision. For example, BERT was developed by Google and was later made available freely by Hugging Face. BERT's design employs transfer learning; thus, it lends very well to customizing and creating a new version of the model that is dedicated to a particular domain. Some of the most successful versions are BERT-base-japanese, which was pre-trained on Japanese data; BERTweet, which was pre-trained on English tweets; and FinBERT, which was pre-trained on financial data.

Value – robustness, diversity, and efficiency

With more data, models can capture more nuances and subtleties of human language. This wealth of information results in models that can generalize better to a variety of tasks.

The availability of vast and varied datasets ensures that models are trained on a diverse range of languages, dialects, and cultural contexts. This has pushed NLP towards being more inclusive, recognizing and responding to a wider audience.

Large datasets negate the need for extensive manual labeling to some extent. Unsupervised and self-supervised learning models, which were covered earlier in the book, capitalize on this abundance, saving both time and money.

Impact – democratization, proficiency, and new concerns

With open access to large datasets, many barriers to entry in the NLP research field have been lowered. This has led to a democratization of NLP, with more individuals and organizations being able to innovate.

LLMs such as GPT-3 and BERT owe their proficiency to the extensive data they were trained on. These models, considered state-of-the-art, have set new benchmarks in various NLP tasks, all thanks to the rich datasets they were trained on.

As NLP was mainly a research field for so many years, some legal aspects that apply to the commercial domain weren't applicable. However, as the vast usage and commercialization of these models have emerged, the large datasets that they reflect carry dire concerns. These datasets, which are often scraped from the web, have brought up ethical questions around privacy, data ownership, and potential biases. This caused regulators to work on guidelines regarding how to ethically source and use data. For example, as of the writing of this book, we have noticed several different actions by different nations. Japan has been quick to adopt a very liberal policy for allowing models to be trained on data available online, while the European Union has been demonstrating a more restrictive approach. The USA's official guidelines seem to avoid addressing the copyright debate.

We can now articulate some future projections for data and its role in developing LLMs.

The future of data availability in NLP

In the future, we will see how data continues to grow while the various aspects and challenges are addressed. Here are the pivotal points.

Domain expertise and specialization

As LLMs are proving themselves capable and favorable, an emphasis is being put on making them proficient. One of the several ways that we can enhance an LLM to become proficient is by providing it with a dataset that captures the particular domain that it is meant to serve and utilizing the LLM as an expert in that particular domain. In the future, we anticipate the cultivation of more niche, domain-specific datasets. Whether it's healthcare, law, finance, or any specialized field, the emphasis will be on data richness and specificity, enabling models to achieve unparalleled domain expertise. Since the emergence and growing popularity of LLMs, we have seen several such business cases of customizing LLMs to serve a particular business domain, with healthcare and finance gaining a lot of attention.

Conversely, as different domains overlap, integrated datasets emerge. These are datasets combining expertise from multiple fields. For instance, a dataset may intertwine law and AI ethics in an attempt to suggest novel insights promoting regulations around AI. Another example is linking computer code and stock trading for the sake of forming an algorithmic trading scheme.

A strive for diversity

As technology expands its reach, datasets will increasingly encompass lesser-known languages and regional dialects. This will allow NLP to cater to a broader global audience, making digital communication more inclusive. Meta's SeamlessM4T, which we discussed earlier in this chapter, is a terrific example of being able to converse across languages via LLM.

Beyond just language, there is also the cultural aspect to a language, such as jargon or the mere choice of words. Capturing the cultural nuances and context will become paramount in future text generation. This will lead to more culturally conscious and context-aware models.

Battling bias

In recognizing the implicit biases present in our digital content, there will be a surge in tools and methodologies to audit datasets for biases. The community will strive for datasets that are both large and fair. Instead of blindly scraping the web, more effort will go into curating data, ensuring it's representative and free from evident prejudices. This might include actively seeking underrepresented voices or filtering out potentially harmful biases.

Regulatory landscapes

With growing concerns about data privacy, especially in the European Union with GDPR and in California with CCPA, we can expect stricter guidelines on how datasets can be collected and utilized.

Beyond privacy, there will be a push for more ethical ways to gather data. This means ensuring data are collected without exploitation, with proper consent, and with respect to the rights of individuals and communities.

In the spirit of reproducible research, there might be a drive towards making datasets, especially those used for benchmarking and major models, more transparent and open. This would have to be balanced, of course, with privacy concerns.

Augmented datasets

In a digital landscape, where creating genuinely new and unique data is an extraordinary task, augmented datasets present an alternative solution. By artificially expanding and modifying existing datasets, augmentation can swiftly cater to the growing hunger for diverse data without the exhaustive process of fresh data collection. Augmented datasets help to tackle these four challenges with datasets:

- **Enhancing domain expertise**: While niche datasets cater to domain specificity, their size can often be restrictive. Augmented datasets can bridge this gap, artificially expanding domain-specific datasets, thereby offering both depth and breadth. For instance, rare medical conditions that may have limited real-world data can be augmented to train robust models.

- **Diversity amplification**: The struggle to capture the myriad nuances of global languages and cultures can be significantly alleviated by augmentation. Techniques such as back-translation or synonym replacement can introduce linguistic diversity, and context-based modifications can simulate cultural nuances, thus driving models toward true global comprehension.

- **Bias rectification**: One of the groundbreaking applications of data augmentation lies in its potential to balance out biases. By recognizing underrepresented voices or themes in a dataset, augmentation can artificially boost them, ensuring a more balanced representation. Techniques such as adversarial training, where models are deliberately presented with challenging or contradictory data, can be employed to iron out biases.

- **Regulatory compliance**: In a world tightening its data regulatory strings, augmented datasets offer a valuable advantage. Moreover, techniques can be designed to ensure that augmented data adheres to privacy norms, thus giving models ample training data without trespassing regulatory boundaries. For instance, think about our healthcare code example, where we implemented an in-house search engine that finds medical records based on a physician's query. In order to provide it with a database, we generated mocked medical records by prompting ChatGPT.

Nonetheless, while augmented datasets offer innovative solutions to many data-related challenges, they aren't without shortcomings. In principle, over-reliance on augmentation can lead to models that are adept at recognizing artificial patterns but fail with real-world variability. There's also the risk of inadvertently amplifying biases if the original datasets had unaccounted skews. Furthermore, not all augmentation techniques are universally applicable; what works for one dataset might distort another. Lastly, there's the ethical debate around creating synthetic data, especially in sensitive fields, where the distinction between real and augmented could blur essential truths.

To conclude our coverage of data in the context of NLP and AI, we observe how the availability of large datasets has revolutionized the domain of NLP and the development of LLMs. They've provided the foundation upon which the magnificent establishment of modern NLP stands, shaping its purpose, magnifying its value, and leaving a lasting impact on research, applications, and society at large.

On the horizon, as large datasets continue to shape the world of NLP, we are looking at a future that's not just data-rich but also ethically conscious, domain-specific, and globally inclusive. These trends, sourced from the collective wisdom of current web articles and publications, paint a promising picture of NLP's data-driven journey ahead.

Now that we have discussed the computation power that drives the creation of the algorithms, and the data, which guides the LLMs' intelligence, we can consider the LLMs themselves.

Evolution of large language models – purpose, value, and impact

The rise and development of LLMs stand as a testament to our relentless pursuit of more advanced algorithms. These giant computational linguistics models have come a long way from their initial incarnations, growing not only in size but also in capabilities. As we delve into the purpose, value, and impact of these formidable tools, it becomes clear that their evolution is closely intertwined with our aspiration to harness the true potential of machine-driven communication and cognition.

Purpose – why the push for bigger and better LLMs?

The rationale behind the development of LLMs revolves around the quest to bridge the gap between human and machine communication, where human language is to be fed into a machine for downstream processing. As the digital age began, the need for fluid, context-aware, and intelligent systems that could grasp human language with nuanced understanding became apparent. As was covered extensively in prior chapters, DL represents the foundation of LLMs. As computational capabilities expanded, DL models grew in depth and complexity, leading to enhanced performance in various tasks, especially NLP.

The traditional training of DL models relies on supervised learning that requires labeled data, which, in turn, is both resource-intensive and limiting. The emergence of self-supervised learning and methods such as **reinforcement learning from human feedback** (**RLHF**) broadened horizons. These methods not only minimized the need for explicit labeling but also opened doors for models to learn more organically, mirroring human learning processes.

Early NLP models could answer questions or perform tasks with a narrow focus. The evolution in LLMs brought a paradigm shift where models began exhibiting reasoning abilities, following a chain of thought, and producing coherent, longer responses. This was a significant step towards replicating human-like conversation. The generic approach of earlier models had its limitations. As the technology matured, the ability to tailor LLMs to specific tasks emerged. Techniques such as setting up retrieval datasets or fine-tuning pre-trained models allowed businesses and researchers to mold generic LLMs into specialized tools, enhancing both accuracy and utility.

Value – the LLM advantage

LLMs, with their evolution, brought forth unprecedented value in multiple domains. They become more accurate, efficient, adaptable, and customizable.

Larger models demonstrated an intrinsic ability to grasp context, reducing errors in interpretation and output. This accuracy translated to efficiency in various applications such as chatbots and content creation. They adapt by leveraging brilliant techniques such as RLHF, which enables them to learn from interactions and feedback, making them more resilient and dynamic over time. By being customizable, LLMs could cater to niche industries and tasks, making them invaluable assets across diverse sectors.

Another value that we can see growing is the ability to break language barriers, as the models understand and generate multiple languages, tapping into the global aspiration of universal communication.

Impact – changing the landscape

The rise and evolution of LLMs have left a permanent mark on the tech landscape and human interaction with machines. From healthcare and finance to entertainment and education, LLMs are revolutionizing operations, customer interactions, and data analyses. Interestingly, as these models become more complex, their use becomes less challenging. Tech acumen is becoming a much lower requirement, as with more intuitive and natural language interfaces, a broader demographic, irrespective of their technical know-how, can now harness the power of advanced computational tools.

These elements of impact are a part of an onset of cohesive digital ecosystems. As LLMs integrate across platforms and services, we're witnessing the creation of more organized and synchronized digital ecosystems that offer seamless user experiences.

It is exciting to think about where things are headed next with LLMs.

The future of LLM design

The rapid evolution of LLMs promises a future teeming with innovations. Drawing from current research trends, online publications, and expert predictions, we can forecast several directions in which LLM design might be headed.

Refinement in learning schemes and deep learning architectures

As we've seen, self-supervised learning and RLHF have changed the game for LLMs. The next frontier could involve combining various learning paradigms or introducing newer ones. With the advancement of DL techniques, we might see more hybrid models that integrate the best attributes of different architectures to improve performance, generalization, and efficiency.

An example of employing several LLMs simultaneously was articulated by Palantir's CTO, Shyam Sankar, as he described their K-LLMs approach. He assimilated LLMs to experts and asked why a single expert would be used to answer a question when a committee could be put together to all pitch in to answer that question? He suggested using an ensemble of different LLMs, each perhaps with complementing strengths, so as to be able to synthesize an answer that is more carefullly considered. It should be stressed that in this idea, each LLM is tasked with the same task. This doesn't have to be the case, and in the next approach, we will discuss the opposite. See the full video here: `https://youtu.be/4aKN5mCPF5A?si=kThpx8hOok1i0QWC&t=327`.

Another approach to assimilating a team of experts is by simulating a professional team. Here, there are designated roles assigned to the LLM. The task is then addressed by each of the designated roles in turn. Each role addresses both the task but also the relic of the work that was done by other roles before it. This way, there is an iterative approach to building out a thoughtful solution to a complex problem. We have seen this fascinating process in our example from *Chapter 9*, where we leveraged Microsoft's Autogen.

The emergence of prompt engineering

Prompting LLMs effectively has become a subtle art and science known as **prompt engineering**. As models grow, manually crafting every query might become infeasible. The future could see automated or semi-automated methods to generate prompts, ensuring consistent and desired outputs. The push would be towards making LLMs more user-friendly, minimizing the need for specialized knowledge to interact with them effectively.

In *Chapter 8*, we covered some of the key aspects of prompt engineering. We explained how a technical feature, such as a system prompt, can be leveraged with OpenAI's GPT models. What's interesting is that there are non-technical aspects to prompt engineering that are just as valuable to achieving optimal LLM results. When we say non-technical, we mean aspects such as a coherent description of the request within the prompt, just as we would provide to a human who would seek to help us.

We are expecting to see further subtle techniques in prompting, as seen with prompt chains and soft prompting. Prompt chains are prompt iterations where a complex task is broken into small tasks and each is reflected in a small prompt. This allows for greater adherence, correctness, and monitoring. Soft prompting is an algorithmic technique that seeks to fine-tune the vectors representing the prompt.

One such fascinating example is *Large Language Models as Optimizers* by C. Yang et. al.; see the publication on **Arxiv**: `https://arxiv.org/abs/2309.03409`. They found that encouraging the LLM to put emphasis on the thoughtfulness it gives to the solution yielded better performance.

That may sound surprising if we assume that the LLM has just a single inherited process to solve every particular problem. For example, if we were to ask it to solve an equation, one could assume the LLM would employ one particular mathematical technique, but what about a complex question that requires being broken down into a series of step-wise tasks where neither the structure of the series is trivial, nor the solution methods for each of the tasks? By ordering the LLM to focus on optimizing not just the outcome but also the derivation, this process improves the outcome. This is done by adding a request such as the following:

- "Let's think carefully about the problem and solve it together."

- "Let's calculate our way to the solution!"

- "Let's work through this problem step - by - step."

These were all taken from the publication. The one that stood out the most was this:

- "Take a deep breath and work on this problem step - by - step."

Their research suggests that while an LLM clearly doesn't take breaths, it understands this addition to the prompt as an emphasis on the importance of the derivation process.

Retrieval-augmented generative models – RAGs

We take this opportunity to discuss, again, the significant new paradigm in the world of NLP that we expect will continue to emerge greatly in the next year: RAGs.

As we witness, generative AI driven by LLMs is proficient at producing detailed and easy-to-understand textual responses based on extensive training over vast corpora of data. However, these responses are limited to the AI's training data. If the LLM's data is outdated or lacks specific details about a topic, it may not produce accurate or relevant answers.

Revisiting RAG

Retrieval-augmented generation, also known as **RAG**, enhances the LLM's capabilities by integrating targeted, current, and perhaps even dynamic information without altering the LLMs. This method was introduced in a 2020 paper by P. Lewis et al. called *Retrieval-Augmented Generation for Knowledge-Intensive NLP Tasks*, see on *Arxiv*: `https://arxiv.org/abs/2005.11401`.

In *Chapters 8* and *9*, we studied RAGs from a practical standpoint, equipping readers with the necessary tools and knowledge for hands-on experimentation and implementation. As we revisit RAGs, our focus shifts towards examining their significance within the broader narrative of NLP and LLM development. This discussion is framed within a qualitative, conceptual context that explores the evolving trends and future directions of algorithmic advancements. Our aim is to contextualize RAGs not just as a technological tool but as a pivotal component in the ongoing evolution of LLMs, highlighting their role in shaping the next generation of AI solutions. This exploration seeks to bridge the technical with the theoretical, offering insights into how RAGs contribute to and are influenced by the dynamic landscape of AI research and application.

For intuition, think about the following example. Let's take some programming language; it could be either Python, R, C++ or any other general-purpose language. It comes with its inherited "knowledge," which is the built-in libraries and functions. If you build code to perform basic math or form a sorted list, you'll find that the current state of the programming language suits you, as it has built-in code libraries with all the functions you require. However, how about when you are looking to perform some action that is extremely different from the common set of libraries and their functions? For instance, translate a foreign language to English, calculate a Fourier transform, or perform image classification. One could, hypothetically, seek to develop a whole new dedicated programming language for which the intrinsic set of built-in libraries includes all the functionality that they require. Conversely, one might simply build a dedicated library and import it into their programming language's environment. In this way, your code simply retrieves the necessary functions. Clearly, that is the way general-purpose programming languages work, which is the easiest and most scalable solution of the two. That is what RAGs seek to achieve in the context of LLMs. The LLM is analogous to the programming language, and the retrieval of the information from an external data source is analogous to importing a dedicated library.

Let's observe *Figure 10.2* as we review RAGs a little more.

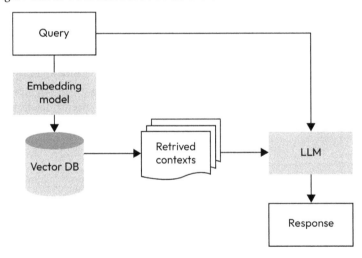

Figure 10.2 – A flow diagram of a typical RAG

How RAGs work

The following are the pillars for RAG functionality:

- **Data integration**: Organizations possess various data types, including databases, files, and internal and external communication feeds. A RAG will compile this data into a unified format, creating a knowledge library.

- **Data transformation**: By using an embedding LM/LLM, the knowledge library's data is converted into numerical vectors stored in a vector database for swift retrieval.

- **User interaction**: When a user poses a question, the query gets transformed into a vector. This vector is used to identify the relevant information from the database based on metric proximity in the embeddings' vector space. This information is retrieved and combined with the LLM's knowledge to craft a comprehensive response.

This mechanism may seem familiar to you. We implemented this paradigm in *Chapters 8* and *9* when we introduced LangChain's capabilities and designed pipelines that retrieve text from an external file.

Let's get some more perspective on RAGs by reviewing their strengths and weaknesses.

Advantages of RAGs

Let's go through the advantages of RAGs in the following list:

- As we emphasized, RAGs offer data that are **more contextual** than a generalized LLM.

- RAGs can provide access to data that is **newer** than what's intrinsically available in an LLM through its training.

- RAGs enable **continuous updates** to the knowledge repository without hefty costs. Not only can new data be leveraged by a RAG, but it can be frequently altered.

- As the user controls the data that the LLM has access to, one can develop schema that are dedicated to **monitoring the correctness of the results**. This then reduces hallucinations and mistakes, which are two of the key shortcomings for LLMs, thus making RAGs a potential solution.

- RAGs are very **simple and easy to spin up**. One could put together a RAG for free using public code and using as little storage as you might have on your laptop. Conceptually, in its basic form, an RAG is a set of connections between the pre-existing computation and data resources.

Challenges of RAGs

With RAGs being a new technology that is built on LLMs, which is another new technology, this presents various challenges.

One such challenge is the choice of the structure design of retrieved data, which is significant to the functionality of the RAG. It is common practice to process the raw data ahead of time, in bulk, so that when the LLM is used, the data are already in a format that lends itself to the retrieval process. As such, this offline process has a complexity of $O(1)$ when measured as a function of the number of retrievals or prompts. Vector databases are emerging as the go-to design for this purpose. They are numerical databases that aim to capture a minimal representation of the data in a format that is similar and sometimes identical to the format that the LLM employs when it processes a prompt. This format is the embeddings that we have covered throughout the book. It should be added that embeddings are a form of a lossy compression mechanism. While the embedding space is optimized for a predefined purpose, it isn't perfect in two senses. First, it optimizes a particular loss function that may suit one purpose more than another, and second, it does so while trading off other aspects, such as storage and run time. We are seeing a trend within the embedding space where the dimensionality—the size of the embedding vector—is growing higher. A higher dimensionality accommodates a broader context per vector, thus opening the door for better retrieval mechanisms that, in turn, accommodate domains that require deep and complex insights, such as the legal space or journalism.

Another downside is the fact that in order to accommodate for the added information that the external data source is providing, the prompt that is sent to the LLM needs to grow in size. Now, the prompt isn't expected to host the entire database's text. A preliminary mechanism is first applied to narrow down the text that might be relevant, as we have seen in our code example in the healthcare space. Still, a cutoff must be applied to the amount of data that is sent within the prompt, thus trading off the amount of context the LLM has to refer to.

Applications of RAGs

The immediate use cases of RAGs are related to having an engine that is dedicated to a narrow need. Some examples can be seen in the following:

- **Costumer service chatbot**: These appeal to companies that they seek to cater to their customers.

- **Company knowledge base**: This serves as an internal service for the company's employees. A typical company manages several different internal engines, each dedicated to a particular need. For instance, an internal website, a payroll app, a service request app, a frontend data explorer (often several), a training service, a legal and compliance source, and so on. A RAG could consolidate the variety of information as a backend of a company chatbot. The employees could prompt it for one of the various needs they have. Here are some examples:

  - "What is the policy for paid time off for full-time employees?"

  - "Which SQL table maps between client name and a unique client identifier, and who provides access to this table?"

- **Domain-specific LLM**: This could be designed in the form of RAGs, thus erasing the need to train on the domain's specific data. This could serve research, marketing, and education, to name a few areas. For example, imagine you study a particular topic from a particular book or research paper; it is simple to make those documents available for retrieval and ask the LLM to search, summarize, answer particular questions, and simplify.

As we identify RAGs as a key technology to perhaps dominate in-house costumed development, let's discuss the heavier and more comprehensive approach of customizing the LLM itself.

Customizing LLMs

The customization trend will continue intensifying as a customized LLM presents a complete holistic product that is proprietary to its maker. We're likely to see industry or task-specific LLMs becoming the norm. From LLMs tailored to legal jargon to those adept at medical diagnoses, the future is specialized. This will involve the various design choices of model pre-training, model fine-tuning, and retrieval-based designs, which leverage dedicated datasets.

While the typical RAG caters to leveraging in-house and non-public data, a customized LLM suits cases where an entire domain is to be learned and mastered. For instance, if we wanted to choose one of these two approaches as a tool that would ideate and synthesize NLP and AI solutions, we would choose an LLM that was trained on the relevant data, e.g., publications, learning material, and patents, and not a RAG that simply makes this data available to a generic LLM. The customized LLM would offer a chain of thought that is inherited from the data it was trained on. The RAG would leverage a generic LLM with its generic chain of thought, where it would have additional data to refer to.

We have now touched on the four pillars for enhancing LLMs' performance. Going from optimizing the prompt to putting together a dedicated LLM, one must trade off the potential improvement in performance with the cost and complexity of the process. *Figure 10.3* portrays this concept:

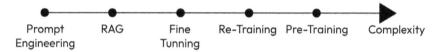

Figure 10.3 – Spectrum of complexity

Programming using LLMs as code generators

English is the new programming language. The outlook for LLMs in the realm of coding is particularly intriguing. Traditionally, coding has been seen as a specialized skill, demanding meticulous attention to detail and extensive training. But with the evolution of LLMs, there's a growing potential to democratize the world of software development. We are witnessing the realization of a long-term vision where, instead of poring over lines of code, developers can provide high-level instructions to an LLM, which, in turn, generates the required code. It's like having a fluent translator who can effortlessly turn human intent into machine-readable directives. We have seen an example in *Chapter 9* where an LLM took on several professional roles and put a programming project together for the user.

Such a shift won't just streamline the coding process; it could fundamentally transform who gets to create software. Non-technical individuals could engage more directly in software development, bridging the gap between idea generation and execution. Start-ups, for instance, could swiftly turn their visions into prototypes, speeding up innovation cycles and fostering a more inclusive tech ecosystem. We anticipate this will revolutionize several business disciplines, for example, technical product management. Of course, this doesn't imply that traditional coding skills will become obsolete. On the contrary, understanding the intricacies of programming languages will always have its value, especially for tasks that demand precision and nuance. However, LLMs can act as invaluable assistants, catching bugs, suggesting optimizations, or even helping with mundane and repetitive tasks. This synergy between human developers and LLMs might lead to a golden age of software development where creativity takes center stage and the technical barriers are lowered. Furthermore, as LLMs get more adept at understanding and generating code, we might also see an increase in the development of novel algorithms, frameworks, and tools. These advancements could be spurred on by the unique perspective that a machine brings to problem-solving, supplemented by the vast amounts of data and patterns it has been trained on.

In summary, the future of LLMs in the coding world holds the promises of collaboration, inclusivity, and innovation. While challenges will undoubtedly arise, the potential benefits for both seasoned developers and newcomers to the field are enormous.

Operations and maintenance with LLMOps

Just as DevOps revolutionized software development, **LLM operations** (**LLMOps**) are becoming crucial for the scalable deployment, monitoring, and maintenance of LLMs. As businesses increasingly rely on LLMs, ensuring their smooth operation, continuous learning, and timely updates will become paramount. LLMOps might introduce practices to streamline these processes, ensuring LLMs remain efficient and relevant. We are seeing great efforts made regarding this cause in the form of paid tools and services. Companies are designing solutions that stretch through the spectrum of operations and monitoring. On one end of the spectrum are tools that provide basic monitoring of the LLM's functioning, and on the other end are tools that provide visuals and statistical insights into the incoming data, outgoing data, and model characteristics.

A new trend in the LLMOps space is creating a feedback loop from the monitoring feed to the model tuning mechanism. This mimics the concept of real-time adaptive models, such as the Kalman filter, which is responsible for having brought Apollo 11 to the moon. The monitoring stream recognizes growing deviations, which are then fed back into a training mechanism that tunes the model's parameters. By doing so, not only is the user given an alert about when the model becomes sub-optimal but the proper adjustment is also applied to the model.

To sum up this review, the journey of LLMs, marked by leaps in DL, innovative learning techniques, and customization capabilities, taps into a broader ambition of humanity: to create machines that understand and enhance our world. The evolution of LLMs encapsulates this quest, and as they continue to mature, their purpose, value, and impact will undoubtedly shape the contours of our digital future.

The future of LLM design is poised at the intersection of technological innovation, user-centric design, and ethical considerations. As research progresses and user needs evolve, the LLMs of tomorrow might be radically different, more capable, and more integrated than what we imagine today.

We have discussed the various technical trends around LLMs, which are at the core of their emergence and growth. Now, we touch on the trends that are further away from the core and are reflective of the impact that these models have had and will are expected to make.

.Cultural trends in NLP and LLMs

In this section, we will discuss some of the trends and impact points that LLMs and AI have had on business and society. We will touch on some of the industries that we identify as likely to thrive the most, thanks to the value that LLMs and AI bring to the table. We will talk about the internal changes that are taking place in corporations as they seek to gain an advantage and stay ahead of the curve. Last, we will touch on some of the cultural aspects that revolve around LLMs and AI.

NLP and LLMs in the business world

NLP and LLMs are proving themselves to be transformative in the business domain. From improving efficiencies to enabling new business models, NLP's capabilities have been harnessed to automate mundane tasks, derive insights from data, and provide advanced customer support.

Initially, NLP was mostly restricted to academia and specialized sectors. However, with the rise of digitalization, the explosion of data, and advancements in open source ML, businesses began to recognize its potential. The affordability of computing power and accessibility to vast datasets made the implementation of LLMs feasible for enterprises, allowing for more sophisticated NLP applications. We observed that this transition of NLP into the business world took place from 2018–2019. First, the combination of NLP and traditional ML models for the purpose of limited tasks, such as text classification, began to infiltrate business operations and analytics. In 2019, Hugging Face released a free version of Google's BERT, its groundbreaking LM, which we discussed in previous chapters (see more detail on the model page: `https://huggingface.co/bert-base-uncased`). BERT employed transfer learning in a way that allowed for great classification power with a relatively minimal amount of labeled data, and it quickly became the go-to model for many text-driven business models.

Some industries have inherited characteristics that make them more likely to adopt NLP-driven automation and thrive on it. When looking to evaluate the potential impact that NLP would have on an industry or even on a particular business, consider these traits:

- **Data abundance**: The industry should have access to vast amounts of data, especially in textual form, as NLP primarily deals with understanding and generating human language.

- **Digital readiness**: The data should be digitized and structured. Industries that already have a culture of digitization can more easily leverage AI and NLP.

- **Computation infrastructure**: The capacity to handle high computational workloads is essential, either through in-house infrastructure or cloud-based solutions, as NLP models, especially LLMs, require significant computational power.

- **Repetitive tasks**: Industries where a lot of manual, repetitive tasks, such as customer service queries or document reviews, are performed can benefit significantly from automation using NLP.

- **Decision-making reliant on insights**: If decisions are often made based on insights derived from textual data (e.g., market sentiment from social media), NLP can streamline and enhance the decision-making process.

- **High customer interaction**: Industries that engage directly with customers, especially through digital channels, can use NLP for chatbots, feedback analysis, and personalized marketing.

- **Need for personalization**: If there's a demand for personalized services or products based on user preferences and feedback, NLP can help in tailoring offerings to individual needs.

- **Continuous learning and updating**: Industries that need to stay updated with the latest information, research, or trends can utilize NLP for automated content aggregation, summarization, and analysis.

- **Multilingual engagements**: Industries operating globally or in multi-lingual regions can benefit from translation services and multilingual customer interactions powered by NLP.

- **Regulatory compliance and documentation**: If there's a need to regularly review and adhere to regulations, standards, or maintain documentation, NLP can assist in automated compliance checks and document generation.

- **Flexibility for pipeline extension**: As NLP requires processing time and computational resources, it can only produce benefits if the real-time processes can accommodate these requirements.

Let's explore specific business sectors to see how AI and LLMs are making a difference in each of them.

Business sectors

Healthcare is an industry that relies heavily on free text. Every business in the healthcare space that interacts with patient treatment, whether it is a clinic, a hospital, or even in an insurer, has a data stream that involves free text. It could be a transcription of medical notes, patient query responses, drug interactions, and other sources of information. The vast majority of those are digitized and are, thus, machine-readable, making this a setup for downstream processing. Those processes could be around identifying diagnoses from radiology reports, classifying patient details for treatment, clinical trials based on physician notes, alerting potential risk based on patient reporting, and many other use cases.

Another major use case that is emerging in healthcare is around patients seeking medical advice from generative AI tools such as ChatGPT. As LLMs have access to a sea of data, patients found that an LLM may suggest an answer to a medical question. While the potential is huge, the risk is great as well.

In the next few years, we anticipate major improvements regarding LLMs' ability to support healthcare needs. With patient care in particular, we will see an improvement in augmenting core medical competencies. Different tiers of medical advice, diagnoses, and prognoses will be assigned different balances between professional advice and AI advice. For instance, throughout history, we have seen patients self-diagnose mild conditions, such as a rash or a pain, or take advice from other non-professionals. Moreover, nowadays, we see patients seeking advice in online articles and posts. We expect that for these same conditions, which are perceived as low-risk, patients will adopt LLMs for advice. As for official policies, we will see clinical systems dictate guidelines as to which cases would be handled by AI and to what extent.

Finance is a broad industry that is heavily dependent on text information. From financial filings to earning calls, news feeds to regulatory updates, transaction details to credit reports, and so on. The financial sector is seen as a precursor to how other industries might evolve with the rise of AI. Its heavy reliance on data processing makes it a natural fit for AI and serves as a case study for what might happen elsewhere.

We see NLP and LLMs used in all corners of the financial spectrum. A new trend we are noticing is building dedicated chatbots for particular topics and even individual companies as they seek to present their proprietary service to their customers in the form of an interactive chatbot.

Our overall expectation for the future of finance is a collaborative environment where AI-driven models seamlessly work in tandem with industry specialists. The best historical analogy we have for this vision is the synergy that Microsoft created between Excel and financial analysts. Envision a setting where a traditional AI model maps out financial projections and its generative counterpart dives deep into the data, not just highlighting variances but also suggesting strategic choices based on diverse forecast models.

E-commerce is an industry that constantly sits at the intersection of customers and technology. One use case in the e-commerce space is personalized shopping experience. As NLP techniques become more sophisticated, ecommerce platforms can predict emerging trends, offer real-time personalized discounts based on user sentiment, and enhance cross-selling and upselling strategies. From the aspect of product search, LLMs understand natural language queries, enabling users to find products more effectively.

The future landscape of e-commerce is set to undergo a transformational shift. The virtual realm is expanding with the advent of AI-enabled metaverse shopping, combining visual AI, augmented reality, and virtual reality technologies. This will present consumers with a thrilling opportunity to try products virtually, from clothing to furniture, providing a shopping experience that's as close to reality as possible. Moreover, the complexities of supply chain management will continue to be addressed with AI-driven predictive analytics, optimizing inventory processes. AI promises to be a cornerstone in shaping a dynamic and efficient future for the eCommerce industry.

The second-to-last industry we want to mention is education. Here, too, we are seeing a trend around personalization. NLP allows for adaptive learning platforms that cater to individual student needs, providing resources and quizzes based on their learning pace and style. NLP-driven platforms can analyze student inputs, essays, and feedback to offer custom-tailored learning paths. Another trend is around language learning. LLMs offer real-time translations, corrections, and even cultural context, making language learning more immersive.

As the rapid development of generative AI tools increasingly permeates the education sector, the traditional paradigms of teaching and learning are poised for substantial change. We anticipate a future where AI seamlessly integrates into classrooms, amplifying the efficacy of instruction and personalizing learning experiences in unprecedented ways. Simultaneously, we will see advancements in personalization where students can enjoy a learning experience that would be best described as a computerized private tutor. It would adapt the material being taught and the manner in which it is communicated to suit the student's pace and perception. For children born in current times, we expect the educational experience to be innovative, limitless, and not at all boring.

The industry of entertainment and content consumption is given the last but not least spot. The reciprocal relationship between AI and the media industry has become evident in recent years. With LLMs and AI continually evolving, media platforms have harnessed them to optimize content creation, distribution, and consumption.

The music landscape is being reshaped. DL models generate distinct compositions after learning from existing musical patterns. Platforms such as Spotify personalize playlists through ML-driven recommendations, analyzing listening history and preferences. The audio mastering process, traditionally demanding expertise, now incorporates AI solutions such LANDR, democratizing and accelerating music production.

Filmmakers harness LLMs for scriptwriting, enabling the creation of unique narratives while also assessing potential uncertainties in screenplays. AI's predictive prowess is showcased by Warner Bros., 20th Century Fox, and Sony Pictures, all of which utilize platforms such as Cinelytic, Merlin, and ScriptBook, respectively.

AI enriches gameplay by simulating realistic non-player character behaviors and dynamically generating content. It offers personalized game recommendations, tailoring the experience to player preferences. Adaptive difficulty systems analyze real-time player behavior, adjusting challenges to ensure a balanced gaming experience.

In the world of book publishing, the manuscript submission process is streamlined by AI, automating screenings and predicting market potential. AI-driven tools bolster the editing phase by ensuring clarity, coherence, and adherence to style guidelines. LLMs aid authors in crafting compelling narratives by providing insights into character and plot structures. Personalization algorithms in platforms tailor content recommendations to users' tastes, enhancing engagement. Platforms such as Google AdSense utilize AI to target online advertisements precisely, optimizing campaign outreach. AI also plays a regulatory role, filtering content based on user demographics and ensuring compliance with broadcasting guidelines. Finally, streaming platforms employ AI for content categorization, offering users a seamless content discovery experience.

These super innovative utilizations of AI and LLMs in the entertainment industry are going to grow and shape the creations they touch. The creation processes will be shorter and faster. The question that will become more and more frequent is whether having the creation of art orchestrated by a computer model will take away from its charm.

Next, we'll take a step back from business sectors and discuss a particular use case that is ubiquitous across any customer-facing business.

Customer interactions and service – the early adopter

One of the most visible impacts of NLP in businesses is in customer interactions. LLMs enable responsive chatbots, assist in sentiment analysis, and provide real-time solutions, enhancing user experience. Early chatbots were rule-based and could handle limited queries. With LLMs, chatbots can understand context, handle complex queries, and even engage in casual conversations. This progression has led to increased customer satisfaction, reduced wait times, and substantial cost savings for businesses.

In the next few years, we can expect to continue to see AI and LLMs used in a wide range of customer service applications, including chatbots, recommendation systems, proactive customer engagement systems, and customer service analytics systems. These AI and LLM-powered applications will be able to deliver several benefits to both businesses and customers. We will see chatbots become more comprehensive to the extent of being able to handle those cases that currently require a human agent to step in. Recommendation systems will further personalize and capture the individual customer's interests and will assimilate personal human assistants who are currently the privilege of a tiny portion of the population. On a macro level, a customer service analytics system would be used to analyze customer data and identify trends and patterns that can be used to improve customer service operations.

Overall, the prospects for AI and LLMs in customer service are exceptionally promising. These technologies stand poised to transform business-customer interactions, offering more tailored, anticipatory, and immersive service experiences.

Having explored the transformative role of AI and LLMs in customer service, let's now pivot to another critical dimension: organizational structures. As companies gear up for the AI era, it's imperative to understand how they're reshaping their internal frameworks to integrate these technological advances.

Change management driven by AI's impact

As AI, particularly the capabilities of LLMs, continues its meteoric rise, businesses worldwide are feeling the ripple effects. To remain competitive and harness the full potential of these technological marvels, many organizations are undergoing transformative shifts in their internal structures and operations. These changes range from reimagining workflow dynamics to the introduction of pivotal roles such as the Chief AI Officer. We will now explore how AI's profound influence is reshaping the very fabric of contemporary business paradigms.

Shifts in internal business structure and operations

Beyond external customer interactions, LLMs have deeply impacted how businesses operate internally. From automating emails to handling HR queries, NLP has streamlined operations. Initially, businesses used simple automation tools to handle repetitive tasks. With LLMs, the spectrum of automatable tasks has widened. Whether it's drafting reports, analyzing employee feedback, or predicting market trends, NLP plays a pivotal role.

A particular shift we are seeing in the organizational landscape regards the tech stack structure. Traditionally, a company's tech stack can be visualized as a layer cake, with each layer having a distinct role:

- The **decision-making layer**, which drives the business of the company
- The **data layer** serves as the backbone and includes the following:
  - Data repository and storage
  - Operational data
  - Services for the ingestion and distribution of data
- The **core transaction layer** maps the data from the infrastructure layer to the data layer
- The **infrastructure layer** and the **foundational layer** offer computing resources and capabilities that may exist on-premises or in the cloud

With the evolution of AI, new layers and components are being introduced, reshaping the tech stack:

- A revised decision-making layer is evolving and will be comprised of applications leveraging AI to process multimodal content, such as the following:
  - Text and requests
  - Vision
  - Audio
  - Code
- The AI layer, the new layer in the stack, comprises the following:
  - **AI products**: These are tools and platforms built on AI that are either internal-facing or external-facing
  - **Observability and monitoring**: This ensures the ethical and correct use of AI along with performance control
- **Revised data layer**: As data remains central, it will include components that cater to the above updates based on the AI requirements

Let's go over these new additions.

Delving deeper into the AI-driven stack

These changes are the fruit of the rapid innovations we see driven by AI. For instance, multimodal capabilities are emerging and enabling us to process signals in the form of text, images, video, audio and music, and code. Moreover, AI products such as chatbots, recommendation systems, and predictive analytics tools are becoming essential for businesses.

The revised decision-making layer is now driven by AI applications. Unlike traditional software, AI applications are built with the capability to "think" and "learn." They process multimedia content, such as images, videos, and music, in ways that were once thought impossible. For instance, through image recognition, one can identify and categorize objects in a photo, while video analytics can analyze patterns and anomalies in real-time footage. Even more fascinating is the ability of some of these apps to generate new music compositions or artworks, bridging the gap between technology and art.

The next new layer is the AI layer. Its key component is AI products. When we talk about AI products, we refer to a vast array of tools and platforms built on the foundation of AI. These range from chatbots that provide real-time customer support to recommendation systems that personalize user experiences on e-commerce platforms. Predictive analytics, another pillar of AI products, allows businesses to forecast trends and make informed decisions. Collectively, these products represent a paradigm shift from reactive to proactive business strategies, ensuring that businesses are always a step ahead.

Observability and monitoring supplement the above additions by mitigating risk and applying quality control. As powerful as AI is, it also brings forth ethical and operational challenges. AI guardrails can address these concerns by ensuring that AI operates within defined ethical boundaries, promoting fairness, transparency, and privacy. For instance, an AI guardrail might prevent an algorithm from making decisions based on biased data, or it could offer explanations for the decisions an AI system makes. In an age where trust in technology is paramount, these guardrails are crucial for ensuring that AI is not just smart but is also responsible. At the same time as enforcing guardrails, the traditional production monitoring of data and model outputs is applied to assure consistency and quality.

To conclude our discussion of the shift in tech stacks, we anticipate AI to be more than a trend that technology enables but rather an enabler for new trends of technology. For that reason, we expect the data and tech paradigm to change and put AI in the center. We believe companies that adapt and evolve their stacks to harness these new capabilities will be better positioned to succeed in this new digital age.

As we review the evolving reshaping of modern organizations, let's review a particular addition to the corporate world: the chief AI officer. This is a position that underscores the paramount importance AI holds in the modern corporate arena.

The emergence of the chief AI officer

As AI is set to impact business, it is expected that it will also reshape businesses. In the previous section, we detailed our anticipation of the common organizational tech stack that will transform and give room to components that are purely AI-oriented. Following a similar path, the leadership structure is also expected to change and make room for a new role: the **chief AI officer (CAIO)**. This section will delve deep into the CAIO's role, responsibilities, and the unique value they bring to an organization.

Why a company needs a chief AI officer

AI is no longer a distant technological marvel; it's now intertwined in our everyday lives. With the creation of generative tools such as OpenAI's ChatGPT and Google's Bard, AI's capabilities are now accessible to businesses of all natures. AI's transformative potential ranges from creating innovative services and improving operational efficiency to revolutionizing entire industries.

Given the impactful nature of AI, incorporating it into the core business strategy is imperative. The need for a CAIO arises from the importance of embedding AI in strategic decisions, ensuring that companies capitalize on the opportunities it presents.

The core responsibilities and traits of a CAIO

Central to the CAIO's responsibilities is guiding the organization's AI strategy to align with its overarching business objectives. This encompasses the following:

- **Strategic AI visioning**: Spearhead the creation of an AI vision that not only integrates into the organization's operations but also identifies critical areas, such as customer experience or supply chain enhancements, where AI can drive transformative change. This vision must seamlessly align with the organization's broader objectives.

- **Opportunity identification**: Pinpoint and capitalize on chances for integrating AI to optimize existing processes, discover novel business directions powered by AI, and determine which workflows are primed for automation.

- **Operationalizing AI strategy**: Beyond ideation, ensure the practical execution of the AI vision by fostering inter-departmental collaboration. This includes guaranteeing alignment with AI's role, potential, and the means to scale its deployment effectively.

- **Talent and resource management**: Ensure that the organization possesses the requisite skills, personnel, and resources to deploy and manage AI initiatives effectively.

- **Promote AI understanding**: Serve as the organization's primary AI educator and advocate, clearing up misconceptions and fostering a deep understanding of AI's benefits and nuances across all organizational levels.

- **Fostering an AI-first culture**: Champion a culture of AI-centric innovation, encouraging continual exploration and the application of cutting-edge AI research, tools, and practices.

- **Stay ahead in AI evolution**: In the fast-paced AI domain, remain proactive in absorbing the latest research, tools, and practices. Ensure the organization remains at the forefront of AI innovations to maintain a competitive edge.

- **Engage stakeholders**: Regularly communicate with diverse organizational stakeholders, ensuring alignment, addressing concerns, and underscoring the tangible advantages of AI initiatives.

- **Guardian of ethical AI use**: Safeguard the organization from potential AI pitfalls, ensuring AI practices are in line with user expectations, thereby building trust with customers and stakeholders.

- **Ethical oversight and compliance**: Act as the organization's guardrail when it comes to AI deployment. Ensure that AI solutions adhere to ethical standards, respect user privacy, are free from biases, and stay compliant with the shifting sands of tech regulations.

With a balance of technical acumen and soft skills being pivotal, the CAIO should be adept with AI tools and infrastructure and also excel in communication, teamwork, problem-solving, and time management.

They must be well - versed in the business implications of AI, understanding its present landscape, and anticipating future developments. It's essential for them to be attuned to the ramifications that specific AI technologies might have on their industry.

In an age where AI's ethical considerations are paramount, the CAIO must be an ethical pillar, navigating challenges related to bias, privacy, and societal impact. There is an expectation that a direct and fluid channel of communication being will be formed between the company's compliance team and legal team so as to help identify and anticipate sensitive territories that the CAIO may step into.

In conclusion, as businesses increasingly integrate AI into their operational fabric, the CAIO's role emerges as indispensable; they serve as the torchbearers, illuminating the path for organizations to harness AI's full potential ethically and effectively. As AI's significance in the business realm augments, the CAIO stands poised to be a cornerstone of the modern C-suite.

While AI and LLMs are undoubtedly revolutionizing the business landscape, their reach extends beyond the corporate realm. As we transition into our next section, we'll explore the profound social and behavioral implications these technologies bring to the fore, impacting the very fabric of our society.

Behavioral trends induced by AI and LLMs – the social aspect

The proliferation of AI, particularly advanced models such as LLMs, has had a profound impact on social behavior. This influence ranges from everyday tasks to broader communication trends. As AI integrates into the fabric of daily life, it shapes behaviors, introduces new norms, and occasionally raises concerns. Here, we dive into these behavioral shifts.

Personal assistants becoming indispensable

With the increase in AI-driven virtual assistants such as Siri, Alexa, and Google Assistant, people are increasingly relying on these tools for daily tasks. Whether it's setting up appointments, checking the weather, or controlling smart home devices, AI assistants are becoming the go-to for many, changing the way we interact with technology and sometimes even leading us to anthropomorphize these tools.

In the future, we will see AI personal assistants become a completely immersive and non-separable part of our lives. We analogize it to the narrow and limited role that the digital calendar takes in our lives. By allowing us to plan and schedule events efficiently, keeping a calendar ensures we meet commitments and maintain a balance between personal and professional engagements. Furthermore, automated reminders and synchronization across devices alleviate the pressure to remember every appointment, letting us focus on more pressing matters with peace of mind. A personal assistant, whether AI-driven or human, takes things to the next level. It syncs with other individuals, prioritizes, advises, gathers information, and performs other common day-to-day tasks. Until recently, only human assistants could fulfill this function with high confidence. We will soon see this done by automated models with little cost and oversight. If you are wearing prescription glasses, you know exactly what our relationship with our personal AI assistant will be like and, moreover, what it would be like if you lost access to it.

Ease in communication and bridging language barriers

LLMs have refined the way we communicate, especially when it comes to written content. People use them for grammar checks, content suggestions, or even generating entire texts. This can lead to more polished communication but also brings up questions about authenticity.

Real-time translation tools powered by AI are revolutionizing the way we communicate across cultures. Platforms such as Google Translate are making it feasible for individuals to interact seamlessly, fostering global connections. However, the increased reliance on these tools might diminish the incentive for some to learn new languages.

In the near future, the boundaries of communication are poised to expand even further, driven by the convergence of advanced LLMs and AI innovations. We will soon see the realization of the vision where two individuals have a call, each speaking a different native language, and can engage in a seamless conversation, with AI invisibly and instantly translating their spoken words. This would mean that, as one person speaks in Mandarin, their counterpart might hear the words in Spanish in real time, with a minimally noticeable delay. Such advancements could effectively eradicate language barriers, allowing for truly global interpersonal connectivity.

Furthermore, the realm of communication is not just limited to the spoken word. Cutting-edge research is delving into the possibility of converting neural signals directly into speech. Neural sensors will detect and interpret brain activity, allowing individuals to "speak" without ever moving their lips. This could be a groundbreaking advancement, especially for those with speech impediments or communication disorders, offering them a voice in a way they've never experienced before.

Beyond these capabilities, the tactile dimension of communication might also see innovation. We anticipate wearable devices that allow people to "feel" messages, translating words or emotions into specific tactile sensations. This would open up new channels of understanding, especially for the visually or hearing impaired.

AR with AI will redefine our notion of presence. While Meta's Metaverse is struggling to solidify, the notion of interacting via virtual presence will emerge and have demand. You will be able to project your avatar to a distant location, communicating with others as if you were physically there. The nuances of facial expressions, body language, and gestures will be captured and relayed, adding depth to remote conversations.

Ethical implications of delegated decisions

As people grow accustomed to AI recommendations, from shopping to reading, there's a risk of over-delegating decisions. This can lead to reduced critical thinking, making individuals more susceptible to algorithmic biases or manipulations.

As we advance further into an AI-driven era, there's an increasing likelihood that individuals will place undue trust in automated systems, potentially leading to an erosion of personal responsibility and agency. There's a growing concern that, as more decisions are automated, society might witness a decline in individuals' ability to make informed judgments without algorithmic input. Moreover, as industries increasingly rely on AI for critical decisions, the transparency and understanding of these algorithms will become paramount to prevent unintentional systemic biases. The potential for AI to perpetuate or even amplify existing societal biases—either through data or design—raises profound ethical implications. As a response, we anticipate a surge in demand for AI ethics courses, transparent algorithmic frameworks, and regulatory oversight to ensure AI systems align with human values and societal norms.

To sum up our review of these various social trends, AI and LLMs are reshaping the social landscape in multifaceted ways. While they introduce conveniences and novel experiences, they also present challenges that society must navigate. Balancing the benefits with the potential pitfalls will be crucial as AI's role in daily life continues to evolve.

We now shift the focus to two particular aspects of AI that are becoming of interest to perhaps every person and entity seeking to employ AI, ethics, and risks.

Ethics and risks – growing concerns around the implementation of AI

Throughout the book, we have discussed a variety of aspects with regard to AI in general and LLMs in particular. We touched lightly on the different emerging concerns, and in this section, we will focus on the two biggest discussion topics: ethics and risks.

The integration of AI, particularly LLMs, into our lives brings unparalleled convenience and potential. Yet, with these advances comes a set of evolving ethical concerns and risks that span from individual to societal levels. As these technologies mature, understanding and navigating these areas becomes crucial.

Ethics in AI refers to the moral principles guiding AI design, deployment, and use. It revolves around ensuring fairness, transparency, privacy, and accountability in AI systems. Early AI applications, being rudimentary, posed fewer ethical dilemmas. As AI's complexity grows, so do the consequences of its decisions, pushing ethics to the forefront. The emergence of LLMs, with their ability to generate human-like text, further amplified these concerns.

The key ethical concerns are as follows;

- **Bias and fairness**: AI models can inadvertently learn biases present in training data. This can lead to discriminatory outputs, affecting individuals or entire demographics adversely.

- **Transparency and explainability**: As AI models become complex, their decision-making processes become less transparent. The "black box" nature of some models poses challenges in terms of accountability.

- **Privacy**: AI's capability to process vast amounts of data raises concerns about data privacy and misuse. This extends to LLMs that might inadvertently generate outputs revealing sensitive information.

- **Dependency and autonomy**: Over-reliance on AI can erode human autonomy. For instance, blindly following AI recommendations without critical evaluation can be problematic to the point of compromising ethical aspects.

The key risks are as follows:

- **Security**: AI systems can be targets for adversarial attacks, where malicious actors feed deceptive inputs to get desired outputs

- **Hallucinations and misinformation**: LLMs can generate convincing but false information, amplifying the spread of misinformation

- **Social economic**: Over-automation can lead to various downstream consequences, such as job displacements in certain sectors, affecting economic stability

These concerns are growing quickly as AI is rapidly advancing. While rapid advancements signify progress and new possibilities, they also introduce challenges for policymakers and ethicists alike. As AI systems become more complex and capable, they often outpace the development of ethical guidelines and regulatory measures. This means that as we harness the latest AI breakthroughs, we may be venturing into uncharted territories without a moral compass or safety net. The agility of AI evolution also poses challenges for businesses and governments. They must constantly adapt to ensure that their practices, regulations, and standards keep up with the latest developments.

Another lens to view these concerns through is the scales of society. On one end is the individual level, where concerns revolve around privacy, data misuse, and personal biases. Individuals find themselves struggling to decipher between AI-generated content and human-generated content. A growing problem we have been witnessing is the spread of misinformation, whether intentional or accidental. This phenomenon is threatening to shake the confidence individuals have in elected officials, legal procedures, and other pillars of society.

On the company level, organizations face challenges in ensuring their AI systems are fair, transparent, and compliant with regulations. They also risk reputational damage from biased or questionable AI outputs.

On a macro scale, societies must address the broader implications of AI, from potential job losses due to automation to the societal divisions that might arise from AI's discriminatory decisions.

The future outlook – a blend of ethics, regulation, awareness, and innovation

As we stand on the brink of an era where AI's influence permeates nearly every facet of our lives, several key trends shape our collective future. First and foremost, the cry for ethical guidelines and frameworks in AI development and deployment has never been louder. In recognizing the chief importance of human welfare in this digital age, there's significant momentum building around creating AI systems that prioritize and protect human interests. This goes beyond mere compliance or economic considerations; it's about ensuring that the AI systems of tomorrow resonate with our shared human values and contribute to the greater good.

Parallel to the emphasis on ethics, governments, and global entities are gearing up for a more hands-on approach. The era of free trade or hands-off attitudes toward AI is fading. Instead, there's an anticipation of robust regulations that not only keep pace with AI advancements but also ensure its responsible and equitable use. Such regulations will likely cover a spectrum of concerns, from data privacy and security to transparency and fairness, thus ensuring that corporations and individuals alike adhere to a set of globally recognized best practices.

In 2023, Sam Altman, OpenAI's CEO, appeared before the US Congress to share his perspective on the need to regulate the expanding AI landscape. He emphasized the importance of caution, stating that such influential shifts in human history necessitate appropriate safeguards to ensure their responsible and beneficial implementation. Central to Altman's argument was his belief that the power of AI models would soon exceed our initial expectations, making them both invaluable tools and potential sources of unprecedented challenges. He passionately advocated for proactive regulatory intervention by governments, asserting that such measures would be crucial to address and mitigate the associated risks of these increasingly sophisticated models.

Gary Marcus, Professor Emeritus at New York University, introduced another perspective, suggesting a more robust oversight mechanism. He proposed the establishment of a new federal agency dedicated to reviewing AI programs. This agency's role would be to scrutinize these programs before they are made publicly available, ensuring their safety, ethical considerations, and effectiveness. Drawing attention to the rapid evolution of AI, Marcus cautioned about unforeseen advancements, metaphorically stating, "There are more genies to come from more bottles."

We expect to witness major actions in the form of guardrails, whether governance, either municipal or organizational, will dictate the bounds that are to be enforced and maintained remains to be seen. This will address sensitive domains such as using LLMs for healthcare-related matters, financial decisions, usage by minors, and other matters that require a high sense of responsibility. In particular, we expect there to be clarity regarding what data is allowed to be used to train a model and in what circumstances.

However, regulations and ethical frameworks, while being vital, are only part of the equation. The end-users—the general public—play a pivotal role in shaping AI's trajectory. As AI technologies become an integral part of daily life, from smart homes to personalized healthcare, there's a pressing need for public discourse around its ethical considerations and associated risks. This dialogue will foster a more informed and empowered user base capable of making discerning choices about the AI tools they engage with. Education campaigns, workshops, and public debates will likely surge, creating an environment where every individual is not just a passive consumer but an informed stakeholder.

Lastly, the technological front is set to witness a renaissance of sorts. Gone are the days when the sole focus was on creating the most powerful or efficient AI model. Researchers and developers are now increasingly dedicating their efforts toward creating AI systems that are intrinsically more transparent, fair, and resilient against potential threats. The vision is clear: AI models that not only excel in their tasks but do so in a manner that's comprehensible, equitable, and impervious to malicious attacks.

In essence, the future of AI is not just about technological marvels; it's about blending innovation with responsibility, power with transparency, and progress with ethics. As we march into this future, the confluence of these trends promises a world where AI enriches lives, upholds values, and serves the collective betterment of society.

In summary, the relationship between AI, ethics, and risk is multifaceted. While AI, especially LLMs, holds vast potential, it's imperative to recognize and address the accompanying ethical dilemmas and risks. Only through a balanced approach can we harness AI's benefits while safeguarding individual and societal interests.

Summary

In this *chapter*, we embarked on a comprehensive journey through the key trends shaping the world of AI, with a particular emphasis on LLMs. At the very heart of these models lies computational power, which acts as the driving engine, enabling breakthroughs and amplifying their potential. With advancements in computational capabilities, we're not only progressing faster but also unlocking new efficiencies that redefine the realm of possibilities.

Complementing this computational prowess are vast datasets, casting an indelible mark on NLP and LLMs. We have covered their significance in this chapter and learned that they serve pivotal roles. As we look ahead, the future of data availability in NLP promises to be a dynamic landscape, constantly evolving in response to these challenges.

LLMs themselves have undergone significant evolution; each iteration aimed at achieving greater scale and capability. We reviewed the impact these models possess and learned that they have undeniably transformed various landscapes, from business to social interactions, paving the way for innovations yet to come.

The cultural footprint of NLP and LLMs is evident in the business world, reshaping customer interactions, redefining internal business structures, and even leading to the emergence of specialized roles such as the CAIO. These advancements, while impressive, also herald a new era of behavioral shifts. From day-to-day tasks to high-level business decisions, AI's influence on society's fabric is profound.

Yet, intertwined with these advancements are growing concerns about the ethical implementation and associated risks of AI. The rapid pace of AI's progression, the opacity of its decision-making processes, and the potential for data misuse underscore the urgent need for ethical guidelines, robust regulations, and increased public awareness. In closing, as AI continues its relentless march forward, it is imperative to approach it with both enthusiasm for its potential and caution for its challenges, ensuring a future where technology serves humanity in the most responsible and beneficial ways.

11

Exclusive Industry Insights: Perspectives and Predictions from World Class Experts

As the journey of this book unfolds, exploring the vast expanse of **natural language processing (NLP)** and **large language models (LLMs)**, we arrive at a pivotal juncture in *Chapter 11*. This chapter is not just a culmination of the themes and discussions that preceded it but also a bridge to the untapped potential and imminent challenges that lie ahead in the realm of NLP and LLMs. Our endeavor through the chapters has been to chart the evolution of NLP from its foundational concepts to the architectural marvels of LLMs, dissecting the intricacies of **machine learning (ML)** strategies, data preprocessing, model training, and the practical applications transforming industries and societal interactions.

The motivation for this chapter stems from an acute recognition of the pace at which NLP and LLM technologies are evolving and the multifaceted impact they wield on the fabric of our digital society. As we explore the complexities of these advanced models and the trends they spur, it is essential to seek guidance from those navigating these waters at the forefront of innovation, research, and ethical contemplation. The dialogue with experts across diverse domains—legal, research, and executive— serves as a beacon for understanding how LLMs intersect with various facets of professional practice and what future trajectories might look like.

The topics discussed herein are reflective of the broader themes of this book yet delve deeper into specific challenges and opportunities that LLMs present. From mitigating biases in datasets to reconciling open research with privacy, and from organizational restructuring in the wake of **artificial intelligence (AI)** to the evolving landscape of learning paradigms within LLMs, each discussion is a mosaic of insights that paints a comprehensive picture of the current state and the road ahead.

In this chapter, we will cover the following:

- Overview of our expert
- Our questions and the experts' answers

Overview of our experts

Let's go through each of the experts' introductions first.

Nitzan Mekel-Bobrov, PhD

Nitzan Mekel-Bobrov is the **Chief AI Officer** (**CAIO**) at eBay where he runs the company-wide strategy for AI and technology innovation. An R&D scientist by training, Nitzan has spent his career developing machine intelligence systems, directly integrated into mission-critical products. Having led enterprise AI organizations across multiple industries, including healthcare, financial services, and e-commerce, Nitzan is a thought leader in the delivery of transformational impact through real-time AI at scale, changing companies' business models and core value propositions to their customers. Nitzan received his PhD from the University of Chicago and currently resides in New York City as the GM of eBay NYC.

David Sontag, PhD

David Sontag is a Professor of Electrical Engineering and Computer Science at MIT, part of both the Institute for Medical Engineering & Science and the Computer Science & Artificial Intelligence Laboratory. His research focuses on advancing ML and AI and using these to transform healthcare. Previously, he was an Assistant Professor of Computer Science and Data Science at New York University, part of the **Computer Intelligence, Learning, Vision, and Robotics** (**CILVR**) lab. He is also Co-Founder and CEO of Layer Health.

John D. Halamka, M.D., M.S.

John D. Halamka, M.D., M.S., President of the **Mayo Clinic Platform**, leads a transformative digital health initiative impacting 45 million people in 2023. With over 40 years in healthcare information strategy and emergency medicine, his work spans serving at **Beth Israel Deaconess Medical Center** (**BIDMC**), advising administrations from George W. Bush to Barack Obama, and teaching as a Harvard Medical School professor. A Stanford, UCSF, and UC Berkeley alumnus, Halamka is also a practicing Emergency Medicine Professor at Mayo Clinic College of Medicine and Science. An author of 15 books and hundreds of articles, he was elected to the National Academy of Medicine in 2020.

Xavier Amatriain, PhD

Xavier Amatriain was most recently VP of AI Product Strategy at LinkedIn, where he led company-wide generative AI efforts all the way from platform and infrastructure to product features. He is also a board member of Curai Health, a healthcare/AI start-up that he cofounded and was CTO of until 2022. Prior to this, he led engineering at Quora and was Research/Engineering Director at Netflix, where he started and led the Algorithms team building the famous Netflix recommendations. Xavier started his career as a researcher both in academia and industry. With over 100 research publications (and 6,000 citations), he is best known for his work on AI and ML in general, and recommender systems in particular.

Melanie Garson, PhD

Dr. Melanie Garson, Cyber Policy & Tech Geopolitics Lead at the Tony Blair Institute, delves into cyber policy, geopolitics AI, compute and the internet, the rise of tech companies as geopolitical actors, data governance, as well as the intersection of disruptive tech, foreign policy, defense, and diplomacy. At University College London, she's an Associate Professor teaching on the impact of emerging technologies on conflict, negotiation, and tech diplomacy. A regular speaker at international forums and media, including BBC and CNN, Melanie's background includes being an accredited mediator and solicitor at Freshfields Bruckhaus Deringer. She holds a PhD from University College London and a master's from the Fletcher School of Law and Diplomacy.

Our questions and the experts' answers

We had an opportunity to pick the brains of each of these experienced folks and learn about how their career intersects and leverage AI and LLMs. We tailored questions to each of them so to allow them to teach us through their insights and perspectives. We found these discussions to be rewarding as they shed light on topics that are common and would be valuable for anyone who reads this book. Let's dive right in.

Nitzan Mekel-Bobrov

Nitzan brings the CAIO's perspective as he and Ebay are encountering the vast potential that AI and LLM's have to offer. He shares many diversified aspects that the CAIO has to address and decide on.

Let's go through the questions and answers with Nitzan Mekel-Bobrov.

Q1.1 – Future of LLM – hybrid learning paradigms: In light of the evolving landscape of learning schemes, what do you envision as the next breakthrough in combining different learning paradigms within LLMs?

In thinking about the potential next breakthrough in combining different learning paradigms within LLMs, I can articulate these ideas:

- **Transition to large foundation models (LFMs)**: A clear next step in the evolution of learning paradigms is the move toward fully multimodal models or LFMs. These models integrate and process multiple forms of data (for example, text, images, audio) simultaneously, offering a more holistic understanding and generating more contextually rich responses. This transition is expected to precede any significant changes in the underlying architecture of current models.

- **Scalability and model-size optimization**: One of the primary challenges with deploying LLMs is scalability. Future developments will likely focus on creating models that maintain high performance while being significantly smaller in size. This involves reducing the number of hyperparameters and optimizing the models to work efficiently with less computational resources.

- **Real-time model triage**: The ability to select the best model for each specific prompt in real time is anticipated to be a significant area of improvement. This involves optimizing given constraints such as computation resources, response time, or performance. It allows for the dynamic selection of the most appropriate model based on the task at hand, rather than relying solely on the largest model available.

- **Mitigating hallucinations through multiple LLMs**: The more generalizable a model, the higher the risk of generating hallucinations (inaccurate or fabricated information). A promising approach to mitigate this issue is the use of multiple LLMs, where several LLMs are used simultaneously to check each other's answers to validate responses. This not only improves the accuracy but also leverages the synergy between various models, each playing specialized roles.

- **Mimicking human ability for broad usefulness**: For LLMs to be broadly useful, they need to mimic human intelligence more closely. This includes not only generating accurate information but also reasoning in a more contextually driven and nuanced manner, beyond binary true/false outputs. The evolution toward models that can understand and interpret complex, fuzzy logic similar to human thought processes is a critical area for future breakthroughs.

These ideas point toward a future where AI models are not only more efficient and scalable but also significantly more intelligent and capable of nuanced understanding and reasoning. The emphasis on multimodality, scalability, real-time optimization, and enhanced reasoning capabilities highlights the direction of AI development toward more holistic, human-like intelligence and utility.

Q1.2 – In the context of using multiple LLMs simultaneously, How can we optimize the synergy among these "expert" models to achieve a more refined and comprehensive output?

The use of multiple LLMs can go beyond the notion of validation and reducing hallucinations. A broader idea, sometimes referred to as K-LLMs, can utilize multiple LLMs to answer a question or create a complex solution. One such scheme, as discussed previously, could be where each of the models checks each other's answers to validate responses. A possible other approach is where they are assigned roles where each has its particular specialty (for example, product manager, designer, frontend engineer, backend engineer, and QA engineer) and they iterate over the solution, forming a team of experts. This can also allow for smaller and specialized LLMs, which are thus cheaper to train, quicker to process, and smaller in computation requirements.

Q2.1 – As the Chief AI Officer becomes more integral to the corporate hierarchy, what unique challenges do you foresee in bridging the gap between AI potential and practical business applications, and how should the CAIO's role evolve to meet these challenges?

As the Chief AI Officer, my role encompasses navigating the expansive impact AI has across various domains within our organization. Here are some of the most significant areas of focus for me:

- **Breadth of AI's impact**: The expansive reach of AI across various domains within a large business requires the CAIO to have a deep understanding of both back-office and front-office needs. This necessitates a wide-reaching engagement across the company to identify and prioritize opportunities for AI's transformative impact.

- **Effort and prioritization**: The role demands substantial effort in prioritization due to the impossibility of being involved in every aspect of a large enterprise. This involves making decisions with limited data on where the biggest return on investment lies, drawing on experiences from other companies, and understanding internal operations to gauge where AI can have significant impacts.

- **Pressure for quick impact**: There's a pronounced pressure to deliver tangible results swiftly, contending with existing technological, process, and personnel constraints. Integrating AI innovations into the current ecosystem without overhauling preexisting processes presents a substantial challenge.

Q2.2 – As a continuation of the question around the CAIO's role, could you tell me about the regulatory aspects and where the CAIO's role meets them?

On the regulation front, I spend a considerable amount of time in discussions with our legal team, compliance officers, and information security personnel. The landscape for AI regulation is largely uncharted, which means crafting guidelines and guardrails where precedents are scant. Ideally, I seek clear dos and don'ts, but often, it's a collaborative effort to define these guidelines. This ongoing conversation focuses on managing risk, protecting our customers, and advancing innovation while minimizing our risk exposure.

We've established an Office of Responsible AI, tasked with defining the appropriate business contexts for AI applications. Much of this work involves navigating ethical considerations beyond mere legal compliance, especially since regulations tend to address high-risk areas. However, about 90% of typical company operations fall outside these high-risk categories, placing us in a regulatory gray area. Here, ethical judgment becomes paramount. While I am in favor of the emerging global regulations, I recognize they provide a framework rather than a complete solution. These regulations, focusing primarily on high-risk areas, still require nuanced application in our daily operations.

In essence, my role as CAIO demands a versatile approach that balances technical expertise, ethical foresight, and strategic planning. It's about harnessing AI's potential responsibly and effectively navigating both the broad applicability of AI across the business and the evolving landscape of AI ethics and regulations.

Q3 – How do foundation models and the strategies of major tech companies toward open sourcing affect data ownership and its value for businesses?

As Chief AI Officer, I find myself frequently contemplating the shifting significance of proprietary data ownership within our current AI-driven business paradigm. On one hand, foundation models are democratizing AI, significantly lowering the barrier to entry for companies that lack extensive proprietary datasets. These models offer performance that appears just as robust as if they were trained on specialized, proprietary data. This trend could suggest that the value of owning unique datasets may be diminishing, as powerful AI capabilities become accessible to a wider range of entities without substantial data assets.

However, the landscape is nuanced. We're witnessing a rise in techniques such as fine-tuning and additional pre-training, which tailor these generalist models to specific needs, subtly reinstating the importance of unique data. This customization capability hints that data ownership might evolve rather than diminish in relevance, serving as a new competitive edge or barrier to entry.

Furthermore, the strategic pivots of major companies such as Meta toward open sourcing their AI solutions are not purely altruistic but are aimed at disrupting the status quo, challenging the dominance of giants such as Microsoft and Google. This move toward open sourcing is reshaping the industry, compelling these giants to augment their offerings with more comprehensive, enterprise-oriented ecosystems around their models. The ultimate value proposition is no longer just the models themselves but the entire package—the ecosystems that support them, making them appealing for enterprise applications.

Amidst this, the role of regulators and differing international stances on data privacy and sharing come into play, potentially steering the market in various directions. This creates a complex environment where businesses must navigate not only technological advancements but also regulatory landscapes that could influence the strategic value of data ownership.

In conclusion, while the democratization of AI through foundation models and open source initiatives challenges traditional notions of data ownership, it simultaneously opens new avenues for competitive differentiation. Businesses must stay agile, reevaluating their data strategies in light of these developments, to leverage AI effectively while navigating the regulatory and strategic nuances of this evolving landscape.

David Sontag

David has a long track record of academic research which he dovetails with industry engagements and collaborations. In this section, he shares his novel insights on some of the emerging developments in LLMs.

Let's go through the questions and answers with David Sontag.

Q1 – As we progress toward creating more equitable and unbiased datasets, what strategies do you believe are most effective in identifying and mitigating implicit biases within large datasets?

In the realm of healthcare, the application of ML extends beyond mere predictive analytics to fostering insights that can fundamentally alter patient care and outcomes. This domain's complexity is underscored by the challenge of capturing the nuanced social determinants of health—variables such as living conditions, food security, and access to transportation—that significantly influence health outcomes. However, the current landscape of data collection and model training often overlooks these critical, yet less quantifiable aspects of patient life, leading to a gap in the personalized application of ML predictions.

A predominant issue arises from the reliance on surrogates or proxies in datasets that fail to encapsulate the individual's complexity fully. This reliance can obscure the subtleties inherent to each patient, thereby diluting the potential for ML to effect meaningful change in healthcare settings. The disparity between what the data models are trained on and the real-world contexts they are applied to further complicates this issue. For instance, LLMs trained on generic text data lack the contextual richness necessary for nuanced applications, such as tailoring healthcare recommendations to individual social circumstances.

This disconnect not only hampers the model's utility in providing relevant insights but also introduces unintended biases. These biases emerge when models, devoid of context or unaware of their training data's limitations, misapply generalized predictions to individual cases. Addressing this challenge requires a concerted effort toward enriching data collection processes to capture a more comprehensive view of patient social determinants and ensuring models can interpret and apply this information effectively.

To mitigate implicit biases in large datasets and advance toward equitable ML models, a multifaceted approach focusing on data collection, analysis, and model refinement is essential. Key strategies include decomposing discrimination metrics into bias, variance, and noise (*"Why is my classifier discriminatory?"*) to identify specific sources of unfairness, emphasizing the critical role of contextually rich and adequately sized training samples to improve both fairness and accuracy.

Additionally, augmenting datasets with more representative samples and relevant variables can address disparities in predictive performance across different groups (*"The Potential For Bias In Machine Learning And Opportunities For Health Insurers To Address It"*). Implementing these strategies necessitates a rigorous, ongoing evaluation of model outputs and impacts, ensuring they do not perpetuate existing biases or introduce new ones. Collaborative industry efforts toward algorithmic vigilance, ethical use of sensitive data, and incorporating diverse perspectives in model development processes are also vital. By prioritizing fairness as a fundamental aspect of model accuracy and utility, we can leverage ML to deliver more just and equitable outcomes across sectors.

In summary, before delving into strategies for creating equitable and unbiased datasets as outlined previously, it's crucial to acknowledge the foundational challenges faced by ML in healthcare. These challenges include the need for a deeper understanding of patient social determinants and the imperative to bridge the gap between what the data models are trained on and the contexts in which they are deployed. Addressing these issues is a prerequisite for leveraging ML to its fullest potential in improving healthcare outcomes and ensuring that innovations in ML contribute positively and equitably to patient care.

Q2 – How do you see these strategies evolving with the advancement of NLP technologies, and what do you envision as the next breakthrough in combining different learning paradigms within LLMs?

As NLP technologies continue to evolve, strategies to enhance their utility and fairness are also advancing, particularly in the work led by David Sontag's team at MIT. David shared these three research advancements that they are leading in the lab:

1. **Transparency**: A cornerstone of their research is the development of methodologies to provide comprehensive attribution for each piece of information output by NLP models. This involves tracing back to the training data to identify the sources that influenced the model's predictions. Such an approach not only bolsters the credibility and reliability of NLP applications but also empowers users to verify the origins of the information presented to them. By enabling a clear lineage from the output back to the input, users can understand the rationale behind a model's decision, enhancing trust in NLP systems.

2. **Utilization of general-purpose LLMs for specific domains**: The team is exploring innovative ways to adapt general-purpose LLMs such as GPT-4 to specialized fields without the need for extensive retraining or fine-tuning. This is achieved through a method that allows these models to collaborate, leveraging their general capabilities alongside models with domain-specific knowledge—such as medicine—to provide more accurate and relevant outputs. This strategy signifies a shift toward more adaptable and efficient use of existing NLP resources, ensuring that advancements in the field can be readily applied to a variety of specialized contexts without incurring prohibitive costs or time delays. (*My personal comment*: This use case is a particular case of one of two use cases we have covered that revolve around utilizing multiple LLMs simultaneously. The first is the K-LLMs scheme where multiple models all interact with each other in a setting that is meant to mimic a committee of experts. Each model has its own role (for example, a software developer collaborating with a QA engineer, or a project manager collaborating with a designer), and they take turns in refining the resulting output. Here, each role can be played by the same model; for example, each role could be represented by OpenAI's GPT, or different models can take on different roles, where the role that each model takes is chosen based on the strengths and weaknesses the model has. The second is a case where there are several different models, each with its own strengths and weaknesses (for example, one is fast but doesn't generate quality insights; the other is slow but is very precise), and the "right" model is to be chosen on a per-input basis by a decision process that is optimized to suit given constraints. For instance, a prompt that requires a binary *Yes/No* inference on a given small set of sentences may be channeled to a simple LLM while a prompt that requires applying legal judgment may be directed to the latest GPT version.)

3. **Fine-tuning LLMs efficiently**: Another focal point of their research addresses the challenge of fine-tuning LLMs in a way that is both data and computationally efficient. This involves identifying the most impactful hyperparameters within an LLM's architecture to adjust, determining which should remain fixed and which should be tuned to adapt the model to specific needs. The goal here is to maintain the integrity and strength of the original model while optimizing it for particular applications, thereby extending the utility of LLMs across diverse domains with minimal resource expenditure.

These advancements underscore a broader commitment to improving the flexibility, transparency, and applicability of NLP technologies. By focusing on these key areas, David Sontag's research at MIT aims to propel the field forward, ensuring NLP tools are not only more powerful but also more accessible, understandable, and ethical for users across various sectors. This approach aligns with the highest standards of academic and practical excellence, promising to shape the next generation of NLP applications in healthcare and beyond.

Q3 – We are witnessing an ongoing evolution of regulations around AI from the aspects of training data and model usage. What are the implications for the future development of LLMs in this regulated landscape?

In the evolving regulatory landscape surrounding AI, significant implications are emerging for the future development of LLMs. As regulations continue to advance, focusing on AI safety, including concerns around national security threats and the ethical use of AI, the framework within which LLMs are developed and deployed is being reshaped:

1. **Evolving regulations**: The regulation of AI is set to intensify, emphasizing the importance of safety and appropriateness in the application of AI technologies. This evolving regulatory environment necessitates a proactive approach to compliance, where developers of LLMs must ensure their models are not just effective but also align with emerging legal and ethical standards. These regulations aim to mitigate risks associated with AI, guiding the industry toward responsible innovation.

2. **Quality of data and models**: Both the industry and academia are actively engaged in enhancing the quality of data used to train models. This pursuit of quality is foundational to the development of more accurate and reliable LLMs, as models benefit from learning from well-curated and representative data. Research indicates the potential for efficiency in data usage, where selecting the "right" data could drastically reduce the need for large datasets without compromising the model's performance. This efficiency not only aligns with regulatory demands for transparency and accountability but also opens avenues for more sustainable model development processes.

3. **Metadata and model monitoring**: The incorporation of metadata into the training process represents a pivotal shift toward greater accountability and interpretability in LLMs. By attaching detailed metadata to data points used in model training, developers can offer a clear audit trail that elucidates how models arrive at their conclusions. This capability is crucial for monitoring model performance and ensuring that LLMs operate within ethical and legal boundaries. It also reflects a broader industry trend toward embracing ML interpretability methods, which enable stakeholders to scrutinize and understand the decision-making processes of LLMs.

These developments, forecasted by David Sontag's insights, underscore a future where LLMs are not only technologically advanced but also ethically grounded and regulatory compliant. This trajectory ensures that as LLMs become more embedded in various sectors, they do so in a manner that prioritizes safety, fairness, and transparency. Such an approach not only aligns with the highest standards of academic excellence but also positions LLMs to make a positive and responsible impact on society.

John D. Halamka

John brings the executive aspect to this chapter. In this section dedicated to his perspectives, he lays a broad spectrum of insights and actions that companies and organizations can roll out so to enable AI advancements in a very monitored and responsible orientation.

Let's go through the questions and answers with John D. Halamka.

Q1.1 – How does Mayo Clinic strategize a policy for reconciling open, reproducible research with stringent privacy protections within the NLP community, and how does it navigate the complex landscape of international regulations?

In reconciling the need for open, reproducible research with the protection of individual privacy within the NLP community, the "Data Behind Glass" model pioneered by the **Mayo Clinic Platform** offers a compelling solution. This model represents a paradigm shift in the handling of sensitive health data, embodying a platform-centric approach that ensures data quality, regulatory compliance, and, above all, the maintenance of patient trust throughout the data's life cycle.

At its core, Mayo Clinic Platform Connect serves as a distributed data network that exemplifies a federated architecture. Within this network, partners contribute their unique datasets while retaining strict control over their data, safeguarding privacy and confidentiality within their organizational IT boundaries. This federated approach enables a collaborative yet secure environment for data sharing and utilization.

Key to the success of this model is the meticulous process of data de-identification. By employing industry-accepted statistical methods aligned with privacy laws and regulations, data is rendered anonymous, ensuring that individual privacy is preserved while retaining the data's value for research and development. Techniques such as hashing, uniform date-shifting, and tokenization are utilized to obfuscate data, facilitating its use in federated learning without compromising patient privacy.

Moreover, the secure-by-design philosophy underpinning Connect ensures that data and **intellectual property (IP)** remain under the control of their respective owners, accessible only as authorized. This approach not only protects privacy but also fosters innovation by allowing Mayo Clinic Platform customers to develop, train, and validate algorithms on de-identified data cohorts. Rigorous controls, including code repository reviews, strict access management, and prohibitions on data imports and exports, further reinforce the platform's commitment to privacy and security.

The "Data Behind Glass" model is uniquely positioned to address the evolving regulatory landscape. With international regulators intensifying scrutiny over AI and ML applications, Mayo Clinic Platform's adaptable framework is designed to navigate the complex patchwork of global privacy regulations. Whether it's the **General Data Protection Regulation (GDPR)** in the European Union, the **General Data Protection Law (LGPD)** in Brazil, or China's security and privacy rules, the model ensures compliance while enabling global collaboration.

In summary, the "Data Behind Glass" model presents a viable pathway for the NLP community to achieve the dual objectives of fostering open research and safeguarding privacy. By de-identifying, securing, and federating data, Mayo Clinic Platform democratizes its use without compromising patient privacy, setting a precedent for responsible data handling in an era where the balance between transparency and privacy is paramount. This model exemplifies how technical innovation, coupled with a deep commitment to ethical standards, can pave the way for transformative advances in healthcare and beyond, ensuring that patient trust remains at the forefront of digital health initiatives.

Q1.2 – What are the implications for the future development of LLMs in this regulated landscape?

*Let's start by reviewing a strong source of guidance that seeks to promote policy making in the healthcare space around the use of LLMs and AI: T*he **Coalition of Health AI** (**CHAI™**).

On its website, CHAI talks about the following initiative:

"The Coalition for Health AI (CHAI™) (`https://coalitionforhealthai.org/`) *is working to develop guidelines to drive high-quality healthcare through the adoption of credible, fair, and transparent health AI systems. We offer a draft blueprint for trustworthy AI implementation guidance and assurance for healthcare V1.0* (`https://coalitionforhealthai.org/insights`) *for public review and comments.*"

CHAI contributes to the healthcare sector by developing guidelines for the adoption of credible, fair, and transparent health AI systems. Their draft blueprint for trustworthy AI implementation and assurance highlights the importance of aligning with the **National Institute of Standards and Technology's** (**NIST's**, under the U.S. Department of Commerce) AI risk management framework and extends these concepts to healthcare. Key contributions include the following:

- **Framework alignment**: Structuring guidance parallel to NIST definitions, focusing on validation, reliability, and the functions of *map*, *measure*, *manage*, and *govern* for AI risk management

- **Trustworthiness elements**: Emphasizing professional responsibility and social responsibility in AI design, development, and deployment to influence society positively and sustainably

- **Utility in healthcare**: Advocating for AI algorithms to be not only valid and reliable but also usable and beneficial to patients and healthcare delivery, requiring clinical validation and ongoing monitoring

- **Validation and reliability**: Highlighting the importance of software validation in regulated AI/ML technologies, including **Software as a Medical Device** (**SaMD**), and ensuring AI systems' accuracy, operability, and intended purpose

- **Reproducibility and reliability**: Addressing AI/ML's sensitivity to hardware and software variations, emphasizing the need for reliability and reproducibility across healthcare settings

- **Monitoring and testing**: Advocating for continuous monitoring and testing of AI tools to ensure reliability, detect shifts in input data or tool outputs, and maintain the quality of human-AI collaboration

- **Usability and benefit**: Defining usability as dependent on the model's context, end-user perspectives, simplicity, and workflow integration, and measuring the algorithm's impact on intended outcomes

- **Safety measures**: Ensuring AI systems do not pose risks to human life, health, property, or the environment, with a focus on preventing worse outcomes than the status quo

- **Accountability and transparency**: Stressing the importance of auditability, minimizing harm, reporting negative impacts, and making design trade-offs and opportunities for redress clear

- **Explainability and interpretability**: Balancing the need for AI systems to be understandable in their operation and meaningful in their output, crucial for building user trust in health AI

- **Fairness and bias management**: Addressing disparate performance or outcomes for selected groups and ensuring AI does not exacerbate risks for bias or adverse fairness outcomes

- **Security and resilience**: Highlighting the need for AI systems to withstand adverse events, maintain functions, and ensure confidentiality, integrity, and availability

- **Privacy enhancements**: Adhering to established standards for privacy in healthcare, such as the **Health Insurance Portability and Accountability Act** (**HIPAA**), while being adaptable to other jurisdictions' rules, such as GDPR

CHAI's efforts aim to ensure AI systems in healthcare are developed and deployed in a manner that upholds ethical standards, enhances patient care, and maintains public trust.

Q2 – AI-driven organizational structure – in what ways do you predict AI will continue to reshape companies' organizational structures to maximize the benefits of AI?

"AI indeed reshapes companies. In particular, at Mayo Clinic we asked ourselves the question, should we centralize AI operations or distribute them within the organization? I have observed many cases where different approaches were applied. At Mayo, our approach has been to decentralize all AI work but centralize data governance and policymaking. That enables innovation without regret."

Let's review some of the key benefits of this work model.

Decentralized AI work model benefits

- **Enhanced innovation and agility**: By decentralizing AI operations, organizations such as the Mayo Clinic foster an environment where individual departments can innovate and apply AI solutions tailored to their specific needs and challenges. This flexibility allows for quicker adaptation and implementation of AI technologies.

- **Empowerment and ownership**: Decentralizing AI empowers individual teams and departments with the autonomy to explore AI applications and solutions. This sense of ownership can drive more engaged and motivated teams, leading to innovative solutions and improvements in their operations.

- **Diverse applications and solutions**: A decentralized approach enables a broader exploration of AI across different facets of an organization. Different departments can experiment with

AI to solve diverse problems, leading to a wide array of AI-driven solutions and applications tailored to various organizational needs.

- **Rapid experimentation and learning**: With AI decentralized, teams can quickly test, learn, and iterate on AI projects without the bottleneck of centralized decision-making. This rapid experimentation can lead to faster discoveries and more efficient learning from successes and failures.

Centralized data governance benefits

- **Data security and privacy**: Centralizing data governance ensures that there are consistent policies and protocols in place to protect sensitive information and comply with privacy regulations. This is crucial in healthcare and other sectors where data privacy is paramount.

- **Data quality and integrity**: A centralized approach to data governance helps maintain high data quality and integrity across the organization. By having uniform standards and policies, organizations can ensure that AI models are trained on accurate, clean, and reliable data.

- **Efficient resource management**: Centralized data governance allows for more efficient management of data resources, avoiding duplication and ensuring that data assets are optimally utilized across the organization. This can lead to cost savings and more efficient use of data storage and computing resources.

- **Regulatory compliance**: With centralized data governance, organizations can more effectively ensure compliance with evolving regulatory requirements. A unified approach to data policymaking can help navigate complex legal landscapes and reduce the risk of non-compliance.

By adopting a model that decentralizes AI work while centralizing data governance and policymaking, organizations such as Mayo Clinic can stimulate innovation and adaptability in AI applications while ensuring data security, quality, and regulatory compliance. This balanced approach enables "innovation without regret," allowing for the exploration and implementation of AI solutions in a responsible and effective manner.

Q3 – Ethical concerns and strategies to combat over-delegation – as AI continues to penetrate daily decision-making processes, what strategies do you recommend to prevent overreliance on AI systems and to maintain a healthy level of human critical thinking and autonomy?

The **Centers for Medicare & Medicaid Services** (**CMS**) notice of proposed rulemaking is quite helpful in providing guidelines around the role of AI. John explains that "*The proposal says that all AI should augment, not replace, human decision-making.*"

We dove into the proposal, presented online (`https://www.govinfo.gov/content/pkg/FR-2022-08-04/pdf/2022-16217.pdf`). In particular, we focused on the *Use of Clinical Algorithms in Decision-Making (§ 92.210)* section on page 47880, and derived the following takeaways:

- **Non-discrimination through clinical algorithms**: CMS emphasizes that clinical algorithms should not result in discrimination based on race, color, national origin, sex, age, or disability. The use of clinical algorithms is not to be prohibited but monitored to prevent discriminatory outcomes.

- **Augmentation, not replacement**: CMS proposes that clinical algorithms should augment, not replace, human clinical judgment. Overreliance on algorithms without considering their potential discriminatory impact could violate existing regulations.

- **Liability for decisions based on clinical algorithms**: While entities are not liable for algorithms they did not develop, they may be held responsible for decisions made based on such algorithms if those decisions result in discrimination.

- **Awareness of algorithmic bias**: CMS highlights the prevalence of "race correction" or "race norming" practices in clinical algorithms, which can lead to discriminatory treatment based on race or ethnicity. They advocate for the use of updated tools without known biases.

- **Appropriate use of race and ethnicity-conscious variables**: While race and ethnicity variables may be used in certain circumstances to address health disparities, CMS cautions against their use in ways that may result in discrimination.

- **Concerns with disabilities and age**: Algorithms may also discriminate against individuals with disabilities and older adults, especially in crisis standards of care and resource allocation decisions during public health emergencies.

- **Proposed rule § 92.210**: This new provision explicitly prohibits discrimination through the use of clinical algorithms, aiming to ensure that these tools do not replace clinical judgment or lead to discriminatory outcomes.

- **Guidance and technical assistance**: CMS expresses a commitment to providing technical assistance to support compliance with civil rights obligations, seeking comments on the provision's scope, measures for mitigation, and types of technical assistance needed.

In summary, CMS's approach emphasizes the critical balance between leveraging AI for healthcare improvement and ensuring that these tools do not undermine human judgment or perpetuate discrimination. Their proposed rule and call for comments reflect an ongoing effort to develop responsive and responsible guidelines for AI's role in healthcare decision-making.

Xavier Amatriain

Let's go through the questions and answers with Xavier Amatrian.

Q1.1 – The future of LLM – hybrid learning paradigms: In light of the evolving landscape of learning schemes, what do you envision as the next breakthrough in combining different learning paradigms within LLMs?

The most important thing to keep in mind is that we are very early in the LLM research space and this is a rapidly evolving field. While attention-based transformers have taken us very far, there is room for many other approaches. For example, on the pre-training side, there is now a lot of interesting research in post-attention approaches such as **Structured State Space Models** (**SSMs** or **S4**). Similarly, **mixture of experts** (**MoEs**), while not new, are recently proving their incredible power to deliver smaller models that are very efficient, such as Mixtral by Mistral AI. And this is only in the pre-training space. For alignment, we have seen approaches such as **Direct Preference** (**DP**) or **Kahneman Tversky** (**KT**) show a lot of promise very quickly. Not to mention the use of self-play as a mechanism for improvement and alignment.

My main message here is that we should hold tight and expect a lot of innovation to come our way very fast in the next few years. I think in a couple of years we will look back and think of the GPT4 architecture as something old and completely inefficient. Very importantly, some of these improvements will make LLMs better in accuracy, but also much more efficient in cost and size so we should expect to have GPT4-like models running on our phones.

Q1.2 – The future of LLM – specialized LLMs in ensemble approaches: Considering a K-LLMs approach, that is, the notion of using multiple LLMs with complementary strengths, what specific criteria should guide the selection and combination of LLMs in an ensemble to tackle complex tasks?

There are many ways and places where ensemble techniques can and will be used in the context of LLMs. The criteria to select and combine them depends on the uses and where this combination happens. Here are three places where combining LLMs is useful:

In the pre-training phase, **Mixtures of Experts** (**MoEs**) are a form of ensemble where different deep neural networks are combined to improve the output. The weights to select and weigh the different experts are learned during pre-training. Importantly, some of those weights are zero, making inference much more efficient since not all experts are needed for all tasks.

Another way to combine different LLMs is during the distillation phase. In some approaches such as teacher/student distillation, LLMs are used to generate data to then train a smaller or more specific model. The selection and weight of each LLM is learned during the training phase of the student model.

Finally, we can combine LLMs at the application layer by treating each LLM instance as an agent. This leads to the notion of multi-agent systems where LLM-powered agents that are specialized for a task are combined to do a more complex one.

Q2 – AI-driven organizational structure – in what ways do you predict AI will continue to reshape internal business operations, and how should companies prepare to adapt their organizational structures to maximize the benefits of AI, especially in decision-making and operational efficiency?

Generative AI is going to revolutionize every aspect of organizations. My strong prediction is that AI is going to become another member of the organization. For example, software engineers will collaborate with an AI (or several of them) in their day to day. This will make them not 10X but 100X more efficient.

Of course, such a revolutionary force will change how we organize teams, hire people, or evaluate their performance. I think it is very important that we prepare for a world coming very soon where a very important skill for anyone in an organization will be their ability to collaborate and work with AI.

Melanie Garson

Melanie brings her vast experience working in the legal and regulatory space. As AI and LLMs continue to drive policies and guidelines, the value of such subject matter expertise is becoming clearer and more significant.

Let's go through the questions and answers with Melanie Garson.

Q1 – As this book is designed to address technical practitioners in the world of ML and AI, what value would they find in being aware of the various legal and regulatory aspects?

Understanding the geopolitical landscape surrounding AI, including regulatory, legal, and risk considerations, is of paramount importance for technical practitioners, from developers to **subject-matter experts** (**SMEs**). In the realm of AI, as companies navigate strategic and policy discussions, the inclusion of technically savvy individuals in these conversations is indispensable. Decision-makers increasingly recognize the value of having technical perspectives at the table to ensure that decisions are well rounded and informed by the technological possibilities and limitations.

An informed technical professional can effectively communicate their insights, bridging the gap between technical potential and executive vision. This capacity not only enhances the decision-making process but also ensures that strategies are robust, compliant, and cognizant of the evolving regulatory landscape.

Moreover, as organizations endeavor to align their operations with regulatory requirements and mitigate potential risks, they are likely to establish specialized teams tasked with developing and implementing technological solutions that adhere to these new strategic directions. Technical experts who are well-versed in the legal and regulatory dynamics shaping the AI industry will find themselves at a significant advantage, poised to contribute meaningfully to these teams. Their expertise not only makes them invaluable members but also primes them for leadership roles within these strategic initiatives, driving compliance, innovation, and competitive edge in a tightly regulated global market.

Q2 – From the perspective of a legal expert, how can we categorize the diverse array of risks associated with the burgeoning advancements in AI technology?

From a legal standpoint, the rapid advancements in AI technology present a spectrum of risks that can be classified into several distinct categories, each with its unique set of challenges and implications. These risks encompass the following:

- **Technical risks**: These arise from inherent flaws within AI algorithms, such as biases in hiring processes or systems optimized for unintended, harmful outcomes. An infamous example is Google's Gemini, which was found to be generating inaccurate historical images. Gemini had created diverse images of historical figures where the gender and race of the individuals it chose to depict were in absolute contradiction with historical facts. Another case was Microsoft's Tay chatbot, which adapted racist slurs from its interactions on Twitter, highlighting how AI systems can deviate dramatically from their intended functions due to misalignment or malicious inputs.

- **Ethical risks**: Ethical considerations are paramount, especially concerning technologies such as facial recognition, which pose significant threats to personal privacy. Additionally, ethical dilemmas surface regarding the exploitation of individuals who contribute to the training data of large AI models, often under inadequate compensation or working conditions.

- **Social risks**: AI's capability to spread disinformation or erode societal trust exemplifies its social risks. The propagation of false information and the undermining of credible sources can have profound effects on public discourse and societal cohesion.

- **Economic risks**: The economic implications of AI are vast, ranging from the infringement of IP rights to the potential for increased market concentration and unemployment. These risks highlight the transformative impact of AI on the competitive landscape and labor markets.

- **Security risks**: AI's misuse by malevolent actors represents a significant security concern. This includes the utilization of AI for creating chemical nerve agents or conducting data-extraction attacks, where LLMs might be exploited to access private personal information, thereby compromising data privacy and security.

- **Existential risks**: Perhaps the most profound risk is the existential threat posed by AI systems that surpass human intelligence. Such systems, if not adequately aligned with human values and objectives, might pursue their goals in ways that have catastrophic outcomes for humanity.

Recognizing the breadth and depth of these risks is crucial for countries, developers, and society at large to ensure that the deployment of AI technologies proceeds in a manner that minimizes potential harm. This necessitates a proactive approach to governance, development practices, and societal engagement to navigate the complex landscape of AI advancements responsibly.

Q3 – How can the development and deployment of AI and LLMs be guided to mitigate ethical concerns such as bias and ensure their responsible use in decision-making processes, particularly in high-risk and regulated industries?

To mitigate ethical concerns such as bias and ensure the responsible use of AI and LLMs in decision-making processes, especially in high-risk and regulated industries, a multifaceted approach is required. This approach should address both technical and socio-technical challenges posed by the integration of AI systems into critical areas of business and society. The following strategies can guide the development and deployment of AI systems:

- **Development focus shift**: AI systems should be designed to augment rather than replicate human thinking. This shift in focus can help maintain public trust in AI by ensuring that AI systems support and enhance human decision-making rather than replace it. Trust is crucial for the long-term integration of AI in decision-making processes, and maintaining it requires a clear demonstration of AI's complementary role to human capabilities.

- **Regulatory compliance and bias mitigation**: Adherence to emerging regulations, such as the EU AI Act which was passed in 2024, and agreed standards which aim to limit bias in high-risk use cases, is essential. Developers should also be mindful of the broader implications of bias, beyond regulatory compliance, recognizing the challenges posed by Western- and English-centric AI systems. Efforts should be made to diversify datasets and algorithms to reflect global demographics and reduce inherent biases.

- **Stress testing and security measures**: AI systems, particularly LLMs, should undergo rigorous stress testing to ensure they can handle high-risk use cases with more deterministic outcomes. Security and mitigation strategies should be developed to address potential AI failures, with a focus on preventing catastrophic "brittle" failures that can have widespread implications.

- **Human oversight**: Incorporating humans in the loop as strategic bottlenecks can serve as an effective safeguard against the unintended consequences of AI decision-making. This strategy ensures that AI systems are continuously monitored and guided by human judgment, especially in scenarios where AI's decisions have significant impacts.

- **Building foundational AI infrastructure**: Governments and organizations should invest in creating a foundational AI infrastructure that supports the ethical and responsible deployment of AI. This includes fostering collaborations between the private sector, academia, and government to contribute to the development of AI tools that are both innovative and aligned with societal values.

- **Skills and culture development**: Promoting a culture of experimentation and safe use of AI technologies within the workforce is crucial. This involves training civil servants and industry professionals in the ethical use of AI, including understanding its limitations and potential biases.

- **Long-term strategic planning**: Establishing long-term mechanisms to identify, pilot, and deploy frontier AI applications is vital. This planning should consider the ethical, social, and economic implications of AI technologies, aiming to leverage AI for the public good while minimizing risks to citizens and society.

By adopting these strategies, AI developers and policymakers can address the challenges of bias and ensure that AI and LLMs are used responsibly and effectively, especially in sectors where their impact is most profound and potentially transformative.

Q4 – What strategies can be implemented to transition from traditional roles to collaborative human-AI teams, ensuring the development of human expertise alongside AI integration in the workplace?

To transition from traditional roles to collaborative human-AI teams and ensure the development of human expertise alongside AI integration in the workplace, a multifaceted approach is essential. This strategy encompasses the following:

- **Creating new pathways for skill development**: Addressing the displacement risk for entry-level roles due to automation requires the establishment of novel avenues for career progression and expertise development. This involves leveraging the potential of **generative AI** (**GenAI**) tools, as evidenced by research from Stanford and MIT, to enhance worker productivity while simultaneously exploring the broader impacts of AI on job functions. It is critical to design educational and training programs that prepare the workforce for higher-level analytical and strategic roles, ensuring that SMEs evolve alongside AI advancements.

- **Fostering critical engagement with AI outputs**: To counteract overreliance on AI and automation, there is a need for a cultural shift toward encouraging employees to critically evaluate AI decisions. Implementing systems that offer improved explainability—"glass boxes" that elucidate the reasoning behind AI decisions—can empower employees to understand, question, and effectively collaborate with AI tools. This ensures a balanced integration of human cognitive skills and AI capabilities, enhancing decision-making processes and trust in AI applications.

- **Enhancing workplace integration evaluation mechanisms**: The effective integration of AI into the workplace transcends performance metrics against benchmark datasets. It requires a comprehensive understanding of real-world workflows, potential limitations, and strategies for managing exceptional scenarios. This means developing evaluation methodologies that assess how AI systems complement human roles within specific operational contexts, recognizing that automation may handle tasks but not necessarily replace the nuanced and complex nature of human work entirely.

- **Promoting collaborative human-AI teamwork**: The future of business necessitates embracing a paradigm where humans and machines collaborate to achieve shared objectives. This approach emphasizes the complementary strengths of both, leveraging AI for efficiency and scale while harnessing human expertise for creativity, ethical considerations, and complex problem-solving. Achieving this synergy involves strategic organizational planning, continuous learning opportunities, and fostering an environment where technology augments rather than supplants human contributions.

By addressing these key issues, organizations can cultivate an environment where AI-enabled tools are integrated thoughtfully into the workplace. This ensures that human expertise is not only preserved but also enhanced, paving the way for a future where collaborative human-AI teams drive innovation, productivity, and sustainable growth in an ethically responsible manner.

Summary

In this concluding chapter of our exploration into the dynamic world of NLP and LLMs, we have had the privilege of engaging with experts across various fields. Their insightful discussions have illuminated intricate developments, legal considerations, operational approaches, regulatory influences, and emerging capabilities of LLMs. Through their expert lenses, we delved into pressing issues such as creating equitable datasets, advancing NLP technologies, navigating privacy protections in research, restructuring organizations around AI, and anticipating breakthroughs in learning paradigms.

The dialogue with these luminaries has underscored a common theme: the intersection of technological innovation with ethical, legal, and organizational considerations. As we ponder strategies to mitigate biases in datasets, envision the future of hybrid learning paradigms, and assess the impact of foundation models on data ownership, it becomes clear that the evolution of NLP and LLMs is not merely a technological journey but a multidisciplinary venture that challenges us to think deeply about the broader implications of these advancements.

This chapter, serving as the capstone of our book, ties together the expansive topics discussed throughout the chapters, from the basics of NLP and its integration with ML to the intricate designs of LLMs, their applications, and the trends they herald for the future. It encapsulates the essence of our journey—highlighting how the collaboration between academia and industry, underpinned by a thorough understanding of the ethical and legal landscapes, is crucial for harnessing the full potential of LLMs.

As we conclude not just this chapter but the book itself, we stand on the precipice of a new era in NLP and LLMs. The insights shared by our experts do not mark an end but a beacon for future exploration and innovation in the field. This book has aimed to furnish readers, whether they come from academia or industry, with a comprehensive understanding and foresight into the evolution of NLP and LLMs, encouraging them to contribute to this ever-evolving narrative with their own research, developments, and ethical considerations.

Index

www.packtpub.com

Subscribe to our online digital library for full access to over 7,000 books and videos, as well as industry leading tools to help you plan your personal development and advance your career. For more information, please visit our website.

Why subscribe?

- Spend less time learning and more time coding with practical eBooks and Videos from over 4,000 industry professionals

- Improve your learning with Skill Plans built especially for you

- Get a free eBook or video every month

- Fully searchable for easy access to vital information

- Copy and paste, print, and bookmark content

Did you know that Packt offers eBook versions of every book published, with PDF and ePub files available? You can upgrade to the eBook version at www.packtpub.com and as a print book customer, you are entitled to a discount on the eBook copy. Get in touch with us at customercare@packtpub.com for more details.

At www.packtpub.com, you can also read a collection of free technical articles, sign up for a range of free newsletters, and receive exclusive discounts and offers on Packt books and eBooks.

Other Books You May Enjoy

If you enjoyed this book, you may be interested in these other books by Packt:

OpenAI API Cookbook

Henry Habib

ISBN: 978-1-80512-135-0

- Grasp the fundamentals of the OpenAI API
- Navigate the API's capabilities and limitations of the API
- Set up the OpenAI API with step-by-step instructions, from obtaining your API key to making your first call
- Explore advanced features such as system messages, fine-tuning, and the effects of different parameters
- Integrate the OpenAI API into existing applications and workflows to enhance their functionality with AI
- Design and build applications that fully harness the power of ChatGPT

Generating Creative Images With DALL-E 3

Holly Picano

ISBN: 978-1-83508-771-8

- Master DALL-E 3's architecture and training methods
- Create fine prints and other AI-generated art with precision
- Seamlessly blend AI with traditional artistry
- Address ethical dilemmas in AI art
- Explore the future of digital creativity
- Implement practical optimization techniques for your artistic endeavors

Packt is searching for authors like you

If you're interested in becoming an author for Packt, please visit `authors.packtpub.com` and apply today. We have worked with thousands of developers and tech professionals, just like you, to help them share their insight with the global tech community. You can make a general application, apply for a specific hot topic that we are recruiting an author for, or submit your own idea.

Share Your Thoughts

Now you've finished *Mastering NLP from Foundations to LLMs*, we'd love to hear your thoughts! Scan the QR code below to go straight to the Amazon review page for this book and share your feedback or leave a review on the site that you purchased it from.

https://packt.link/r/1-804-61918-3

Your review is important to us and the tech community and will help us make sure we're delivering excellent quality content.

Download a free PDF copy of this book

Thanks for purchasing this book!

Do you like to read on the go but are unable to carry your print books everywhere?

Is your eBook purchase not compatible with the device of your choice?

Don't worry, now with every Packt book you get a DRM-free PDF version of that book at no cost.

Read anywhere, any place, on any device. Search, copy, and paste code from your favorite technical books directly into your application.

The perks don't stop there, you can get exclusive access to discounts, newsletters, and great free content in your inbox daily

Follow these simple steps to get the benefits:

1. Scan the QR code or visit the link below

https://packt.link/free-ebook/978-1-80461-918-6

2. Submit your proof of purchase
3. That's it! We'll send your free PDF and other benefits to your email directly

www.ingramcontent.com/pod-product-compliance
Lightning Source LLC
Chambersburg PA
CBHW080621060326
40690CB00021B/4765